TOM P'S FIDDLE

•———————————————•

A TRUE TEXAS TALE

TOM P'S FIDDLE

A TRUE TEXAS TALE

BY SHERRI KNIGHT

LANGDON STREET PRESS

Langdon Street Press

Langdon Street Press
212 3rd Avenue North, Suite 570
Minneapolis, MN 55401
1.888.645.5248
www.langdonstreetpress.com
Order online: www.TomPsFiddle.com

ISBN 10: 978-0-9799120-7-8
ISBN 13: 0-9799120-7-5
LCCN: 2007941606

Book sales for North America and international:
Itasca Books, 3501 Highway 100 South, Suite220
Minneapolis, MN 55416
Phone: 952.345.4488 (toll free 1.800.901.3480)
Fax: 952.920.0541; email to orders@itascabooks.com

Cover Design by Julie Moeller
Interior Design by Andrea Horne

Printed in the United States of America

AUTHOR'S NOTES

Tom P's Fiddle is a narrative account of a man who lived in north central Texas in the late 1800s. While dialogue and narrative were added, no deviation was made from Tom's real story. The truth was a much wilder tale than any yarn that could be spun by a storyteller's imagination.

Through extensive research which took the author from Hillsboro to Austin to West Texas, the Panhandle, and on to New Mexico and Oklahoma, the true story emerged out of court records and documents, prison records, newspaper accounts, census records, and autobiographies, along with family stories and interviews. Information gleaned from all these sources provided a clear picture of the events that would shape and impact Tom P's life. Putting Tom into the context of his times helps the reader understand how forces beyond one's control can shape a person's life. One such force in Tom's life was how the stories printed in the newspapers took on a life of their own outside of the facts of his case. Fighting against the public image of himself reinforced by exaggerated, unsubstantiated rumors, Tom learned that the truth can be buried beneath the force of a public bent on believing everything they read in the papers.

Much thanks is given to the Cellblock Museum in Hillsboro, Texas, where two of Tom P's fiddles along with a framed copy of one of his original compositions are on display. Mr. Richard Greenhill, docent, was very helpful and accommodating.

The author's research could not have been completed without the help of so many, such as Jerry Templeton, Rita Briley, Irene Norman, Stephen and Libby Bodio, and my brother Mike Stephens. Invaluable were the files and books at the Dick Smith Library at Tarleton State University, the Texas Collection at Baylor University, the University of Texas at Austin Libraries, Texas State Archives, Hillsboro, Stephenville, Waxahachie, Socorro, Magdalena, and Fort Worth Public Libraries, and the amazing, indexed archives of the *Dallas Morning News*. Cover graphics and photo restoration was done by Julie Moeller, www.legaseekeepsakes.com. And finally, this project could not have been completed without my editors: my husband, Arden Knight, and Jeanie Crane.

For those interested in more information along with copies of actual documents, photos, and other research treasures related to Tom P and the time in which he lived, a blog has been set up to give more of the back-story and information about the people and events surrounding Tom P. Readers can post questions or simply enjoy learning more about this incredible story. Go to: www.TomPsFiddle.blogspot.com.

When I started this project, I simply sought to separate fact from fiction, truth from the oft-told family stories. As I delved into Tom's life, digging deeper, I became aware that Tom P Varnell had reached across the divide to draw me in. I knew early on that his was a story that needed to be told.

The following is the true story of Tom P Varnell, my great, great uncle.

—Sherri Knight

This book is dedicated to my husband, Arden Knight,
and to my cousin, Don Templeton.

Tom P Varnell (1) and his friend George Walker

CHAPTER ONE

26 July 1903

Looking into the mottled mirror hanging above the oak dresser, Tom P Varnell quickly shaved. A drooping mustache neatly outlined his mouth, hiding the slight downward turn that appeared when he was contemplative, the residue of the hard years he had spent in prison. Tom pulled on his clean, long-sleeved white shirt and charcoal gray vest, then reached for a dark blue cravat to tie around his collar.

Buttoning up his trousers, Tom walked over to the window that framed his world. The family-owned private horse track came into view. No longer used, it still brought to mind the time many years before when John Wesley Hardin, passing through Hill County, stopped at their ranch when Tom was not yet ten years old...

A handsome man, clean-shaven with dark brown hair well hidden under his wide-brimmed gray felt hat, Wes Hardin leaned up against the unpainted wooden fence alongside the dirt race track. Chewing on a piece of yellow straw, he talked easily of good horseflesh and successful breeding techniques with Tom P's father, Isaac Varnell.

Hardin was a bit of a legend already. Even so, judgment for his past deeds, including the killing of several men, was suspended. He had relatives, Ann and Westin Hardin, who lived in Hill County. No one would be alerting the sheriff. It was an unwritten law.

Reconstruction Governor Edmund Davis had replaced the Texas Rangers after the Civil War with his State Police, made up mostly of carpetbaggers, scalawags, and freed slaves. Wes Hardin became the target of these sanctioned vigilantes early on. Escaping raids, meant to deprive him of his life, earned Hardin the reputation as one of Texas' most notorious shootists. Word spread rapidly among the country folk that Hardin would be at the Varnell ranch that afternoon. Keeping a respectful distance, excited onlookers gathered to watch Hardin as much as the races.

Young Tom's eyes were drawn to Hardin's Colt .45 peeking out from the special vest he wore. Visible, also, were the carved notches on the handle. Tom watched Hardin flex his expressive hands, which never seemed to be very far away from his six-gun. Curiosity finally got the better of Tom. Unafraid, he went over to where his father stood with his guest.

"Mr. Hardin, can I see your pistol?" Tom bravely asked. Hardin quickly turned to look down at the earnest youngster. Isaac Varnell intervened.

"Tom P, it's not polite to ask to see a man's gun. Now run along and get Sunny Boy ready for Mr. Hardin to see for possible stud service."

"Yes, sir," Tom replied, crestfallen. He stepped away but did so slowly, his blue eyes still on Hardin. Even at his young age, Tom P was learning how to take the full measure of another man, a skill needed on the Texas frontier.

Tom finally headed for the stables but was still close enough to hear his father say, "Sorry about that! Tom P has a fascination with guns. He's spent a lot of time practicing the border shift with wooden pistols he carved himself because he wants to be able to shoot with either hand. No offense was intended."

"None taken! I'm sure your son will make a fine marksman. He has a look of confidence few men ever acquire. You should be proud he can already look a man square in the eyes," Wes Hardin replied before turning back to the track in anticipation of the next race…

Running his hand through his bed-ruffled, dark curly hair, Tom returned to the present. Wooden pistols had long since been traded for the real thing. Tom had fond memories of his youth, at least until his father was murdered.

Tom took the time to study his own hands. Keeping them clean had become a habit, especially after the dirty, squalid conditions he had endured while at Rusk Penitentiary. The rope calluses across his palms came from working on a horse ranch. His long, tapering fingers were those of a musician. The fiddle was the one positive constant in Tom P's life, besides his mother and older sisters, Lina and Rosa. His ability to skip across the strings had always provided an escape from daily challenges.

Family loyalty was something he could always count on. Through all of his troubles, Tom had found family by his side. Their belief in him provided the anchor he had needed to survive a press-fueled public bent on his destruction.

Raising the window, Tom spied the windmill that pumped well water into the wooden trough for the horses and other livestock. When Tom was younger, he spent many a happy afternoon throwing rocks at the turning blades. He'd probably hit every single one of them. One time he used them for target practice with a six-shooter 'borrowed' from his father. His mother, Frances La Docia Varnell, put a stop to that. Tom chuckled, remembering the amused look on his father's face even though he wisely did not intervene in Docia's discipline. Tom could see that one blade still sported the bullet hole he had put through it. Tom heard the windmill creak and groan as the morning breeze started moving the blades round and round, spinning, spinning...

Breaking Tom's reverie with its squawking, a blue jay flew by, taking a dive at the barn cat. The family birddog, Princess, loped across the yard toward the kitchen door. Tom was once again struck by the resemblance Princess had to her deceased dam, Queen, the family's much-beloved pet and watchdog. Turning back from the window, Tom realized it was time to finish dressing. Today he had some things he wanted to get done in Abbott.

Taking the same care in brushing his hair as he did when brushing his horses, Tom liked to keep his dark curls clipped at the neckline. His good looks and polite demeanor lulled many into misjudging him. Tom's quiet but affable mannerisms belied his wiry confidence and inability to back down from a fight. At age forty-one, Tom's clear blue eyes hid a hard side in their shadows. When his eyes flashed, it was time to leave him alone or suffer the consequences.

Tom lived by his own code of honor, forged in the fire of his father's death, which did not necessarily adhere to existing laws. He believed in hard work and self-reliance for survival, since trusting others except for family was risky. Tom learned at a young age that justice and protection from the law didn't always happen.

Hearing his mother in the kitchen admonishing Glory, the Negro housekeeper, to get breakfast ready, Tom walked over to his dresser to pick up the gold watch and chain that had belonged to his father, whom he and his siblings had affectionately called Pap. Attaching it to his vest pocket, a look of sadness passed briefly over Tom's countenance. Turning, he picked up the piece of paper that was a deed to land located not far away from his mother's ranch—but far enough. Tom eyed his pearl-handled pistol in the holster hanging on the bedpost.

"Tom P, are you up yet? Your vittles are ready," called his mother.

He had been called Tom P all his life. It was like the 'P' was a part of his first name, although it really stood for Powhattan. No one seemed to know for certain where the name had originated. Was it an indication of a familial native connection or some distant relative's fascination with American Indians? Tom wasn't sure, as its origin was lost to the family. What he did know was that he could always tell when his mother was angry because Tom P turned into 'Thomas Powhattan' spoken in a much harsher tone, and she would give him that determined, dark look. Then he knew his mother meant business. Time to listen, even if he had no intention of giving in to her demands. Tom's love for his mother was real and abiding. Her strong will matched his own.

Tom entered the kitchen. Planting a quick kiss on his mother's cheek, he settled down to flapjacks, scrambled eggs, and grits. To round it out, Glory brought him a large tin cup of the hot black coffee he loved so much.

"Thanks," he offered up between scalding sips. He smiled and winked at Glory who grinned back before turning away to start on the dirty dishes in the sink.

"Tom P, we've a lot of horses needin' a workout today!" hinted Docia, whose gruff manner belied the soft spot she had in her heart for her youngest and only offspring remaining in her home. She had lost her two oldest sons, Augustus and Napoleon, many years before when they were young. Of her three married daughters, Adeline, Rosa, and Henrietta, only Rosa still lived in Hill County. Henrietta (Etta) had moved to Florida and Adeline (Lina) to West Texas.

Behind the tiny frame, Docia Varnell, of French descent, was no shrinking violet. Widowed for many years, Docia successfully managed the family ranch of more than a thousand acres, showing the resilience and fortitude that any woman needed to survive and prosper alone on the Texas frontier. Delegating most of the cooking and cleaning to hired help, she preferred to talk politics and horseflesh. Well known in the community for hostessing barbecues so she could give the local elected officials a piece of her mind, Docia was held in high esteem, even though women did not have the right to vote. In town, she was often invited to sit up on the platform at political rallies for the Southern Democrats.

"I hear ya, Mother," replied Tom. "I've an errand to run in Abbott. Then I'll be back to work the horses. Have Jethro and Mack get started." Touching lightly the hidden deed in his vest pocket, he hoped she wouldn't probe further.

Docia interjected, "You know the hired hands need someone to supervise 'em or they'll fritter away their time spittin' and scratchin'. Besides, I won't be able to get 'em up 'til mid-afternoon. I heard 'em come back pretty late last night. Come to think of it, so did you!"

Docia's eyes narrowed. "What business could you possibly have in Abbott? It's the Lord's Day. Are you courtin' some farmer's daughter and not lettin' me know?"

Tom smiled. "Mother, ya know you're the only gal for me! I won't be long. You can count on it. Tell Mack I'll let him ride Solidad when I get back if'n he's taken care of the rest of the herd. That should get him movin'!"

Tom scooted off the wooden chair, grabbed his Stetson and tan leather gloves, and was out the kitchen door before Docia could think of another question. The window framed him striding across the yard on his way to the stable. Watching him put the Mexican saddle on 'Cane (short for Hurricane), his favorite black stallion, her frown turned slowly into a smile. Her son was a handsome man, strong and capable. She admired him on many different levels, even though he had brought her a lot of heartache as well. But that was in the past. The future was what she wanted to concentrate on now for her son.

Despite the years he'd spent in prison, Tom still had that lanky, vulnerable air about him and twinkling blue eyes that drew admiring glances and bold female conduct. Women had been a source of trouble for Tom throughout his life. Even with his bad reputation, Docia had lost count of the number of young ladies who stopped her to ask about Tom when she went into Hillsboro. Only last week, pretty Sallie Jameson deliberately crossed the street in front of an oncoming one-horse buggy to have a word with Docia.

"Afternoon, Mrs. Varnell. Good to see you in town," Sallie had called out breathlessly.

"Hello, Sallie. How have you been?" Docia had responded.

"Fine, Mrs. Varnell. Say, how's Tom P doin'? I've not seen him for awhile and was hopin' he would be at the Methodist Church supper Sunday."

While Mrs. Varnell studied her, Sallie blushed. Docia figured that this girl, like so many, was sweet on her son. She'd heard too many stories of hurried kisses and expectant hearts from those who loved to spread town gossip. Tom'd always had plenty of female attention from which to choose. Yet, he hadn't. Docia still hoped some day he'd meet the right girl.

"Sallie, I don't much keep up with Tom P's social calendar any more. I'll tell him you inquired," replied Docia.

Sallie blinked. "Uhh... Thank you, Mrs. Varnell. I `preciate it." Sallie moved away quickly.

Docia never told Tom about the encounter. It just wasn't 'fitting or proper.' Still, she understood why young ladies vied for her son's attention. The air of danger created by Tom's checkered past only seemed to increase the attraction of the local unmarried girls hoping to capture his heart.

Watching Tom strap on his spurs through the kitchen window, Docia suddenly remembered something. She ran out the back door after him.

"Son, I hope you're not carrying a pistol! You don't always seem to remember it's against the law to have one in public."

"No, Mother. I don't have a gun with me. It's not that kind of errand," Tom P turned around. "Mother, I ..."

"What, Tom P?"

He paused, looking at his mother for a moment. "Nothin'. I'll be back before you know it."

"You best be. Don't tarry!" she admonished.

Satisfied, Docia gave a final wave and headed back toward the house. Tom realized he'd almost spilled the beans but backed off in time before telling his mother he was making plans for his future. He meant to build his own house and maybe, just maybe, take a wife! Hurried kisses and fondling willing partners, married or not, ceased to have the allure it once did when he was a much younger man. So why hadn't he told his mother of his plans? He decided there was no need to answer the questions she was sure to ask until he was all set.

Moving `Cane onto the main road after crossing Ash Creek, Tom made a mental note to check out the quarry at Hooker's Cave, located close to where stagecoaches used to stop to deliver mail to area residents just south of Abbott. He wanted rock for building a solid foundation. His smile, never far away, returned. Tom started whistling the melody of one of his recent uncompleted compositions, knowing instinctively how it would sound on his fiddle.

CHAPTER TWO

1 January 1876

Two men squatted low, keeping out of sight on the high bluff located above a sharp turn along the Bynum Road. They had been there most of the day keeping a lookout. Both their muskets were loaded, ready for use. Occasionally, one stood up, peering into the distance. From the bluff, they could see for several miles the surrounding rich farmland of Hill County.

Heading home from Hillsboro, Isaac Varnell moved the buckboard wagon slowly along after successfully selling some stock horses. He shivered and pulled his brown wool coat closer, making sure all of the buttons were securely fastened. He could not remember a colder winter than this one. He knew he had a lot to be thankful for on this frosty New Year's Day. Nearly sixty years old, he had been in Texas for over thirty years, arriving in 1847 from Mississippi soon after Texas became a state. He had prospered after moving from Walker to Hill County back in `61. Yes indeed, lots to be thankful for.

Isaac was anxious to get home. Docia hadn't much wanted him to go into Hillsboro. She pointed out it was too cold and a holiday, but Isaac had promised to deliver the five horses to Sam McGregor. Business was business.

Tom P asked to come with him, but Isaac decided to let him sleep in since they had stayed up late to celebrate the coming of the new year. Isaac made a quick deal on the horse sale. Afterwards, he stepped over to a mercantile store he was lucky enough to find open and bought coffee and sugar Docia said she needed if he insisted on going into town.

Soon enough, Isaac headed back home. The rhythm of the horses' hooves lulled him into a reverie. Isaac paid little attention to the road. The horses pulling the wagon knew the route to take to the ranch without much prodding from him. Isaac started humming one of the fiddle duets he'd heard Tom P and Docia play the night before. Thinking about his son's future, Isaac wondered if he could get Tom interested in the new Texas Agriculture and Mechanical College at Bryan he knew was opening later this year.

Lost in his thoughts, Isaac did not see the two men who rose up from the top of the bluff just enough to get a good aim on him. When the horses slowed down to negotiate the turn in the road, Isaac caught the movement and shielded his eyes from the sun's bright glare, but he couldn't quite make out who was towering above him.

One of the men raised a musket and, without warning, fired. Isaac grunted in surprise as the minnie ball and buckshot struck him in the chest. Before he had time to think, another minnie ball struck him in the shoulder. Isaac stood up but immediately started falling off the wagon. He managed to catch himself by grabbing the end of the seat. It slowed his descent, but he still fell hard to the ground.

Isaac did not hear his attackers take off. He remained conscious long enough somehow to ease off his heavy coat and make a pillow. Hopefully, someone would come along soon to offer him aid. Was that fiddle music he was hearing? Looking down the road, he could see someone walking toward him even though his vision was fading. Why, it appeared to be La Docia, looking as young as the day he first met her! She was the most beautiful woman he had ever seen.

Jamie and Hal Tyson poked along on their farm horses, heading home mid-afternoon. Both of them had headaches as big as the cold blue sky above, so they mostly watched the ground go by rather than look into the bright afternoon sun. Drinking too much whiskey the night before, they'd crawled off into the hay barn after a rousing party to sleep it off. Ma and Pa were going to be misput with them if they didn't get home in time to take care of their daily chores, but neither had the energy to get their horses past a slow walk.

Hal finally raised his eyes to see if they were getting any closer to the turn-off to their home place. What he saw was pretty peculiar. A hitched wagon was up ahead, stopped in the middle of the road. No one seemed to be around. Then he spied something or someone lying on the ground.

"Hey Jamie! Look ahead. Who do you think that is?" exclaimed Hal, slapping the reins to get his horse moving.

"I have no idea. Pipe down! My head is splittin'!" replied Jamie, so intent on nursing his noggin he wasn't interested in his brother's chattering.

"Jamie, somethin' terrible has happened here!" With that, Hal raced ahead. Arriving at the wagon, he slid off his horse and ran over to the man lying on the ground. Jamie came out of his reverie when he realized that Hal was more than excited; his brother was scared.

"It's Old Man Varnell. He's been shot! I think he's dead!" Hal exclaimed. He looked all about but saw no one lingering. Hal turned back to the murder victim.

"Oh my lord," whispered Jamie, no longer aware of his headache. "Hal, we have to do somethin'. I'll go to the Varnell place. You go for the constable! Hurry!"

Hal needed no further instructions. He took off. Jamie covered Isaac Varnell up the best he could with an old brown horse blanket he found in the back of the wagon. He tied the reins to a large rock to keep the horses from trying to take the wagon home. Then he headed for the Varnell place to let them know. He didn't want to stick around the murder scene in case the shooters came back to make sure Isaac Varnell was dead.

From a short distance away, things seemed far too normal to Jamie as he arrived at the Varnell ranch. Kind of quiet really. Why did he have to be the one to bring the storm their way? He turned into the entry and trotted his horse on down to the main house, following Queen, whose bark brought Docia to the porch to meet the rider.

Fourteen-year-old Tom P never forgot seeing his father lying on the cold, hard ground, his sightless eyes turned as if he were looking at something or someone down the road. This was the worst day in Tom's life, but he dared not cry. Tom remembered a sob trying to rise up from somewhere deep in his chest. He'd swallowed hard to control his emotions. His mother needed him, and he would be there for her.

Docia and Tom managed to get Isaac's body home and laid out on the kitchen table by the time Constable Johnson and his posse arrived. They investigated the scene of the shooting, but no tracks were visible along the rocky terrain of the bluff. The men did not have a clue in which direction the culprits had gone. Johnson stood on the porch where Docia Varnell met him.

"Ma'am, we're awful sorry about your troubles. We're here to see if you could shed some light on this terrible crime."

"You find A. P. Fisher and Isaac Livingstone. They're the ones who did this," stated Docia firmly.

"Who are these men? Why would they want to kill your husband, ma'am?" asked Johnson.

"I overheard them arguing with Isaac just a few days ago

about a horse trade. They said Isaac cheated `em. I can tell you that's not true, but Isaac couldn't convince `em. Fisher and Livingstone were so angry they yelled Isaac better watch his back, as it could get filled with holes. I'd say that's a threat, wouldn't you, constable?" Docia retorted.

"Ma'am, what about a robbery? Wasn't Mr. Varnell carrying some money? I heard he just sold some horses in town," Johnson queried.

"Of course, I'm sure. Isaac still had his money pouch on him – untouched," she responded.

"Well, ma'am, we'll take care of this then. I'll get back to you," stated Constable Johnson. He and his men left shortly, all riding back in the direction of Hillsboro.

A few days later, Jamie Tyson rode over to bring the Varnells a newspaper. "Your husband's death made the *Waco Examiner*, Mrs. Varnell. Thought you'd like to see it," announced Jamie.

"Thank you," Docia replied, spreading the newspaper out.

The Varnell Murder

On New Year's day Mr. Isaac Varnell, an old gentleman about sixty years of age, was found by the roadside about six miles east of Hillsboro, dead, with eighteen buckshot and two Minnie balls in his body, notice of which was previously published.

Mr. A. P. Fisher and Mr. Isaac Livingstone were arrested on suspicion of having committed the deed, and were undergoing a preliminary examination. There being no jail in Hill County, they were sent to this County for safe keeping, arriving here on Sunday evening last, in

*charge of Deputy Sheriff John J. Trott, and others, but
on account of the crowded condition of our jail, they were
not received, and at the time of this writing are still in the
hands of the Hill County officers…*

"I wonder what has happened to those two?" asked Docia
out loud.

"Well, that's just it, Mrs. Varnell. I heard they let `em go as
there was not enough evidence to charge `em," Jamie replied.

Docia was furious, especially since the constable had promised to keep her informed, and young Tom P felt a rising rage at
the incompetence of the law. Finally calming down, Docia told
him not to fret. They would bide their time. Texans knew how
to take care of matters themselves if necessary. Some day, some
way, those men would get their reckoning. While great sympathy
was shown by neighbors and friends, both Docia and Tom held
onto their resolve. The law be damned! Some day, some way!

Eventually for the Varnells, life went back to some sort of
normalcy. Tom's remaining sisters got married, Rosanna to John
Sweeney and Etta to Dr. Abbott. The Abbotts soon moved to
Florida. Tom's older sister, Lina McGee, already married to Jasper, stayed to help at the ranch.

Tom took on a careless attitude that got him into trouble.
He was always game to participate in pranks either he or his
friends thought up. One night they passed a church meeting and
decided to shoot off their guns several times into the air outside.
They quickly melted into the darkness of the night, laughing
at the chaos they caused as people poured out of the building.
Fearless and never willing to back down from a challenge, Tom
was popular among the other young men who congregated regularly at the Varnell ranch, often for horse racing and games of
skill with guns or rifles. A natural leader, Tom was always willing
to give pointers on how to improve one's aim or handling of

firearms.

Invariably, concerned neighbors stopped by to let Docia know about Tom's escapades. She thanked them and gave assurance that Tom P was acting up because he missed his father. She was loath to reprimand him too much since the pain of that loss was still too raw. Docia relied on Tom. Sooner or later he'd grow out of his foolishness, which seemed to be his only outlet besides his interest in playing the fiddle and composing songs. In her estimation, he'd settle down before too long.

Docia enjoyed the long, cold evenings when she and Tom would pull out their fiddles, rosin up the bows, and try to outdo each other on hoe-downs and reels. Tom nearly always managed to continue after Docia would laughingly sit down exhausted, her arms aching. She remembered the time Tom brought home the tail of a large rattlesnake and poked it inside the cavity of the fiddle. Most fiddlers knew a rattler's tail kept small creatures, varmints, and even spiders from nesting inside.

Four years later life took an unexpected turn. In the Varnell mail one day was an unsigned letter stating that one A. P. Fisher was back in Hill County, living close to the small community of Brandon, east of Hillsboro. The informant claimed that Fisher was seen in a local saloon bragging about the killing, saying Varnell deserved being shot full of holes. Docia put her hands up to her eyes. Four long lonely years and now this scoundrel was bragging? Well, the time had come. Time for a reckoning.

"Tom P, come here!" Docia yelled out the back door.

Sitting on a fence watching the horses being exercised, Tom practically fell off in his haste to get down. During his eighteen years, his mother had not often yelled like that. Arriving in the kitchen, he took one glance at the determined look on her face and in her eyes. He knew his mother was more than just agitated.

"Calm down, Mother. Tell me why you're so worked up!" spoke Tom, shutting the back door.

"Tom P, our time's come," announced Docia. "How'd you like to help me take care of one of the men who killed Pap?"

"Maybe you'd better tell me what you have in mind," Tom replied.

"Just got word A. P. Fisher's back in the county, braggin' about Pap's death. Just can't abide that. If'n the law won't do nothin', I certainly will," Docia decreed vehemently, wringing out a wet rag over the sink as if it were a chicken's neck.

"Mother, too much time has passed for us to hope the law will get involved. Those men dry-gulched Pap, but we have no evidence to prove it."

"I know, Son," replied Docia wiping off the kitchen table. "Time to mete out our own justice. That man walks around braggin' while Pap's six feet under."

"As much as I'd like to plug Fisher, I don't think the law will take kindly to us forming our own vigilance committee," cautioned Tom, feeling both excitement and uneasiness mingling in his stomach.

"We don't need anyone else. Enough time's passed. They won't suspect us," exclaimed Docia, knowing Tom would not need much in the way of convincing.

Docia finally sat down. As she outlined her plan, Tom went from being skeptical to nodding his head. They chose a Saturday morning. Tom scouted the area and reported back that he'd found the place where Fisher was living. White Creek was close by the man's house and still running from the spring rains.

When dawn arrived on the appointed day, Docia carefully mixed ashes and buttermilk until the consistency was perfect. She took one of their bay mares and went to work 'painting.' When she finished, the bay looked like a mottled gray mare, unlike any horse on the Varnell ranch.

Tom saddled up and waved one hand at his mother, taking off down Ash Creek. He disguised himself in old, cast-off clothing and a greasy, gray felt hat he'd found among some belongings a previous hired hand had left behind. In this disguise no one would recognize him since he was known to be a snappy dresser when out in public. Tom tried to control his nerves. He felt he owed both his mother and his father to do this. He needed a cool head and steady fingers. All that target practice made him feel confident, but this was no childish prank.

Tom hummed a tune that he had worked out as a fiddle composition a couple of years before – "Some Day, Some Way." This was the day. He hummed the tune repetitiously, which served to calm his nerves at last.

The intended house came into view soon enough. Tom stopped and hid along the banks of White Creek, waiting for the sun to get higher in the sky. As morning daylight filtered through the tree leaves, Tom left his hiding place, riding slowly to the hitching post as he would on any ordinary day. Remaining in the saddle, Tom wiped his sweaty palms on his pants. He pulled the loaded pistol out of its holster.

"Hey, Fisher, you in there? Can I have a word with ya?"

Tom deliberately kept his tone friendly to make it seem like a neighbor had stopped by. He lowered the gray hat over his brow so the shadow made by the sun partially hid his face.

Fisher came out, closing the door behind him. He stepped off the porch toward Tom who lifted his six-gun at that very moment. Tom didn't say a word. He just fired, staying only long enough to note that Fisher was hit dead heart center.

Feeling dazed, Tom put away his father's gun and turned the bay quickly toward the road leading into Brandon. When he got out of sight of the Fisher place, he turned back toward White Creek. He hoped that anyone who caught a glimpse out a window or from a distance would not be able to describe his face, upon which he had smeared dirt to look like a day old beard. Tom ran the horse through the water in White Creek a ways. He jumped off briefly and, using a brush, got the rest of the 'paint' off. He quickly washed his own face, then changed his clothes and hat from a saddlebag he'd left earlier on the creek bank. Taking off for home, Tom had traveled only a couple of miles along the main road when an excited farmer passed him, riding hard.

Turning back, the agitated man yelled, "Did ya see a scruffy lookin' cowboy, wearing a blue flannel shirt and an old weather-beaten gray hat, ridin' a gray mare?"

Tom just shook his head. "Can't say as I did. What's the trouble?"

The farmer didn't tarry. He continued on, hollering something about a shooting and that he had to get the sheriff.

Tom turned his face to feel the warmth of the rays of the morning sun as he traveled back home. He felt satisfaction for completing the task necessary to avenge his father's death but also sensed that on this day he had left his childhood irrevocably behind.

Tom and his mother kept an eye on the front gate for several days thereafter, but no one appeared to ask questions. Neither did the Varnells inquire as to the health of Fisher. Tom finally had a fiddle tune no longer needed in his repertoire.

Tom P shook the long-ago memories loose, noticing 'Cane stood still at the crossroads. How long had he sat there? Well, he was in no hurry. To the right, Tom could see the road his Pap had traveled the day he was murdered.

Tom stored away his memories and turned 'Cane to the left heading toward Abbott. Even after all these years, he still missed his father. He started whistling again. Maybe by the time he arrived in Abbott, he'd have the melody worked out to his new composition.

CHAPTER THREE

2 December 1881

Nine-year-old Guy McGee knelt down in the dirt. Sticking the tip of his tongue out the corner of his mouth, he concentrated on drawing a perfect circle with a stick. Ed, his seven-year-old brother, watched while holding the precious bag of glass marbles their Uncle Tom P had brought them from Fort Worth the previous month. Their three-year-old brother, Alf, was also attentively looking on.

"Got it!" exclaimed Guy, reaching for the leather marble bag.

Ed was too quick for him though, upending the contents into the circle and grabbing the blue and red taw that was his favorite shooter.

"No fair!" protested Guy. Being stronger, he knew he could wrestle the marble away, but he didn't want to fight with his younger brother. His mother had fussed at him the last time, reminding him that he was supposed to set an example. While he didn't much care about that, Guy did not want to face the hickory stick his mother kept in the pantry for the times when her lectures didn't get the desired results. Besides, he'd be able to get that taw another time.

"Hey, can I play too?" asked Alf, squatting down next to Guy.

"You're too little, Alf. Jist watch `n learn," commanded Guy, the self-appointed leader.

Alf's bottom lip quivered. He said no more but did grumble a bit under his breath. Ignoring Alf, Guy continued to set up for a game of 'keepsies,' while also watching his grandmother's house. He had heard raised voices several times. He knew his mother was telling Grandmother Docia the news that they would be moving to West Texas soon. Pa had taken off to see about it, leaving Mother the task of telling her own mother. Guy could tell from some of the loud talking that Grandmother was not taking it too well. He turned his attention back to the marble game. Noting that Ed wasn't holding the shooter quite right, Guy gave in to wanting to show his superior ability. He leaned over.

"Ed, hold the shooter this way, between your thumb and first finger to aim it right; then put your knuckle down before you flick," he instructed while demonstrating. Ed managed to knock two marbles out of the circle on his first try.

"Gee, thanks!" Ed exclaimed.

Guy realized too late he might have made a mistake. Queen wandered by but quickly moved away when the boys slapped at her to protect their marble circle. She ambled over to the fence where eleven-year-old Gus McGee and Tom were watching the hired hands work. One of the four-year-old blood bay stallions had just been brought into the corral.

"Time to break that one to the saddle," commented Tom to his nephew while scratching Queen behind the ears.

"How do you know when to do it?" queried Gus.

"He's four years old. We'll put him up for sale soon, and we can get a much better price if he's saddle broke."

"Why're you selling him?"

"We don't keep many stallions around here, only the ones we want to use for stud service and personal use. Our ranch herd's mostly made up of brood mares along with growing colts.

This stallion has good, clean straight legs, a short back, and long, sloping shoulders. He'll make a good saddle horse at fifteen hands in height," explained Tom patiently.

Gus watched as Matt, the hired hand, lassoed the blood bay from the center of the wooden corral. Matt pulled the rope tight next to his leather chaps with his gloved right hand. He let the horse continue to run around the corral a few times, snapping a saddle blanket toward him. Dale, his backup, stood by with another lasso in case it was needed. Matt finally tied the bay to a post, and with Dale's help, they got the hackamore, blanket, and saddle on, adjusting the cinch. The stallion was less than cooperative. Dale finally twisted the horse's ear to keep him still. Placing his boot in the stirrup, Matt reached for the horn and hoisted himself onto the saddle, signaling for Dale to turn the stallion loose. Dale quickly retreated to the top of the fence.

"Now, the real fun begins!" declared Gus, in anticipation, and he wasn't disappointed. The horse quickly tried to throw his rider off, leaping and bucking. Often all four hooves were off the ground at the same time.

"One of these days you'll be able to do that," offered Tom.

Gus's eyes widened. He watched Matt holding on for all he was worth.

"But not for a few years," Tom hastily added.

"How come Matt doesn't have his spurs on?" asked Gus.

"Whilst some cowboys use spurs, we don't. Many times it makes a horse pitch somethin' fierce. It's really not necessary when breaking a horse to the saddle," Tom answered, who then called out good naturedly, "Hey, cowboy! You're pulling leather like a tenderfoot."

Matt was forced to make a hasty dismount, landing in the dirt. Dusting himself off while retrieving his hat, Matt let Dale go after the bronc.

Wiping his face with his kerchief, Matt hollered back at Tom, "I'd like to see you ride that one. I bet I'd see you git throwed and bite the dust, too!"

"I wouldn't want to deprive you of the pleasure!" called back Tom, who had ridden his share of unbroken horses already. Nowadays, he left most of the horse breaking to the hired hands he personally trained.

"How long does it take to break a horse to a saddle?" asked Gus, amazed that Matt could be laughing after taking such a hard spill.

"Just depends. Some're easier than others. Can be done in a day but usually takes a few days or even weeks. The ones we're workin' with now we'll take into the Waco market."

"Can I go?" pleaded Gus earnestly.

"As much as I'd love for you to come along, you know it's not up to me. You'd better ask your mother. It's an all-day trip," Tom replied.

Gus's face fell immediately. "I know what she'll say. With Dad away checking on that land west of here, she's already told me I have to do his chores as well as mine. I'm surprised she let me come over this mornin' with her."

Tom had caught wind of the impending move from his brother-in-law, Jasper McGee, the last day before he left for his trip to West Texas, but Tom had wisely kept his mouth shut to his mother. When he saw his sister, Lina, arrive earlier that morning, he had vacated the kitchen fast enough. He wasn't about to get caught in the crossfire between the two strong-willed women.

"Tell you what! I'll see if your mother will let me take you into Hillsboro on Saturday to see the MKT train station," Tom promised.

"Really! You're the best, Uncle Tom!" Gus whooped, looking at his uncle through shining eyes. "What does MKT stand for?"

"Missouri, Kansas, and Texas Railroad. Most everybody just calls it the Katy Railroad though," replied Tom. "Runs from Fort Worth through Hillsboro and on down to Waco. I've heard it goes all the way below Austin. Railroads will soon enough take people all over this great state. I'll come visit you in West Texas."

"You promise?" asked Gus.

"You bet," Tom answered readily.

"I've not seen many trains. Maybe one'll be coming into the station whilst we're there. Can't wait. Thanks!" Gus added, "Hope we don't have to take my little brothers."

Laughing, Tom's eyes softened as he looked at his young nephew. He reached over and tousled Gus's dark blond hair knowing without a doubt he would miss Gus when he moved.

"We'll see if'n we can make that happen," Tom offered, turning his attention back to the corral where Matt was leading in a four-year-old sorrel. The sun was bright on this late fall day, and it actually felt warm. They were having a bit of what his mother called an Indian summer, which he hoped would last. Except for short cold spells when a norther came through, they rarely had much in the way of winter weather before January.

In the house, Lina McGee was in a heated discussion with her mother. Occasionally, she glanced out the window to make sure Guy, Ed, and Alf were still getting along. She didn't have to worry about five-year-old Rosa Belle who was in the parlor playing with her favorite rag doll.

"I just don't understand why you and Jasper are so bent on leaving Hill County," Docia continued her complaint. "We have plenty of work right here to keep Jasper busy."

"That's just it, Mother. Jasper wants his own place with room to grow. So do I in a way. I want to make it clear that I support him in doing this. Land's too expensive here. The seventy acres you and Pap gave us isn't enough for our growing family."

"But why Tom Green County, Lina? You'll be moving hundreds of miles from here," objected Docia.

"It's a golden opportunity with the new law. They're selling off land in West Texas at fifty cents an acre for all un-appropriated public land. We want to take advantage before all the good land's gone," Lina explained. "That's why Jasper's gone to Tom Green. He's heard of some good land close to the Concho River, and there's talk of a new community close by. So we wouldn't be that far from civilization."

"But what about Indians? You'll be settling on land they believe belongs to them."

"Trouble from the Indians ended since Fort Concho and Camp Elizabeth were established. Most of the Indians have been pushed westward or placed on reservations. I'm more concerned about the ranchers with large spreads. They don't seem happy with newcomers, but Jasper says we're not the only ones moving to Tom Green. He thinks these ranchers will get used to us once we arrive. This new barbed wire that's being used is certainly creating a stir among the ranchers. They're used to all the open range that up until now has been public land. Jasper's heard there's been some fence cutting going on," Lina stopped, realizing she may have said too much.

"Doesn't sound too safe to me, Lina," Docia complained.

"Mother, I will miss you, but we have to seize this opportunity. You and Pap took a chance coming to Texas. Hill County didn't have many settlers then, either. It'd have been safer for you to stay in Mississippi. We're simply doing the same thing by moving west. Besides, Tom P's nineteen years old. Pap always meant for him to take control of this ranch. It's his birthright. Is it so hard to understand why Jasper wants his own ranch? We have our own boys to consider," argued Lina.

"Well, you make sense, but I don't have to like it. Just seems so far away," mumbled Docia, not quite ready to accept the inevitable. "Still think Tom P needs a guiding hand from a male relative like Jasper. He won't get that if you two leave. You know as well as I do that Tom P and Jasper speak the same horse language."

Just then, Guy, Ed, and Alf ran into the kitchen struggling to see who could get through the door first. They shouted in unison, "We have company!"

Docia looked out the window in time to hear Queen barking her announcement of the imminent arrival of a visitor. The front gate was far enough away that they could always see visitors coming before they arrived on the front porch.

"George Walker. I'm sure he's here to see Tom P. I wish he wouldn't come around so often. I don't think he's a good influence on Tom," Docia stated, watching George skirt around the house on his way to the corral.

"Isn't he Henry Walker's son?" asked Lina.

"Yep! Henry's a fine man. He and Elizabeth have six sons, including George," commented Docia. "He's always around when Tom P gets into a scrape."

"No need to worry," replied Lina. "I know Tom P has been a bit wild lately, but that's just a part of growing up. If he could find a good woman soon, I think it would do him a lot of good," Lina offered.

"I don't think good women are the kind he has on his mind right now," Docia stated, matter of factly.

"Mother!" Lina was shocked, especially since Guy, Ed, and Alf were still standing there. "Boys, go on outside and play. We'll be leaving soon! Have a feelin' the three of you are going to need an extra scrubbin' when you take your weekly bath tonight."

At the tone in their mother's voice, the three boys scooted out the door. Then Lina did something she rarely had done. She put her arm around her mother whose tense shoulders spoke volumes. Out the window, Docia could see Tom P and George laughing at some joke one of them had made. Only time would tell, but right now, her daughter's pending move was uppermost in her mind…

Docia realized as she crossed the yard to the barn where the hired hands bunked that her mind had been reliving the time right before her daughter had moved to West Texas, twenty-two years previously. She hated to admit that the move had suited Adeline and Jasper just fine. They had truly prospered. As Lina had predicted, the new community of Sterling City had been established along with a new county carved out of Tom Green, named Sterling.

Knocking loudly, Docia stood at the door to the workers' quarters. "Jethro? Mack? Are you up yet? Tom P has gone to Abbott this morning, but he wants you to get started on exercising the horses!" Docia shouted. "Tom said once you're done, you can ride Solidad. So get crackin'!"

Her persistence finally paid off when Mack stuck his hair-tousled, sleepy-eyed face out the wooden door.

"Morning, Miz Varnell." Mack rubbed his eyes and yawned again. "Sorry 'bout that. Sorta made it a late night. We'll get up shortly. Does Glory have a hot cup of Arbuckle's left?" he added hopefully.

"Maybe, if'n you two don't take too long gettin' up," admonished Docia. "And wash up 'fore you come into the kitchen!" She added for good measure.

"Did you say Tom P went into Abbott?" Mack asked.

"Yes. Why're you askin'?" Docia countered.

"No reason 'ceptin' I heard last night that the Ferguson boys have a bone to pick with him. I'm just surprised he'd go to their part of Hill County," Mack answered.

"What kind of bone are you talking about?" Docia asked briskly.

"Somethin' about their sister. Didn't pay too much 'tention to it. They're hot-heads anyhow. I'm sure Tom P wouldn't have headed that way if'n there was goin' to be trouble," Mack offered.

"Hmm. Well, the two of you need to git on up!"

Docia left the barn knowing there was only a 50/50 chance of those two getting up any time soon. She shaded her eyes against the glare of the sun as she peered down the road. What a hot July day it was going to be! She wondered again for the umteenth time what Tom was about to tell her before he left. Not much telling, though. He didn't share much of his personal affairs with her anymore like he did when he was younger. She sighed. Tom P still seemed to invite girl trouble. They were drawn to him like bees to honey, and he always returned their attention regardless of the consequences.

As she walked across the yard, Docia spied the corral. Pausing, she could still mentally see George and Tom so many years before talking and laughing by the fence. So much had happened between those two since then. She knew George was living in Waco now. She also knew that the Walkers had practically disowned their wayward son. Such a shame, since he'd been a good friend to Tom when it counted. She headed back into the house to check if Glory still had some coffee on the stove for Mack and Jethro.

CHAPTER FOUR

10 May 1882

George Walker and Tom P rode side by side as they made their way south to Waco on a Monday morning. Pleasant looking but far from handsome, George was slightly taller than Tom P, though neither of them could be considered big men. George's dark hair was always giving him problems because of two inconveniently located cowlicks. When necessary, though, he used some pomade to good effect. He usually just kept his hat on his head except when it was too impolite, like when his mother insisted on him going to church. As he grew older, he managed most Sundays to make himself scarce before she had time to tell him to get dressed.

George realized early-on that he did not have any desire to spend his life busting sod or raising cattle. His pa called him lazy and good for nothing, but George just didn't see the reason for working so hard. One thing George did know for sure was that his brothers were too serious-minded. They seemed to side with Pa on everything. So any excuse he could come up with to go over to the Varnell ranch was welcomed. He enjoyed being known as Tom's friend because of his popularity with the girls. George couldn't play a fiddle like Tom, but he knew he was pretty good in the saddle.

"What did you tell your mother before you left?" asked

George.

"I told her I needed to check the market before taking some horses down to sell. She was so preoccupied with my sister's move to West Texas, I'm not sure she was even listening," replied Tom.

"Speaking of horses. How's that horse doing that the Ketons got aholt of?" asked George.

"He's doing better."

"So what really happened?"

"You know the Keton boys have hated me for a long time. It goes back to a horse deal they changed their minds on after it was sealed. I've heard from several friends that they've been spreading stories about me. I don't give a damn, but this was a bit much. They demanded Pretty Boy in exchange for the horse they bought. When I refused, saying a deal was a deal, they waited until I was in town to sneak in and take Pretty Boy. They skinned him up and sent him back to us as pay-back. They probably figured he would die because of exposure."

"How'd you save him?"

"Mother coated him with a mixture of turpentine, coal oil, and lard," Tom answered. "It was a sorry process. We weren't sure he'd make it for a while, but he did. We can't sell him, as he'll never grow back his hair, but we can still use him for stud."

"What say we take care of the Ketons?" George offered.

"We'll see. I want to wait a bit. They're lookin' for a dust-up right now, probably even hoping to trap me. I know how to bide my time," Tom answered.

"Whatever you say," agreed George. "I'm lookin' forward to a little action in Waco, if you know what I mean. Did you hear about Deputy Autry?"

"What does he have to do with Waco?" asked a puzzled Tom.

"A lot!" George laughed. "Sheriff Cox sent him to the

McLennan County Jail to bring back Ben Hooker who's been charged with seduction here in Hill County. Instead of bringing him straight back, Autry decided to visit Two Street."

Tom laughed, "I guess Autry couldn't resist having himself some fun in Waco. But what happened to get him in trouble? Going to a prostitute ain't exactly illegal."

"It's in all the papers," replied George. "Autry went to Stella Hartridge's place and left Hooker downstairs with a friend he brought along. After drinking and visiting upstairs with a whore named Belle Talley, Autry kicked up such a row by drawing a pistol on Belle and smashing a mirror that Stella sent for the law. The city marshal found Hooker downstairs, drunk and watching the girls parade around. The marshal arrested all three and proceeded to take them to the calaboose. Right as the lawman was unlocking the door, Autry made a wild break for it. He must have been full as a tick from drinking whiskey `cause he ran down a blind alley and fell flat on his face, before the law collared him again."

"That's funny. I bet Sheriff Cox was embarrassed," Tom chuckled.

"Yep! Constable Stovall of Waco refused to turn over Hooker until Cox sent a more reliable deputy. I'm sure Cox wishes the papers never caught on to the story," laughed George.

George and Tom P were still chuckling about Sheriff Cox's embarrassment when they arrived in Waco. They crossed the bridge at the Brazos River, heading for the town trade square.

As it was First Monday Trade Day, the open market area was busy with buyers, sellers, and those just observing the action. Ranchers and farmers showed off their horses, mules, milk cows, and other stock. Making a deal, be it for cash or for an upgrade, was a bit like being actors on a stage. Each man took his role seriously, which was important if he hoped to make the best deal possible. Also important was not letting the other party see you sweat. Most could tell many a tale of besting others while keeping quiet about the times they ended up on the short end of a deal gone awry. Surveying the crowd, Tom spied J. C. Centervale over to the side. Waving, he sauntered over with George following behind.

"Howdy, J.C.!" greeted Tom shaking the older man's hand while looking at him eye to eye.

"Hey, Tom P. Come to town to do some tradin'?"

"Just observin', like you. See anything that's catchin' your fancy?" Tom asked nonchalantly. For once, he was glad he was dressed neatly in dark trousers, a white shirt, and buttoned gray vest. His long coat gave off an air of prosperity just right for conducting business.

"Naw. Not much. Mostly crow bait here today. When are you going to bring a bunch in? I'd like to look them over. I may be needing some good saddle horses soon," J. C. commented.

Just then two well-dressed ladies strolled by carrying parasols to protect them from the sun. The three men tipped their hats to them. No words were exchanged, but one looked at Tom a little longer than what was socially acceptable. He grinned back at her. Tom noted a smile tugging at the corner of her mouth. Blushing, she quickly averted her eyes as they moved away.

Turning back to Centervale, Tom offered, "Why don't you swing by the ranch? I'll give you a look-see before I haul my next batch over here. That's as good as having first crack at the best I have. Even so, I've got some government agents stopping by soon. If you come by first, though, I'll make you a deal, beings you've been a good customer in the past."

"Might just do that if I have time," J. C. stated. "How's that fine mother of yours? I haven't seen her in awhile."

"She's doing all right. Staying busy like the rest of us. She'll probably be at the next Democratic rally in Hillsboro. Think I'll go check out that bay filly over next to the fence. Good seeing ya," Tom replied.

Tom moved away, figuring he'd probably be seeing Centervale in a few days. He'd always been able to read people, except maybe when he'd had one too many whiskeys.

"Come on, George," called Tom after making a show of looking at a few horses. "Let's go down to Two Street."

The men turned their horses toward the Brazos River, working their way over to Waco's red light district. The brothels in the Two Street area had achieved quasi-legal status since 1879. Matilda Davis opened the first licensed house with ten single women working for her. Their occupation on the city records was listed as actresses. Soon rival establishments sprang up. The city council quickly passed an ordinance that confined the girls to an area dubbed the Reservation in an effort to keep vice confined to a small specific location.

"Before we go to Matilda Davis' fine establishment, let's get our photograph taken. How often do we dress up when we come into Waco?" Tom exclaimed.

"I guess so, if you're buying," quipped George, not entirely sure he wanted his picture taken. "I'm saving my money for a $2.00 whore."

"Wouldn't have offered if I didn't intend to do so. Say, do you want to go to Matilda's or try out Stella Moran's place later?" asked Tom.

"I guess it doesn't much matter. One whore's about the same as another," replied George with a controlled expression, trying to hide his excitement. He was happy that Tom P always seemed to be flush with a little extra cash to spend.

"Don't you sound jaded," shot back Tom laughing again.

George prophesied, "Tell you what. Some day, I'm going to own a saloon right here in Waco. And upstairs I intend to have the prettiest whores around."

"Well, I'll be damned but you sure aim high," laughed Tom.

"I'll be expecting to get a cut-rate when you get set up."

"Naw, I'll be chargin' you double," shot back George.

"You probably would," chuckled Tom.

"Let's get a wiggle on, cowboy," replied George, whose mind was already past posing for a photographer and on to sampling red lips and soft white thighs. He forced his mind back as he did not want his obvious anticipation to show up in the photograph.

Tom dismounted to tie his horse to the hitchrack, with George following suit, grabbing the bit of pomade he carried in his saddlebag for just such an occasion. With that, the two friends strolled into Jones' Photography Studio.

CHAPTER FIVE

26 July 1903

Tom P looked out across the cotton fields as he worked his way toward Abbott. The cotton bolls were starting to ripen early. The fields were richly green, promising a good crop for this year. With a little more rain, the harvest would be abundant. Tom and his mother had some land under cultivation, but his first love was still his horses. Business had not been quite as good as it had once been. While his mother still garnered a great deal of respect in Hill County, Tom's reputation was irreparably lost. He didn't give a damn what others thought of him. Even so, Tom would be the first to admit he had made mistakes, but he still believed to his very soul that nothing he had done should have cost him so much.

The events that forever changed his life and made trouble one of his constant companions happened twenty years earlier on a fair and balmy March evening in 1883. Spring was in the air, and he was only twenty-one years old . . .

Tom P and George Walker arrived at the railroad station in Hubbard City on the four o'clock from Waco. They retrieved their horses and headed for Sweeney's Saloon.

"Thanks for going to Waco with me," commented Tom. "My sister, Lina, and my brother-in-law, Jasper McGee, need my help in getting their horses shipped out to them. When they moved to Tom Green County last year, much of their stock was left here. Maybe you can help me drive the mares to Waco next Saturday."

"Be glad to, Tom P. I'm always looking for a reason to get out of the house. Pa can think of more chores for me than there are fleas on a birddog in the summer time," replied George. "Besides, I'm looking into moving to New Mexico and wondered what it would cost to ship stock there. If you weren't so tied to your mother's ranch, you could go on this little adventure with me."

"I'm surprised you're considering New Mexico. Thought you were going to open up your own saloon in Waco," Tom said teasingly.

"I'll need some start-up cash before I can open a saloon. Thought I'd run some cattle out there and maybe do a little prospecting. Of course, if you want to invest in my proposed business in Waco, I'd be set," George offered. "And you wouldn't have to pay for samplin' the wares."

"As inviting as that prospect might be," Tom laughed, "I'll have to pass on Waco for now. The ranch keeps me plenty busy."

"Suit yourself, cowboy," George quipped.

Walking into the saloon, Tom and George bellied up to the bar, and each ordered a beer. With the crowd being fairly thin inside, they could hear themselves without having to talk loudly.

"We made a good deal on that pair of .44 pistols we bought today," George stated, putting his beer mug down on the bar.

"I agree. Although I inherited Pap's gun, I'm glad to have my own pistol. I'll need it when I go out to West Texas with the horses. I probably won't tell Mother I have it for a while. She'd just fuss," said Tom.

"Well, a man's got to have protection now and again. Your

father might still be alive if he'd had his pistol with him that New Year's Day, and a man certainly needs a gun out west," interjected George.

Tom took a long sip. Thinking about Pap was still tough, even though seven years had passed. Zack Taylor entered the saloon. Seeing Tom and George over at the bar, he headed their way.

"Howdy, Tom P, George," Zack greeted them.

"Hey, Zack! Want a beer?" offered Tom.

"Naw. I don't have time for a beer. Thanks anyway. I just stopped in for a minute. Say, are you two goin' to the party the Land girls are throwin' this evening?" Zack asked.

"Are you talkin' about Emma Land?" asked Tom. "I didn't know they were havin' a party. Who all's invited?"

"Anyone who wants to come. Emma told me to spread the word," Zack answered.

"Well, we may join you later," responded George.

"See ya then." With that, Zack left out the swinging door.

Tom asked, "George, have you met the Land girls?"

"Naw. How well do you know them?" George asked.

"I've talked to Emma before. She was right friendly as I recall. I think her sister's name is Ella, though I don't know much about her," grinned Tom.

"Sounds like it might be a fun dance tonight. I say we go," responded George. "Do you know how to get out to their place?"

"I think so. I at least know the general direction. It's about three miles southwest of town. We can ask along the way if need be," Tom added.

After George and Tom finished their beers, they ordered another round plus a couple of bowls of stew with chunks of cornbread. They did not want to go to the party on empty stomachs. It was late afternoon when they set out for the Land farm.

As George and Tom neared the farmstead, the shadows were starting to lengthen and blend together into darkness. It was the point in the evening when one could no longer see clearly what lies ahead. Getting closer, they saw that lights were blazing through the windows of the sturdy farmhouse framed against the purpled sky. Laughter drifted out, floating across the evening air. The party was already in full swing, not in the main house but in a vacant tenant house nearby. George and Tom tied up their horses to the hitchrack. Putting their new pistols in their belts, they headed for the door. It was for show, as neither gun was loaded.

Although the door was open and they could see the young people inside, George and Tom knocked anyway. Answering the door was a pretty young woman. Her blond hair was swept back into a bun with just enough tendrils escaping to frame her face becomingly. Dark blue eyes stared at Tom and George.

"Hello and welcome," she greeted them.

"Howdy, miss," responded George.

"Evening, Miss Emma. We meet again," greeted Tom.

"Hello, Tom P," Emma smiled. Turning to George, she added, "And you are?"

"George Walker. Zack Taylor told us you were having a party. Hope we're not intruding?"

"Not at all. Any friend of Zack's is welcome. I'm glad you're here," Emma responded.

Emma shook George's outstretched hand, then looked past him at Tom. Her stare seemed to bore a hole through him. Undaunted, he cocked his head to the side and grinned back at her. Emma withdrew her hand from George's. Before she could speak to Tom again, a short, stocky man walked up behind her.

"Who's arrived, Sweetheart?" he asked.

"Arch, I'd like to introduce you to George Walker and Tom P Varnell."

Reaching past her, Arch shook their hands. He put his arm lightly across Emma's shoulders. "Howdy. I'm Arch Beasley. Miss Land and I are engaged to be married," he announced.

"Congratulations, old boy," George offered.

Tom noted a look of annoyance that flitted across Emma's face. Knowing Arch Beasley's fiancée was attracted to him, Tom continued to grin back at her. Arch squeezed Emma's shoulder, causing her to look away from Tom. To cover her momentary lapse, Emma immediately ushered the young men into the room where the party was taking place. Many of the young people standing about already knew George and Tom, who had frequently played his fiddle at other dances in the area. Talking stopped for a moment as they entered. Tom was surprised at how few girls were present. He did not have much time to puzzle through it, though, as Zack crossed the room to shake their hands. Edna Tidwell beat him to them.

"George, Tom P! I'm so glad you're here. Say, Tom P, did you bring your fiddle? I'd love to hear you play!" she exclaimed.

"No, I didn't, Edna. We weren't aware of this get-together until this afternoon. Sorry to disappoint you," replied Tom.

"Oh, but you don't have to disappoint us," stated another young lady who had also walked up to the new arrivals. "We have a fiddle if you're willing to grace us with a tune or two."

Tom turned toward the young woman, with the idea of declining. He only liked to play his own fiddle. Looking back at him was a female who looked a lot like Emma who had met them at the door. This girl was pretty and plump. She wore her abundant blond hair loose and cascading down her back. A button of a nose and long lashes framing her hazel eyes completed her soft round face.

"How could I refuse someone as pretty as you?" Tom replied. The young lady blushed and laughed at the same time.

Tom added, "Who might I have the honor of

addressing?"

"I'm Ella Land, and you're Tom P. I heard my sister greet you at the door," she smiled.

"Well, Miss Ella. I'll play this time just for you," Tom teased.

Handing the fiddle to Tom, Ella offered it in such a way that their fingers touched as Tom took it. He tested the strings and checked how well in tune it was. Tom then turned back to the crowd and started with a foot stomping reel. No one worried about dancing with a partner as there were so many more guys than girls. The music was too good not to move with it. Some of the guys had already drunk enough whiskey to lose any inhibitions they might have had before they arrived. The three girls present were Emma, Ella, and Edna, and they had a sip or two as well, when Mr. Land was not in the room. Tom's boots kept rhythm on the floor as he entertained the crowd. When he finished, the partygoers started making requests.

Playing a few more tunes, Tom followed Ella around the room with his twinkling eyes. Every time their eyes locked, Ella blushed. Tom's fingers flew across the strings while he used the bow to pour forth the passion he felt for the music. Tom finished by playing a soulful ballad full of yearning and sadness. The crowd clapped their appreciation while begging for more.

"Y'all, I have to take a break. Surely, someone else can take up the fiddle and play a tune," Tom announced. "Here, John, I know you play well."

Grinning, John Hardy stepped up to take a turn. Tom gratefully handed over the fiddle while looking around. He spied Ella over to the side. She had her back to him while talking to a young man he didn't know. Tom could tell by the look on the young man's face that he was clearly smitten. Tom decided to bide his time. He knew Ella was interested in him but was pretending indifference. He had played this courtship ritual too many times before not to be able to read the signals from the fairer sex. He moved around the room talking and laughing. Emma Land found Tom off to the side enjoying the music.

"Hey, Tom P, want to dance?" she asked.

"Naw, I'm just enjoying the music. Since we last met, you've acquired a fiancé," Tom teased. "I'm not too sure he'd appreciate me cutting in on his territory."

"Arch is more serious about us being a couple than I am. He's older you know. I told him I'd seriously consider his proposal. He was being a little possessive, I guess. Besides, I haven't seen you since you stole that kiss from me a couple of months ago," Emma accused.

Tom leaned toward Emma. Curling his fingers into a loose fist, Tom tilted her chin up slightly. "Stole? I don't quite remember it that way. Want to get reacquainted? I'm willing to give Arch Beasley a run for his money."

"You're so wicked, Tom P," laughed Emma leaning closer.

Looking up, Tom watched Arch Beasley rapidly cross the room. Arch grabbed Emma by the hand and pulled her onto the dance floor without saying a word to Tom. Emma glanced back at Tom, who chuckled at her fiancé's obvious jealousy. Emma sure didn't seem to want to be with her future husband, he thought.

Tom moved away. He wasn't really interested in watching Emma and her fiancé dance. He walked over to Ed Bryant, who passed him the jug of whiskey. Taking a big swig, Tom said, "Thanks, Ed. I needed that! I may be needing more later."

Tom headed back across the room as a line dance was just about to get started. He found Ella, finally alone and in between partners. He pulled her off to the side.

"You surely do play a fine tune on the fiddle, Tom P," offered Ella coquettishly.

"Thanks for the compliment," Tom commented. "I had to

quit playing for awhile since it does seem mighty hot in here."

"I do believe it's a bit cooler outside," Ella replied in a flirtatious manner.

Tom grinned, "Then, how about you and me taking a stroll outside?"

"I don't know. I don't much think I should leave my guests." Ella's manner belied her voiced hesitation.

Tom looked around the room. Her earlier admirer was now engaged in conversation with Zack Taylor, and Emma Land was nowhere to be seen. Even George was not in sight. The timing was just right.

"They're all busy and won't miss you right now," Tom commented. "I kept watching you while I was playing the fiddle, and I decided you're the prettiest girl I've seen in a long time. It's too crowded in here for us to get better acquainted."

Ella smiled, excitement turning her cheeks rosy. Tom cupped his warm hand under her elbow and quickly steered her out of the room, leaving out the side door into the shadowy night. Only the glow of lanterns from inside provided a faint light as they strolled into the darkness.

CHAPTER SIX

6 March 1883

Walking across the yard, both Tom and Ella breathed in the cool night air, talking little but enjoying each other's company. Tom pulled Ella's arm through his. They headed away from the sounds of frivolity in the party house.

"It's after midnight. I love staying up late, don't you?" Ella finally spoke.

"Of course. I understand your family moved to Texas from Wisconsin recently," Tom offered conversationally.

"Why yes," said Ella. "I was born in Wisconsin. My parents actually came from Illinois. We had a farm, but it was just so cold in the wintertime. I like Texas better. I wasn't sure when we first arrived because, well, we just didn't know anybody. But then everyone just seems so friendly. I don't miss Wisconsin at all. At least not now." Ella paused in her chatter. Taking advantage, Tom leaned in and kissed her lightly on the nose.

"Why'd you do that?" she laughed.

"Because you are so pretty. I'm surprised you don't already have a beau, but I'm glad," responded Tom.

"My sister has to marry first. I haven't really thought about having a steady beau," Ella answered.

Tom replied, "Maybe I'll just apply for the job." They both laughed. When they got far enough away from the party house that the lights no longer shone on them, Tom stopped and turned Ella toward him.

"You seem so relaxed with me. I like that. Have you ever been kissed like a man should kiss a woman?" he asked.

"Well," Ella started.

Before she could say anything else, Tom placed his hands on either side of Ella's face. His kiss on her mouth was gentle. Tom put his arms around her, drawing Ella close. Tom could feel her trembling, while tasting the slight residue of whiskey on her lips. He was pleased when Ella kissed him back, softly at first, but the kisses soon became more and more passionate. She seemed to fit perfectly within his embrace. She put her arms around his neck. Emboldened, he ran his fingers upward along the side of her dress. As he lightly caressed her warm body, Tom felt her shiver, but she did not move away.

The strain against the buttons of his pants told Tom he was fast approaching the point of no return. He decided to find out just how far she was willing to go. He placed his hand on the small of her back and eased her down onto the grassy ground, half expecting resistance but pleased when there was none. As Tom's embrace grew more insistent, Ella matched his caresses. Time ceased for the couple as desire and fulfillment became their reality.

Inside the house, Emma quickly moved from room to room. She found Arch in the small area for refreshments near where the others were dancing. He was eating some bread and butter.

"Have you seen Ella?" she asked.

"Why no. Is there something wrong?" Arch replied, finishing his last bite.

"I don't know," Emma responded irritably. "I haven't seen her for awhile. Tom P Varnell is missing as well." Emma abruptly turned to leave the room, bumping immediately into George

Walker in the doorway. Arch was close behind her.

"Have you seen Ella or Tom P?" Emma asked briskly.

"Not lately. Don't worry. They'll show up soon enough," George replied.

Emma, exasperated at his nonchalant attitude, explained, "I have to find them before Father does! I shouldn't have told him they were missing. He is really upset."

"Well, that wasn't very smart. I guess I'd better help," offered George. "What do you think your father will do if he finds Emma and Tom P together?"

"I'm not sure," Emma hesitated. "He's liable to do anything when he's angry. I saw him leave the party. I think he headed for the barn. We have a chance to find them before he does."

"Did you say something to get him upset?" asked George. "I don't understand why your father is already so angry."

Emma ignored the question she didn't care to answer. "Would you just go look for them? I don't think either Ella or Tom P will want to face Father's wrath if he's the one to find them first."

George headed outside. The initial search yielded no results. Frustrated, Emma announced she was going back into the party to look. While Arch followed Emma, George stayed in the yard. A few minutes later Emma came back out with Arch trailing behind. Spying George, she headed in his direction.

"Any luck?" she asked tersely.

"Not yet. I found Joe Phillpot asleep on the ground. I guess he had too much whiskey," George replied.

Emma went over to the man and nudged him with her foot. "Get up. What are you doing sleeping out here?" Emma spoke harshly.

George interrupted, "Listen. I think I just heard some low voices from over near that other empty house." Emma took off in the direction George indicated.

On the ground about a hundred yards from the search party, Tom held Ella in an embrace. He was so intent on her that he had not heard anyone calling their names.

"Tom, I'm worried. If Father finds out what we've done, he will kill me," Ella whimpered after a few moments.

"I think not, honey," Tom replied trying not to show his vexation at her getting remorseful so quickly. He stroked her hair. "I'll protect you. He'll have to answer to me first."

"But we've been gone too long from the party."

"Don't worry so much. We'll go back pretty soon," Tom replied, deciding it might just be time to go.

Before Tom could get up though, he heard a voice, "Ella? Is that you?" Emma arrived where the couple lay on the ground. "What is the meaning of this?"

"Oh, my god, Emma!" called Ella in a stricken voice. "Get him off me! I haven't been able to make him quit!"

Tom was too surprised at Ella's changed demeanor to say anything. Before he could react, Tom felt himself being yanked off the ground by his hair. The cold air on his exposed skin had a sobering effect.

"What the hell do you think you're doing?" Tom objected.

Emma yelled, "Tell me first what you were doing with my sister!"

"I'd say it's none of your business!" Tom snapped back at her. "Why didn't you just leave us be?"

Thankful for the darkness, Tom reached to pull up his pants. Emma grabbed his arm, keeping him off balance. As he staggered, Tom saw Arch standing next to Emma.

"Damn it, what the hell is he doing here?" Tom challenged.

Neither Emma nor Arch answered. Instead, Arch Beasley backed away. Then, he quickly turned and walked rapidly back toward the party house without looking back. Emma was left with George, Ella, and Tom.

Ella stood up quickly, shaking her clothes back down into place. "Emma, don't be angry. Help me. Where is Father?"

"He's heading this way, you fool. You're in big trouble. You'd better get to the house before he finds you here," snapped Emma.

Lifting her skirts, Ella took off running for the house. Fixated on a clearly agitated Emma, Tom barely noticed Ella leave. He and Emma glared at each other. George moved closer to Tom's side but did not speak.

"How could you do this after what you said to me inside?" Emma cried, still clutching Tom.

George urged in a low voice before Tom could answer Emma's accusation, "I think we'd better get out of here, old boy. Our horses are right where we left them."

"I can't until I find my pistol. I dropped it somewhere," protested Tom. He grabbed Emma's arm, trying to extricate himself from her hold on his sleeve, giving the appearance of being in an embrace.

"Let go of me, Tom P. My father will be angry enough to kill both of us if he finds us like this!" Emma hissed at him.

"I would never let that happen!" exclaimed Tom.

With little time left, George urged both of them, "Mr. Land is headed this way. I think the less said about this the better."

Tom turned back toward the party house just as Jonah Land arrived, carrying a lantern in one hand. Tom noticed something in Land's other hand, but he couldn't quite make out what it was. The shadows along with the bright light in his face obscured Tom's vision. What he could see was the angry expression on Mr. Land's face.

"Daughter, you'd better explain! What's going on here?" yelled Jonah Land.

"Father, calm down," pleaded Emma, finally moving away

from Tom. "It's not what you think."

"I'm well aware of what's happening here. Go to the house where you belong. I'll take care of you and your sister later," Jonah commanded.

"What are you going to do?" Emma asked in a fearful voice. Jonah pushed Emma aside, getting closer to Tom.

"What is the meaning of this!" roared Jonah. "You son-of-a-bitch! You have defiled and ruined my daughters. How dare you come to my home and do this?"

Before Tom could answer, Jonah raised his arm. Tom did not have time to react as the wooden handle of an axe came down on him. His arm caught part of the blow that was aimed at his face, but he was not able to deflect it entirely. As pain exploded, Tom realized that this man intended to inflict serious harm.

"Get back, sir! I am a desperate man!" warned Tom, glancing around for anything he could use to protect himself.

Standing close by, George called, "Tom, here! Catch! It's loaded."

Tom caught the .44 six-gun, neatly wrapping his finger around the trigger. He turned back toward Jonah, intending to issue another warning. Jonah Land was already coming at him. With no time to think of an alternative, Tom pumped a bullet into Land at close range. In a reflexive action, he squeezed the trigger a second time.

Tom knew immediately that he had mortally wounded Jonah Land, who fell to the ground without saying a word. The impact caused the axe to be flung a distance away. The lantern rolled to the side. With a sputter the light went out.

Shortly after the second shot rang out, the young people poured out of the party house. Screaming, Emma rushed to the side of her father. Tom and George moved away from the gathering crowd.

"We'd best be leavin' this scene, Tom P. You're not goin' to be safe when the others find out what happened here," George urged.

Tom and George ran for their horses. Landing in their saddles quickly, they melted into the night as the cloak of darkness folded over them. The yelling and screaming soon faded into the distance.

After hearing gunfire, Ella returned to the site where so recently she and Tom had been in a warm embrace. In her hurry to find out who had been shot, Ella did not look at the grassy spot where she had lain with him. Only the stars and the faint light from the distant windows aided her as she arrived.

"Father!" Ella screamed, seeing him on the ground. "Is he dead?" she cried to Emma before fainting.

"Arch, light that lantern. Then get Ella back into the house!" commanded Emma, regaining her self-control. "Zack, go into Hubbard and get the sheriff or a deputy. Tell them my father has been murdered by Tom P Varnell."

Milling around, the crowd started murmuring in great surprise. They talked about Tom's reputation for being a bit wild, but few ever thought him capable of being this dangerous.

Elizabeth Land arrived and turned her husband over onto his back. She was softly weeping at the devastation to her husband caused by the bullets. She knelt down and cradled his head.

"I never wanted to come here. I told Jonah I had a bad feeling. I told him," Elizabeth mourned. She rocked back and forth holding her dead husband. She kept whispering, "I told him. I told him."

"Mother, let's get Father into the house. The sheriff will be here soon," coaxed Emma.

"Do you really think we should move his body, Emma?" asked Arch, having just returned from the house.

Emma glared at him. "I will not leave my father out here. Are you going to do as I ask or not?"

With the help of several of the young men, Arch carried Jonah Land into the house and laid him out on the kitchen table. Emma put her arm around her mother, who was still crying, and led her toward the house. She looked up at the cloudy night sky. The darkness was pervasive, hiding the aftermath of the evening's disastrous turn of events. Emma shivered. She turned to her mother.

"I swear Tom P Varnell will pay for this," she vowed. "Whatever it takes! This I swear!"

CHAPTER SEVEN

6 March 1883

Tom P and George moved as quickly as possible through the midnight-shrouded countryside in an effort to put miles between themselves and the sudden nightmare of events neither could have predicted earlier. Their progress was hampered because of the cloudy night. Both had grown up in Hill County and knew the back roads and pathways well. They also knew the chances of a posse coming after them before morning were pretty slim, but they stayed off the main roads to keep their movements hidden to anyone traveling late at night. Shock settling in prevented much conversation between the two friends for the first few miles. Haste was their companion, but they were forced to slow down in an effort to protect their horses from stepping in holes hidden in the dark shadows cast across the plowed fields. Tom P finally pulled up next to a small stream so that his stallion could get a drink.

"Do you really think we should be stopping?" queried George.

"No need to tire our horses out unnecessarily. We don't want to end up on foot. Plus, I need time to think," Tom replied.

George asked, "Where can we go? Certainly not to your ranch or to my father's place. We're in a fine mess now."

The conversation stopped for a few moments as the enormity of their situation settled upon them like an unwanted blanket. Each wanted to breathe deeply, but neither seemed able to do so. Tom P stared out at the night-covered landscape as he sorted through possible directions they could take. Finally, Tom led as they took their horses upstream for a distance to shake off any trail scent, and then, he headed north again.

"It would help if you'd tell me where we're going," complained George.

Tom replied, "I had to figure out who lives the closest that we can trust. That person is G. W. McNeese. He'll be able to help us."

Silas Barber and his wife, Mary, moved along in their buggy through the dark night. They were close neighbors and good friends to the Lands. Their oldest daughter, Maryann, had been invited to the party. They had been puzzled when she declined. Now they were thankful she had not attended.

Silas and Jonah belonged to the local Masonic Lodge. Word of the shooting reached the Barbers just after midnight. Mary awakened Maryann to tell her they would be gone and not to expect them back for several hours. Mary gathered supplies to help with visitors who would be paying their respects, and they set off for the Land place.

As the farmhouse came into view, the only indication that things were not as they should be was the blaze of light shining from the kitchen windows, although it was well after midnight. As they got closer, Silas and Mary spotted a few people milling about. Mary was the first to alight, heading for the main residence. Silas took his time hitching the buggy securely, but soon enough followed his wife.

Mary rushed into the house and over to Elizabeth Land's side. After hugging her, Mary, without asking anyone, busied herself stoking up the fire in the stove and starting some coffee to boil. Silas went over to Emma and Arch. "Miss Emma, is there anything I can do?"

"Thank you, Mr. Barber, for coming. Not much we can do until the law arrives," replied Emma. "Won't you have a seat while we wait?"

Several hours passed before Deputy Harrison and his men arrived. After investigating the scene of the tragedy as best he could in the lantern-lit darkness, Harrison entered the house. The deputy allowed most of the young people who were still present to go on home. He could question them later if need be.

"Mrs. Land, Miss Land, I'm so sorry to hear about your troubles. Sheriff Morrison has been sent for. Do you mind if I ask some questions? It will help in our investigation," inquired Deputy Harrison.

"You don't need to ask any questions. I'll tell you everything you need to know. We had a party this evening. Tom P Varnell and George Walker came unannounced. Some time during the party when I was occupied elsewhere, Varnell forced my sister Ella to go outside with him. She resisted, but I think he may have pulled a pistol on her. Otherwise, I don't think she would have gone outside with him. While outside, I believe that Varnell forcibly committed an outrage on her. When my father confronted Varnell, he shot my father twice. End of story!" cried an impassioned Emma.

"Could I talk to your sister?" queried the deputy.

"No! You cannot! She is far too emotionally distraught. She was violated by that horrible man who killed our father. She did not see Tom P Varnell shoot our father, but I did. I'm the one you need to talk to!" Emma's eyes flashed.

"Where do you think Varnell was headed?" asked Deputy Harrison.

Arch Beasley interjected for Emma, "We have no idea, but he and George Walker left together. I saw them hightailing it out on a couple of fast horses."

"And who are you?" asked Harrison.

"Arch Beasley, sir. Miss Emma and I are engaged to be married," replied Arch.

"What did you witness?"

"Not much. I did go outside to help Emma search for Ella earlier when she and Varnell disappeared. When I became aware Emma had found her sister, I decided it was best if I returned to the house. So I left them alone to sort things out. I only went back outside when I heard gunshots," Arch replied.

"What does Walker have to do with all this?" asked Harrison, turning back to Emma.

"George Walker threw Varnell the gun he used to kill my father," Emma explained, finally trying to calm down.

"I thought you said Varnell used a gun to force your sister outside. Why wouldn't he use his own gun?"

"Before my father arrived, Varnell said he lost his gun on the ground," retorted Emma annoyed at Harrison.

To get ahold of herself, Emma walked over to Elizabeth Land and put her arm around her mother again. She wanted to emphasize they were the victims.

Mrs. Land had gotten a wet cloth and was washing off the blood from her husband's face and hands. Clearly, she was in shock. Mrs. Barber was also trying to comfort Elizabeth while offering cups of Arbuckle coffee to the deputy and others. Silas stood up and moved off to the side to listen without being in the way.

The younger children stuck their heads in the door of the kitchen. They rubbed their eyes and looked at their older sister, Emma.

Minnie asked, "What's Pa doing on the kitchen table?"

Emma rushed over and guided them back out the door. Deputy Harrison heard her say, "It's all right children. We didn't mean to wake you up. I'll tell you all about it after the sun comes up. Right now, I want you all to go back to sleep."

"But we don't …" Nathan started.

"Go to bed! Now!" Emma's tone brooked no more interruption. Mary Barber went over to take the children out of the kitchen and back to their bedroom.

"Mother, why don't you lie down and rest?" Emma urged. Elizabeth ignored her daughter and continued to wash Jonah.

"Who else saw what happened?" asked Harrison.

"No one except Varnell, Walker, and myself," replied Emma. "Ella and Arch had gone back to the house. Why aren't you going after those men? Why are you plying me with these useless questions? My father is dead. Murdered! I've told you who did it! Why are you still here?" Emma felt herself getting very close to hysteria again.

"It's too dark right now to try to find the culprits. We'll have a posse out in the early morning when we can get a good look at the tracks. If need be, we'll bring in bloodhounds. Varnell won't go too far. His mother owns property over by Massey. He's well known to us. I'm not too worried about finding him, or Walker either, for that matter," Harrison replied calmly.

"Varnell will be miles away from here by morning!" Emma cried in despair.

"I don't think so. My guess is he'll find a place to hole up. We'll locate him and his crony, Walker, soon enough," promised Harrison. "One more question. One I have to ask. Are you sure your sister was violated by Varnell? Murder is one thing, but did Varnell really commit an outrage on your sister?"

"How can you ask that? My sister is only sixteen years old. She's never even kissed a boy before Varnell showed up here with his sweet-talking ways. He used his fiddle playing to lure her into thinking he was safe to be around. He's a villain who took advantage of her innocence," declared Emma, not entirely sure of the veracity of her statement, but she had to protect her sister and the family honor.

Deputy Harrison headed over to the door. "Again, I want to extend my condolences, Mrs. Land." He paused and then turned back to Emma Land. "Did your father by any chance have a weapon with him outside?"

"The only thing I saw in my father's hands was a lantern. No, I saw no weapon, deputy," Emma answered firmly.

"The coroner should be here shortly. Sorry, but it is necessary that someone in an official capacity testify on this matter before a grand jury. Hope you understand," stated Harrison.

"Of course, I do," replied Emma. "I have vowed that Varnell will pay for what he did to my father and my sister."

The entire burden of the night's events seemed to be sitting squarely on Emma's shoulders. Ella had a lot to answer for, but not now. Elizabeth Land's grieving had crippled her. Emma struggled with her own role in the tragedy, but she knew she had to be strong. She mentally went back through what she had told the deputy. She knew the details were not as important as seeing justice done for her father's death.

Tom P and George continued their flight quietly among the deeper shadows of the night. They listened to familiar sounds of the night symphony. An owl hooted in a nearby tree. The rustling in the bushes was most likely a red tailed fox or a skunk. The movement of wings attached to black dots in the sky were bats hunting for their nocturnal meals. Tom and George felt a heightened sense of sound. Each listened intently for noises not normal for a March evening. They heard none.

Finally reaching the McNeese farmhouse, the two men knew they could no longer put off talking about what happened and what they had to do next.

"Is there a chance Old Man Land might not be dead?"

George asked.

"He's dead all right. He banged me up pretty good before I shot him. I can't believe he kept coming at me," Tom answered. "Never wanted him to end up dead, but he meant to kill me if he could."

"It appeared that way to me too. Are you hurt?"

"I don't know, but my face doesn't feel too good, and my arm has been throbbin'," Tom replied. "I guess we should have stayed to explain our side of things to the law."

"Maybe, but it was a bad scene. Besides the law hasn't been your friend lately," George stated.

"That's true. I got into that fight at the Old Rock Saloon in Hillsboro a few months back, and the sheriff felt he had to arrest me after that tenderfoot annoyed me so much I shot over his head, because he wouldn't shut up. Sheriff Cox has been watchin' me ever since. But this is worse, much worse."

"You have that right," agreed George. "What were you thinking?"

"It's obvious I wasn't thinking. Except I had a drink or two, and I wasn't going to say no to a warm and willing partner. She seemed a bit too forward to me. Not shy at all. I badly misjudged everything, including her sister and father. I don't think Land would have come looking for us with a weapon in his hands if Emma hadn't riled him up," Tom answered.

"Emma did act all crazy-like when she realized that you were outside with her sister. I tried to stall her, but she was hell-bent on finding you two."

"Your help was invaluable. I don't know where I lost my own damn gun. I guess I had my mind on other matters," Tom said sheepishly. "Hope I can pay you back some day. I wouldn't be alive if you hadn't been there."

"I couldn't stand by and do nothing. I think we're both in a heap of trouble," declared George.

"We'll think of something. Let's get McNeese up," Tom replied.

"I'm going to stay out here. You'd better go on inside first and explain things. I'll hang around out here and keep a look-out," George stated.

"Okay, I'll let you know when it's safe to come in," promised Tom, who went up to the back door. He knocked, calling McNeese's name, and identified himself.

Finally, the door opened. G. W. McNeese was holding a lantern he had taken time to light. He set it down on the stoop and continued to button up his long-sleeved shirt while flipping his suspenders into place.

"Tom P? What are you doin' here in the middle of . ." McNeese's voice trailed off after having gotten a good look at Tom. "Whatever happened to you? Here, come on inside."

"G. W., I need your help. I'm afraid I'm in big trouble," Tom replied.

"What kind of trouble are you talking about? You have blood on your face. Let me get a wash cloth."

"I'd better tell you what happened," Tom stated. Without going into too many details, he told McNeese the events that led up to his arrival.

"Are you alone?" asked G. W. McNeese.

"No. George Walker is with me. He stayed outside to keep a lookout," Tom replied.

"Go on out and put your horses in the barn for now. I'll have Sallie bring something out for your face."

"G. W., I appreciate your help. I do have a favor to ask. I have to get word to my mother," Tom stated. "I don't want her frettin' too much before I get a chance to talk to her."

"Tom P, I'll see that your mother knows you are okay. We'll work something out," G. W. McNeese replied.

"Thanks," Tom replied, feeling some relief. He headed for

the kitchen door but then turned back. "G. W., it was self-defense, but I'm not sure the law will see it that way."

"Get a little rest. We'll try to sort it out in the morning," G. W. answered.

CHAPTER EIGHT

6 March 1883

As the early morning dawn lifted the darkness that obscured the previous evening's events, Silas Barber left the Land's kitchen. At the small house where the party had taken place, he found several flasks and bottles. He lifted one up and sniffed—whiskey. Some bad business had happened here. That was for sure. Leaving the ill-fated party house, Barber soon found the spot where Land was killed. He noted an axe sunk into the area close to the blood soaked ground.

Inside the home, Emma sat drinking her fifth cup of coffee. Arch was over to the side dozing a bit in a chair. Mary had finally gotten Elizabeth to lie down to rest. Emma contemplated that soon more neighbors would be stopping by to pay their respects and give their condolences while also satisfying their curiosity. Before anyone else arrived, she knew she had to talk to Ella. She got up and headed down the hall. Opening the door to the bedroom she shared with her sisters, Emma saw Ella lying on top of the quilt covering their bed.

"Ella, we have to talk," Emma spoke as she sat down on the bed. Ella opened her eyes but said nothing. "I need you to get ahold of yourself. We must present a united front, regardless of what happened outside. I blame only one person, Tom P Varnell. I know you did not go outside willingly with him. All you have to do is tell the deputy that when he comes back. I've already told him Varnell forced you at gunpoint to go with him."

Emma paused. Ella's eyes looked at her but seemed so flat, haunted in appearance. Ella made no reply at first. She finally asked in a voice so low Emma barely heard her, "Is Father really dead?"

"Yes, Ella. Father is dead," Emma confirmed. Ella put her hands to her face and sobbed. She rolled over in the bed with her back to Emma.

"Ella, we have no time for self-pity. What is done is done. You need to get yourself together. People will be arriving. You must present yourself properly. You're acting like you're guilty, not Varnell."

Ella moaned, "Emma, what have I done? I will never forgive myself for this. What have I done?"

"Dry up those tears, Ella. You have done nothing. It was Varnell. He's the one who will pay," admonished Emma who was close to exasperation. Ella started sobbing again. Emma gave up and left. She would see that Ella stayed in her room for now.

Jeff Hale arrived in the early morning daylight. He told Emma and Elizabeth Land that he was there to dress Mr. Land's body and act as coroner. Working with the help of Elizabeth, Jeff started undressing Jonah Land. He found a large opened jackknife in Jonah's coat pocket. He held it up, but no one offered an explanation. He put the knife aside and proceeded with his task.

The next few days passed in a haze for the Land family as they set about to bury Jonah and deal with the notoriety brought upon them. They waited for word that Varnell and Walker had been captured, killed, or had turned themselves in. No word came. Ella continued to be distant and uncommunicative. Emma was concerned but annoyed as well.

Emma and Ella were soon called into Hillsboro to act as

witnesses before the inquest into the death of their father. The trip seemed to last forever. They had to change trains in Waco. Emma could feel the curious eyes of everyone staring at them. Ella kept her eyes down, and little seemed to register with her. Only Emma gave testimony. She repeated what she had previously told the sheriff. Because of her condition, Ella was excused from being questioned, especially since she did not witness the killing. Everyone seemed quite sympathetic. At the end of the inquest, both Tom P Varnell and George Walker were charged with murder in the death of Jonah Land. Warrants for their arrest were issued. Tom was also charged with the rape of Ella Land, even though Ella did not testify.

Newspapers from Waco to Fort Worth and Dallas printed story after story. Each one painted Tom as the worst kind of villain who raped a farmer's daughter and then killed the girl's father when he had tried to intervene to save her virtue. Most of the newspapers had articles like *The Waco Examiner* which ended their story called "Murder Most Foul; a Daughter Outraged & Her Father Murdered" with:

> *The citizens are fearfully incensed at the outrage that has been committed, and Judge Lynch will be up to hold a special term of court if Varnell is caught in the neighborhood … Hanging is too mild a punishment for such a villain …*

Tom and George sat at the kitchen table at G. W. McNeese's farm. At G. W.'s invitation, they had remained there to keep from moving about while posses roamed the countryside. They had stayed mostly out-of-sight in the recesses of the barn. Only in the early morning hours did they venture out to the kitchen to get the latest news and drink a cup of Arbuckle's.

Both men read the various accounts of the events at the

Land farm. Putting down the last paper, Tom raged, "How could the newspapers get things down so wrong? They say nothing about the axe Land was using on me. With us hiding, there's no one to set the record straight. Ella hasn't said a word, but it is assumed from Emma's testimony that I raped her. I've never raped anyone, much less Ella Land. I am damned and doomed."

"It really doesn't look too good for you, Tom P.," agreed George. "I was charged with murder as well."

"Neither one of us committed murder. Damn it!" exclaimed Tom, his hurt shoulder throbbing.

"That may be, but we've already been convicted, at least in the newspapers," George replied.

"Most all of what they've printed are filthy lies," Tom responded.

"The worst of it is that if you turn yourself in so you can clear your name, you're liable to get lynched by a mob before you get the chance to tell your side of the story," McNeese stated, getting up to get another cup of coffee.

Tom turned to Walker. "George, I've been thinking. You should turn yourself in."

"And leave you to face this alone?" replied George. "I'm not doing that."

"But you could clear your name while also gettin' my side of the story out to the press," Tom responded.

"Even if I did, I'm not sure but what I'll be convicted of at least helping you," George answered.

"You're not really an accomplice. I was the one who pulled the trigger," Tom said.

"But I let you have the gun. A jury might see it differently," commented George.

"Tell them I took the gun from you. That's the truth or close enough to it. Should I ever testify, I'll back you up. Besides, in court it will be your word against Emma's," Tom replied.

"I still don't like this," George mumbled.

"Look at it this way. We can't stay with G. W. any longer. I can move around more quickly by myself. There's no sense in both of us trying to outwit the law. The longer you stay with me, the more likely they'll see you as guilty of what Emma has said. You don't want to be on the dodge forever like I may be. I want you to go. No more arguments," Tom asserted.

Arch Beasley and Emma Land sat at the barren kitchen table. A week had passed since the ill-fated party on March 5th. A gloom had settled about the house. People barely spoke above a whisper. Everyone seemed to be waiting for news too long in coming.

"Arch, do you still want to get married?" Emma asked suddenly.

"Yes, but I guess we'll have to wait awhile out of respect for your father," responded Arch.

"Father would understand," Emma exclaimed. "I need your help. If we were married, you could be here all the time."

"Are you sure, Sweetheart?" Arch asked.

"Are you trying to back out?" asked Emma impatiently.

"Of course not," blanched Arch.

"Then we'll do it right away," Emma replied satisfied. "I want everyone to see me as a respectable married woman."

"I don't understand," puzzled Arch.

"It's like this. I've heard whispers questioning why there were only three girls at our party when there were fifteen young men. They make it sounds like we were asking for trouble. Our marriage will stop all that talk," Emma explained.

Before Arch could say anything else, the door opened to the kitchen, and Silas Barber entered. "Morning, Miss Emma. Arch."

"Good morning, Mr. Barber. Any news?" asked Emma.

"No news of Varnell's capture. He's still hiding somewhere. Some wonder if he's even in Hill County. Not many have been able to evade the law like he has. George Walker has turned himself in to the sheriff, though. He's going to plead not guilty, or so I've heard. I do have other news. Governor Ireland has issued a reward for the capture of Varnell. This will get detective agencies and bounty hunters involved. I don't believe it will be much longer before Varnell will be in custody or better yet – dead."

"I hope so!" cried Emma vehemently.

"I also want to present to you and your mother a Resolution."

"What is it?" asked Emma.

"As you know, your father was a member of the Masonic Lodge. We want all Masons to know about his murder and our efforts to bring Varnell to justice. Here it is."

Emma read the resolution to herself but one part really stood out:

> *...we tender his bereaved family and Friends our most sincere sympathy and promise to aid in bringing Tom P Varnell to justice. And we hereby ask the Fraternity throughout the land to assist us in doing so...Resolved that a copy of these Resolutions be presented to the Family and one copy to the Hubbard City News...to publish.*

"This will be published in the newspapers. You can be sure that all Masons will know and make it their objective to see Varnell does not get away with his dastardly deed," announced Silas.

"Thank you so much, Mr. Barber. You have been a great source of strength to me and my family," Emma replied. "If I could impose, I need your advice on a family matter."

"I'll help if I can, Miss Emma," responded Silas.

"I hate to admit it, but Ella is not getting any better. She cries most of the day and refuses to respond to any of us," Emma explained.

"Sounds serious. Have you taken her in to see Dr. Waller?" asked Silas.

"Yes, but she wouldn't answer his questions. He said she just needed more rest. I don't think he knew what to do either," answered Emma.

"Miss Ella must have been really traumatized by what happened to her. Has she talked about being outside with Varnell before your father was killed?"

"Not at all. At first when I brought up the subject, she'd get a panicked look in her eyes and run out of the room," Emma answered. "Now she acts like she does not hear anything we have to say. I'm afraid she is going to just waste away."

"The best suggestion I can make is to get Miss Ella away from here for awhile. If she is not talking nor reacting to any of you, she would be a candidate for the Deaf and Mute Asylum in Austin. Such a shame really. If you want me to do so, I'll make inquiries to see if we can get her in for treatment," Silas offered.

Emma brightened considerably. "Mr. Barber, that sounds like an excellent solution. Thank you so much."

"You're welcome. I'll get along and see what I can do. Give my regards to Mrs. Land," Silas said, while getting up to leave. He gave a final tip of his hat and headed out the door.

Emma turned back to Arch with a smile, "Now, let's get busy with those wedding plans."

CHAPTER NINE

30 July 1883

The summer heat shimmered across the cotton fields of Hill County. The occasional electrical storm brought a little relief but only when not accompanied by crop-destroying hail. So far, most of the county had escaped this fate. Butterflies fluttered among the wildflowers while cicadas punctuated the quiet with a cacophony of dissonant sounds, rising and falling rhythmically.

Tom P preferred the daylight hours to the nights. Sound sleep eluded him most of the time. Often when he did sleep he woke up in a cold sweat after dreaming about his own death while being captured. Rarely in the nightmares did he manage to escape the posse closing in on him before anxiety would rip him back to consciousness. At these moments Tom wished mightily for the comfort of his own bed back at the ranch.

Tom spent most of his days that summer along the back roads and creek beds, frequenting all the areas he used as a youngster when he wanted to make himself scarce. One day sitting on his horse next to a stream, Tom listened to the water as it traveled across pebbles and stones.

Finally dismounting, Tom sat under a leafy tree, splashing some water over his face and neck, both to cleanse and to cool. He doused his kerchief in the water and tied it back around his neck. Settling back against the tree trunk once again, Tom's thoughts turned to his mother. Two weeks after his flight from the Land farm, Tom had had a tearful reunion with her at the McNeese home, where he had come to feel relatively safe ...

Tom had met his mother outside as she arrived in the family buggy. Stepping down to the ground, Docia said nothing but wrapped her arms around her son.

"Mother, I've never been happier to see someone. I know you must be very angry with me," Tom spoke first.

"Hush, Tom P. You do not need to say any more. I know you were provoked to use such deadly force. What's done is done. I'll get the best lawyers for you. We can fight this," Docia stated.

"Mother, you have to know something. If it had not been for George Walker, I might not be alive. Old Man Land kept striking at me. But the papers make no mention of it. Everyone believes I'm the worst kind of villain," Tom exclaimed. "I've given it much thought. I won't be turning myself in. Too much hullabaloo over Land's death. Many are calling for my immediate hanging. I'm not sure I'd be safe in jail."

"Then, Son, you need to leave Hill County. I'll gather some money for you," Docia continued to plan out loud.

"I may have to do that, but not yet. I've been thinking about something, Mother. Since I don't know what the future will bring, I want to deed my portion of the ranch I inherited from Pap to you so you can run the place in my absence or in case I..."

"Stop talking like that," interrupted Docia. "I cannot bear to think that something might happen to you!"

"Mother, I'm just trying to be practical. Aren't you always drumming that into my head? If you have full ownership, you can transact business when I'm not there," Tom stated reasonably.

"All right, but some day it will be yours again when all this blows over. It is your birthright," Docia reminded him.

"I heard my brother-in-law, Jasper, is here from West Texas to get his stock. Have him meet me at John Park's place in three days with the deed so I can sign it. I'll be relieved when you're set," Tom said.

Docia changed the subject. "Tom P, I just want you to know your friends know the true story."

"I'm afraid that few will ever know the true story," sighed Tom.

"Probably not. Rumors of your arrest show up daily in the newspapers. They can't seem to get anything right. One such rumor had Sheriff Cox going all the way to Fort Bend County in southeast Texas, only to find out it wasn't you after all," Docia exclaimed. "I've also heard that someone sent the story along with your picture to the *National Police Gazette* out of New York City. It breaks my heart the things these men write."

"Nothing I can do about that now. You should ignore the newspapers. They will only upset you," Tom advised. "Do you know if George's trial has been set?" He nervously got up from the kitchen table where they were seated to look out the window.

"Not yet. It probably won't be until this fall. He hopes to get it transferred to McLennan County," Docia replied.

"That's good. He should get a fair trial there," replied Tom. He turned to G. W. McNeese. "I won't be coming around here for awhile. I have a feeling you will be called as a witness for George's trial. I owe you a debt I can never repay." Tom extended his right hand.

McNeese replied while still shaking Tom's hand, "Tom P, all I can hope is that somehow things will turn out all right for you. Both your father and you have been good friends to us for many years. I'd do it again. I wish you the best of luck."

Tom walked his mother out to her buggy. He kept his arm around her shoulders as long as he could. For that brief moment she allowed him to comfort her.

"No need to say any more, Tom P. We'll fight this the best we can. Stay safe. Don't take any chances."

"I won't, Mother. Your standing by me means more than I can say." Tom kissed her on the forehead before she pulled herself onto the seat of the buggy.

"Don't worry about the ranch. You know I'd rather be running the business end than doing housework. It'll be there for you when all this trouble is over," she replied. "Tom, do stay in touch. I need to know you're all right."

"Good-bye, Mother. I know you'll do just fine, and I'll be around when I can," bid Tom firmly.

As Docia took off, Tom watched until she rounded the corner and was out of sight. He turned back to the barn to gather up the rest of his gear and head out. Tom knew in no uncertain terms that his old life was gone forever.

Tom P got word early in August that John Sweeney, his brother-in-law, was back from Wisconsin and wanted to have a meeting with him. Tom slipped into Hillsboro under the cover of darkness. They met in the back of Sweeney's Blacksmith Shop where anyone wandering by would not see them. J. L. Crain, a local attorney who had accompanied Sweeney to Wisconsin, arrived and, seeing Tom, got right to the point.

"You were right, Tom P, when you told us that you thought maybe the Land girls were more experienced than most farm girls tend to be. John and I heard some things you are not going to believe. We've pulled it together into an advertisement I think we should run in the paper. This should counter some of the negative news articles that have besmirched your character," he stated emphatically.

J. L. handed the document to Tom, who immediately read through it silently.

Tom P Varnell

The Other Side of the Land Matter

Being employed to defend in the case of Tom P Var-nell and George Walker charged in the District Court of Hill county with the murder of Jonah Land; and seeing there was great excitement, and I thought prejudice against them, on account of an alleged outrage perpetrated on one of the daughters of the deceased, I felt it to be my duty to investigate the characters of Miss Ella, the much injured innocent, and Miss Emma, the principal witness for the State.

I just returned from Green county, Wisconsin, where the Land girls were raised. I met scores of men and women who had known them from childhood. And when I say that they are base and shameless wantons, I only utter the uni-versal openly expressed verdict of that whole community, without a single exception.

The old man was considered a good man by ev-erybody, and it was declared that his girls were his real murderers, and it was solely on account of the shameless conduct of his daughters that he sacrificed a good home and abundance there to come to Texas. I have the word of Dr. Leroy Cutler, Thomas Howe, John White, Mr. Burley, Tom Bedford and many others.

Tom P Varnell, a citizen of Hill county, born and raised here, though wild, is no wilder than a thousand boys raised in Texas who have made good citizens and useful men. He was never accused of a dishonorable act before last March. Was he not the constant companion of the virtuous girls of Hill County? Is he not respected by every pure girl who knows him?

*No one regrets more than I do the death of old man
Land, but I have to make the above facts known for the
purpose so that justice may be done.*

J. L. Crain

*I was with Mr. Crain and can attest to the validity
of all the above statements concerning the Land girls.*

J. W. Sweeney

Tom P handed the account back to J. L. saying, "You're
right. I'm not surprised at what you found in Wisconsin. Emma
flirted with me openly at that party, even though her fiancé stood
not far away from us. I thought she was more upset with me for
not taking her outside than the fact I was with her sister. But I'm
not so sure this is the right thing to do."

"Why ever not?" asked Crain.

"Smearing those girls' reputations to save my own is not
what I intended. Besides, people have already made up their
minds. A paid advertisement probably won't change it for many.
Couldn't you just get a reporter to print a story?" asked Tom.

"I tried. They're not interested. They said that you are
a desperado on the run while the Land girls have suffered the
loss of an irreplaceable father. Emma Land has not hesitated
to blacken your name. She has told the law and the press very
damaging lies. Sometimes you just have to fight back using your
enemy's own tactics," J. L. replied.

"Maybe, but Ella has not spoken out against me," Tom
countered.

"But her silence has been even more harmful to your cause.
The newspapers have really played on that. People believe every-

thing they read; then they pass it along to others who don't read but believe the press wouldn't lie. The reporter told me that if you were so innocent, you would have turned yourself in long ago like George Walker did," John explained.

"These are the same people who are calling for Judge Lynch as well, I suppose," Tom stated. "I just hope that this paid-for account doesn't backfire."

J. L. replied, "What do we have to lose? It's the truth. If enough people change their opinions, maybe we could get you a fair trial."

"I'm not convinced," stated Tom, but he decided to allow Crain to go forward with publishing the advertisement. It was his only hope to turn the tide of public opinion seemingly etched in stone.

A definite chill in the air along with a stiff breeze caused the last of the autumn leaves to release their hold on life and drift down into untidy piles of tan and brown, accumulating on the ground. Many wondered if a long hard winter was in store for central Texas.

George Walker's trial had been going on for several days in Waco during the first week of December 1883. Tom's mother helped George obtain a former district attorney, Major C. B. Pearre, to fight the charge of murder against him. The defense's case rested almost entirely on George Walker's testimony.

As the crowd filed back in after a recess, few noticed an additional spectator who sat down near the back of the courtroom. He was a scruffy-looking cowboy wearing a gray felt hat, faded pants, and a long-sleeved plaid shirt. Dust clung to his clothes and face, giving him a rather unkempt appearance. People who sat close by averted their eyes and moved away from him. George, seated in the witness box, surveyed the visitors' gallery only to find himself looking into those familiar blue eyes.

George turned back as the judge called the trial to order. Major C. B. Pearre walked over to George. "Before the break, Mr. Walker, you were describing the events of the evening of March 5th. Let's continue. Were you present when Mr. Land was shot by Tom P Varnell?"

"Yes, I was there," replied George.

"Describe what you saw."

"As I said, Emma Land and Tom Varnell were arguing when Mr. Land arrived."

"What were they arguing about?" prompted Pearre.

"She was mighty peeved at Varnell, if you ask me, for going outside with her sister, Ella."

"Objection," shouted the district attorney.

"Sustained," answered Judge Rimes.

"Was Ella Land still there while they were arguing?" Pearre walked over to the witness.

"No. She ran off toward the house as soon as Emma pulled Tom P off the ground," George replied.

"Did Mr. Land say anything when he arrived?" queried Pearre.

"He asked Emma what was going on, but he didn't much wait for an answer before he struck at Varnell."

"Struck at Varnell? What did he use?" Pearre turned toward the jury.

"I'm not sure. It looked like an axe handle. It was hard to see out there in the dark," answered George.

"Is this when Varnell asked you for the gun?"

"Yes, but I told him no."

"What happened next?"

"He didn't much wait for an answer. I was close enough he just reached over and took my pistol. It was right quick like." George demonstrated with a hand motion.

"And then?" Pearre prompted, looking back at George

once again.

"It looked like Mr. Land was going to hit Varnell again. So he shot him twice," George responded.

"You're saying Varnell shot Land twice. Right?" Pearre encouraged.

"That's right," answered George.

"Did you at any time know for a fact that Tom P Varnell was going to shoot Mr. Jonah Land?"

"No. Of course not," replied George.

"Thank you, Mr. Walker. No further questions," stated Pearre.

District Attorney Taylor stood up at the prosecution's table. He appeared to be deep in thought. Then he turned to the defendant. "Now, Mr. Walker. You have already heard Mrs. Emma Land Beasley testify that she saw you throw the gun to Tom P Varnell. Are you saying that she lied?" challenged Taylor.

"I don't rightly know what Emma thinks she saw, but I did not throw anything that night, much less a gun," George stated vehemently.

"So if, as you say, Varnell grabbed your gun, why didn't you grab it back?" Taylor challenged.

"It all happened so fast..."

"So fast you probably don't remember throwing the gun. Right, Mr. Walker?" Taylor interrupted.

"I've already said it. I did NOT throw the gun. I meant it happened so fast I don't think Emma, I mean Mrs. Beasley, saw Varnell grab my gun. That's what I meant," George clarified.

"And you would have the court believe that you would refuse to give your good and true friend, Tom P Varnell, a gun if he asked? I find that hard to believe," Taylor turned to the jury. "Don't you?"

"Believe it or not. That's what happened," declared George.

"Well, if you are so innocent, Mr. Walker, please tell the court why you left the scene with the murderer Varnell?"

"Sure. In my mind Mr. Land's death, while unfortunate, was the result of self-defense. I would not have left with Varnell if I thought he had deliberately shot down an innocent man. I was surprised to hear there was a warrant out for my arrest. That's the reason I turned myself in," George responded.

"When's the last time you talked to Varnell?" asked Taylor.

"Not since I surrendered to Sheriff Morrison last summer. If he's around, I wouldn't know it." George didn't dare glance at the visitors' gallery.

"The facts remain that it was your gun that was used to murder Jonah Land and you were friends with the murderer. You made no move to prevent Varnell from using your gun." Taylor paused. "I submit that Mrs. Emma Land Beasley's version of the events is much more believable."

Major Pearre got up to object, but Taylor beat him by saying, "I have no further questions."

"You have no right..." George began.

Taylor interrupted, "I said I have no further questions."

"Mr. Walker, you may stand down," ordered Judge Rimes.

Clutching his hat, George stood up. He glared at the district attorney but said no more as he walked back to the table where his own attorney waited for him.

After closing arguments from both attorneys, the jury filed out quietly. The spectators stayed in their seats, waiting. The jury did not stay gone long before sending a message to the judge that they had reached a verdict.

The jury re-entered the expectant courtroom. Judge Rimes, looking at the jury, asked, "Have you reached a unanimous decision?"

"Yes, we have," responded Dixon Connally, the jury foreman, passing the written verdict over to the bailiff who promptly turned it over to the judge.

After silently reading it, the judge passed it back saying, "The defendant may rise. The verdict may be read now."

Dixon Connally stated clearly, "We, the Jury, find the defendant, George Walker, not guilty."

As noisy pandemonium issued, the judge pounded the gavel in an effort to bring back order. A relieved George turned to give the scruffy, dust-covered cowboy a brief glance. Their eyes locked. The cowboy smiled, nodded, and raised his arms slightly. His curled right hand crossed back and forth over the left arm held out from his body. Playing an invisible fiddle was a sign of victory only the two of them understood. The cowboy quickly slipped out the back as others were rushing to the front of the courtroom, still shouting their amazement or displeasure with the verdict. George sat back down smiling, allowing others to congratulate him. It was a good day.

CHAPTER TEN

2 February 1884

The long months of the winter drifted into the early spring. Tom P had led the life of a fugitive for almost a year. He hated hiding in cold, dirty dugouts and abandoned cabins but did not feel safe enough to stay at the Varnell ranch at night. His long-time friends rallied around him, creating a safe zone that the law ceased to try to penetrate during the daytime. While he moved about on the back roads of the eastern portion of Hill County somewhat freely, Tom did not venture into Hillsboro or any other small town.

A couple of months after his acquittal, George came to see Tom. They met on the Varnell ranch down by Ash Creek. Because of the system of signals that had been set up, Tom knew George was heading his way long before George's arrival. Tom stepped out from under the shade of a tree.

"Howdy, George!"

"Tom P! You're a sight for sore eyes," George exclaimed.

"It's been awhile," Tom replied as the two friends briefly hugged and slapped each other on the back. "What have you been doing since I last saw you?"

"I've moved to Waco. I've been staying as far away from Hill County as I can get. Some folks did not accept the verdict of the jury. Right now, I'm working as a bartender in a saloon but hope in a few years to run my own, down on First Street," George explained.

"I don't see myself frequenting any saloons right now, but I'm glad to see you landed on your feet," Tom responded.

"Any time you want to knock on the back door, I'll let you in. I can even obtain some female companionship if you want," offered George.

"While I appreciate your offer, females have brought me nothing but trouble," responded Tom ruefully.

"I know what you mean," George agreed. "Say, that advertisement your lawyer ran in the newspapers sure caused a firestorm. I heard the town folk think it's a bunch of lies. In fact, many called for that attorney, Crain, to be run out of town. Besides that, editorials showed up in the newspapers lamenting the fact that you have not been captured. I have one right here from last fall." George handed over a crumpled, stained clipping he pulled out of his pocket.

Tom could only make out parts of the editorial from the *Waco Day*:

> *People who visit Hill County say that Tom Varnell who murdered old man Jonah Land, near Hubbard City makes his home on his native heather almost as unconcernedly as before he stained his hands in innocent blood. It is an open secret that he spends most of his time about the Varnell ranch, and is occasionally seen riding over the country looking after his stock of horses. He is always accompanied by one or two armed friends or sympathizers in the section where he lurks... .*
>
> *It is a disgrace to the State that this audacious young murderer is permitted to remain, un-molested and un-arrested, in a settled and populous county like Hill.*

"It's never gonna to end, is it?" Tom P sighed.

"Probably not," George agreed.

"Getting a fair trial won't happen for me. I'm just glad you did," Tom commented. "I'm going to leave this hellhole soon."

"Well, if you do decide to leave, I have a suggestion for a good place to hide out," George offered.

"Where?" Tom asked.

"It's a little place kind of off the beaten path in New Mexico. Name's Magdalena. It's a little west of Socorro where I thought I might go at one time. I've been hearing about some prospecting going on there, and the railroad will be reaching it soon. You should be able to blend in with the others arriving. I'll draw you a map to a cave with running water I was told about."

"I'll keep that in mind. Thanks for the advice," Tom replied. "That night seems so long ago now. Even so, I spend a lot of time thinking. I've little else to do. I have been puzzled about something, George. When we arrived at the Land place, neither one of us took in a loaded gun, but when you threw me your pistol, you said it was loaded. When did you have time to do that?" asked Tom.

"While I was outside with Emma looking for you, I saw Old Man Land in the distance with a lantern in his hand and something else in the other hand. I guess we know now it was that axe. I could tell by his demeanor that trouble was a-brewin'. Emma had admitted to me she told her father about you and Ella. When I went over to check our horses, I managed to load my gun before continuing to look for you," answered George.

"I have to say I sure am grateful you did load that .44."

Tom looked across the barren winter fields. Turning back to George, he opined, "We had some good times, didn't we?"

"We surely did," answered George.

The two friends visited for another hour or two, mostly reminiscing. When they parted, both knew it would be a good while before they met again. They also knew there would always be a bond between them. It went unspoken but was cemented by their shared involvement in the Land shooting.

Spring brought warm weather. On Wednesday, May 14, the school exhibition was about to begin. Professor William Griffin and his students enrolled at Massey Normal School prepared for the evening's entertainment. Most of the small community accepted the invitation to attend. Each student chose a song, a poem, or a reading from a classic story, famous speech, or document to present orally. Little Charlie Menger asked if he could tell some jokes. Professor Griffin gave in to the request.

The windows were opened to allow for a breeze to cool the crowd in the school meeting hall. People fanned themselves with paper they folded back and forth into homemade fans. All of the students received a hearty round of applause, no matter how prepared or unprepared, eloquent or nervous they sounded during their presentations.

Even Little Charlie got lots of laughs, so he launched into another joke. "A tornado hit near Farmer Smith's land. His neighbors rushed over and asked if the tornado did any damage to his barn. Farmer Smith replied, 'I don't know. I haven't found it yet.'" The crowd laughed again.

Professor Griffin sat by one of the open windows to the side of the stage. Around 10 p.m., he felt a tap on his shoulder. Turning, he saw Tom Varnell standing at the window.

"Hey, Will. I see your students are doing quite well. I know most of them," Tom commented.

"Tom P! While I'm happy to see you, aren't you a little concerned about attending such a public event? The governor has issued a pretty big reward for you," Will replied.

"What's it up to now?" asked Tom.

"I heard it's up to $500. And some detective agency in

Waco is starting to take a serious interest in your case. They've been asking questions around here, but no one's talking," Will answered.

"Thanks for the warning, but I think I'll stay if you don't mind. I've already surveyed the crowd. I see no officers of the law or anyone I don't know. I grew up around here. No one's going to turn me in," Tom replied.

"Suit yourself, Tom P. I just don't want any trouble," Will warned.

"Won't be. I see my mother over to the other side. I'll sit with her. Thanks, Will."

Tom waited until the audience was clapping loudly as Little Charlie's performance ended before slipping in and sitting next to his mother. No one seemed alarmed. Docia slipped her arm through his. Together they sat quietly watching the rest of the students. The bulge of a small pistol in Tom's vest could be seen by those seated close by.

In between each student's presentation, people came over to Tom and shook his hand. No one referred to his troubles, and he did not bring it up. When Mattie Henson finished the evening's program with a rousing reading of the *Preamble* to the *U. S. Constitution*, Tom leaned over and kissed his mother on the cheek and quietly slipped out the back. He waved at Will as he left.

Word got back to the *Hillsboro Mirror* that Tom attended the school function. They could not resist printing a story and even embellished it by including a rumor that a local deputy was there. The unfortunate deputy, J. W. Smalley, had to declare publicly that he had not attended Professor Griffin's exhibition.

On a chilly Saturday morning in October, Deputy Tom Bell stood up on the platform set up for political speeches by candidates in Hillsboro. He was running for sheriff of Hill County. Up against the popular incumbent, Sheriff Cox, Tom Bell dressed carefully for the role he hoped to obtain. He adjusted his new Stetson hat on his head and walked over to the podium. He wore his Colt .45 in a leather holster buckled around his hips. A dark blue vest covered his white, long-sleeved shirt. His size, over six foot in height, commanded respect among the townspeople of Hillsboro.

"Ladies and gentlemen. It is time to bring law and order to our community and to our county. We have living in our midst a man who is a fugitive from justice. All of you know me. I am a simple man. But I am also a man of my word, and I give you my word and my pledge. Elect me, Tom Bell, sheriff of Hill County, and I promise you that I will arrest Tom P Varnell so that he will be forced to pay for his crimes. He should not be roaming our fair countryside free as a bird. I know ALL of you would rest easier at night if Varnell were out of circulation. If I am elected and do not fulfill my promise, you have my word that I will NEVER run for sheriff again. This is my solemn vow and promise to you, the law-abiding citizens of Hill County. Thank you!"

As Tom Bell's eyes flashed, the crowd applauded uproariously. The town's people had long felt the pressure from other areas of the state concerning the fact that Tom P Varnell was still on the loose. If Tom Bell could get the job done, they'd certainly vote for him.

By November, Tom P made the final decision that he had to leave. With Tom Bell, the new sheriff, hellbent on fulfilling his campaign promise, any future in Hill County Tom had hoped for was now gone. Tom's sister, Lina McGee, lived in Tom Green County in West Texas. He meant to go there first before deciding what to do next.

Tom hastily settled his business affairs as best he could. He packed down a sorrel mare with provisions and rode his best stallion, Midnight. The rest of the herd he left with his mother. She managed to scrape together a small stake for him to take. Their parting was hard on both of them. Tom promised to send letters to Lina so that they could be forwarded to Docia. He told her to depend on John Sweeney, her son-in-law, to help out.

Both Tom and his mother lapsed into an uneasy silence. They were loath to make the final good-byes, as neither had an inkling when they would see each other again, if ever.

Docia suddenly said, "Wait!" She rushed back into the house. It wasn't long before she emerged carrying Tom P's fiddle in a case. "You're not leaving without a way to make music."

Tom reached for the case, not saying a word. Instead, to keep the strong emotions from coming to the surface, he busied himself strapping it on top of the rest of his supplies. The only thing left was a hug and a kiss. Docia clung to Tom as long as she dared.

Facing west, Tom turned back one last time to wave at the woman who had given him birth. She seemed so small, but he knew better than any not to underestimate her. Docia lifted her arm in farewell.

Sheriff Tom Bell sat at his desk, getting the feel for his new position of importance in the community. The door opened, and Deputy Jacob Green entered. He quickly delivered his message that impressed upon Bell that his promise to the voters of Hill County would not be easily kept.

"What do you mean Varnell's left?" demanded Bell.

"Just what I said," replied Green. "They're talking about it over at Sweeney's Saloon. He's been gone a couple of days. I guess Varnell realized it's too hot for him to stay around here."

"Damn it!" Bell exclaimed. "I was pulling together an all-out effort to nab him."

"I guess he heard about it," offered the deputy.

"Well, I'm not giving up. I can't leave here right now though.

Green, pull some men together and go after Varnell. Bring him back. Dead or alive. I don't care which," Bell commanded.

"Yes, sir. We'll leave in the morning. I have a good idea where he's headed. He has a sister out in West Texas. Reckon he'll go there," Green replied.

"Get on it then," said Bell, dismissing the deputy who headed out the door. Bell slammed his fist down on his desk, then turned to look out the window. His anger soon cooled into hardened resolve. Tom P Varnell would be caught. Of that he had no doubt.

CHAPTER ELEVEN

1 December 1884

Jasper McGee and his son, Gus, worked their way home from a full day on the range with their stock. Both were bone tired. Some of their horses had gone missing that morning, so they spent the whole day tracking them down. All but two were located in the scrub. Jasper noted with satisfaction that several of the mares were carrying foals. It would be a good spring in the upcoming year.

The McGees' first couple of years in Tom Green County had been challenging, with dust storms plus the growing tensions between settlers and the big ranch outfits over water and grazing rights on the prairie. Several times Jasper had been ready to give up, but each time Lina reminded him their lives were bound to get better, and they had.

As father and son topped the last gully about a half-mile from the house, Jasper stopped suddenly. Gus, not paying attention, kept on going until he sensed the absence of his father. He finally pulled up to a stop before turning to trot his pony back.

"Why'd you stop?" he queried.

"We have company, Gus," Jasper replied. "It's your Uncle Tom P."

"How do you know? We can't even see the house clearly from here," exclaimed a surprised Gus.

"I just know," replied Jasper looking toward the ranch house.

"Yippee," Gus yelled, slapping his pony with the reins.

Inside the farmhouse, Tom was cooling his heels at the kitchen table drinking a hot cup of Arbuckle coffee while his sister worked at getting supper ready. Belle and Alf played with a wooden spinning top in the corner with their brother Dee, who was three years old, and baby sister, Docia, who was just one year old, while Guy and Ed finished up their chores outside.

"I was wondering when you were going to head this way," Lina spoke, stirring the stew she'd started at noon.

"I lingered in Hill County longer than I should have," Tom admitted. "I kept hoping that something would happen so I could stay. I really thought I might have a chance until that new sheriff was elected."

"I can't help but wonder why you didn't just turn yourself in, Tom P.," mused Lina putting the pan of biscuits in the oven.

"I thought about it several times, but the newspapers have everyone believing I'm some kind of hardened desperado, except for those who already know me," Tom answered.

"Well, you probably won't ever be able to go back again. You know that, don't you?" she prophesied.

Tom sighed, "Yes, I know, Sis. I hated leaving Mother to run the ranch alone."

A moment of silence dropped between the two. Tom took a long sip. He'd always loved his sister's coffee. He rose to look out the window, seeing Jasper and Gus as they rode up.

"I don't mean to be so hard on you," Lina softened her tone. "I'm just concerned about Mother."

"I understand. Don't think for a moment I haven't berated myself already, over and over again. I can't change the past, though," Tom replied.

"At age 22, you've already lived a lifetime, haven't you, Tom P?" Lina sighed.

The door burst open, and Gus entered the room. He rushed over to give his uncle a big hug. Tom held his tin cup high to keep the coffee from spilling during the onslaught of affection from his nephew.

"You said you would come for a visit," Gus chortled in his excitement. "Are you staying long?"

Tom smiled at Gus but also caught the look that passed between Lina and his brother-in-law as Jasper entered the kitchen. "Hello, Jasper," greeted Tom.

"Tom P," Jasper nodded, walking over to the kitchen table to sit down.

Tom turned back to Gus, "I probably won't be staying too long. Maybe a few days. I'm headed for New Mexico. Say, your mother told me you have a new blood bay you're training. Why don't you show me?"

The two left out the kitchen door. Lina turned back to the stove. Jasper picked up the cup of coffee she had poured for him.

"You know it's not safe for Tom P to be here," Jasper commented, breaking the uneasy silence.

"Do you honestly expect me to turn away my own brother?" Lina asked, vehemently. "Well, I can't do that."

When Jasper didn't say anything, she walked over to look out the window. Tom and Gus, obviously deep in conversation punctuated by laughter, were heading for the corral. She picked up plates and silverware from the cupboard, then walked to the table.

"How do we know he wasn't followed?" Jasper countered.

"We don't. Tom P knows he can't stay long," Lina said, trying to be reasonable.

"Well, I, for one, believe it is not safe for him to be here. I understand he shot that man in self-defense, but he's putting us in danger." Jasper wasn't giving up his protest.

"I'll talk to him. Please be patient." Lina stepped over to the kitchen door and rang the dinner bell, essentially closing out their argument. The younger boys came running, but she turned them around again to go wash up. Talking about horse breaking techniques, Tom had his arm across Gus's shoulders as they re-entered the kitchen together.

The next day, though cloudy, was still mild for early December. After breakfast, Tom left with Jasper and Gus to work the stock. They found the two missing mares by mid-morning. In the afternoon, Jasper re-shod Midnight for Tom while Gus buzzed about the grown men, looking for ways to help. Tom was thankful, with Gus about, that his troubles never became a topic of discussion. Working together finally eased the tension between the two brothers-in-law.

"Seems awfully dry out here," commented Tom looking out at the arid landscape, so different from north central Texas.

"It can be. We have to be careful with what water we do have. I'm putting up another windmill soon. What we have out here that's plentiful is wind," Jasper laughed.

"I see you've begun building a smokehouse," observed Tom.

"Yep. Lina's been after me to get that done. Your sister keeps a long list of projects for me," Jasper admitted.

"That sister of mine is an organizer, all right," stated Tom agreeably.

"I guess she's always been that way. Did I ever tell you about the time she outwitted me while we were still in Hill County?" Jasper offered. Tom shook his head.

"Well, it was an early morning in September. The cotton crop was in, and I was getting ready to go into Hillsboro with a couple of bales. Lina said to me 'Jasper, I need the money from this cotton to buy bolts of cloth for our winter clothes.' I told her 'Not this time, Lina. I have some bills to pay. Maybe next time.' I loaded up the heavy bales onto the wagon. 'Oh, bosh,' I heard her say as I was leaving. I should have known she would not be satisfied with my answer. Lina took our children into the backyard to play. She tied a rope around the waists of Guy and Gus so they wouldn't wander off. The other end of the long rope was tied to a stake under a tree. Placing a jug of water close by, she put Ben, our birddog, to guarding them. Leaving them in the house, she said later, was out of the question, and she didn't have time to get them over to her mother's abode. Then she saddled Sunshine and arrived in Hillsboro long before I did in my slow-moving wagon. She told Napoleon Stroud at Stroud Brothers Mercantile she was going to pick out some bolts of cloth and that I would be in shortly with a couple of bales of cotton to pay for it. After she picked out what she needed, Lina did not tarry but got right back home to the boys. I arrived myself back at the farmhouse a few hours later with those bolts of flannel and wool.

"Neither one of us discussed it until much later. She always seems to know how to get the best of me," Jasper chuckled, finishing his story. Tom laughed, heartily, pleased at the obvious love his brother-in-law had for his sister.

Soon, Lina called everyone in for supper. The men trooped into the house companionably after washing up at the well. Lina noted the absence of tension and was pleased.

"I'll be looking for some work in this part of the state or the Panhandle," Tom spoke up as everyone started eating Lina's steak, beans, and biscuits.

"Plenty of work for an experienced cowboy, but I wouldn't suggest you use your real name. Some folks will do anything for a little cash," Jasper advised.

Tom nodded. "I've already thought of that. I'll be going by Charles Crawford or Bob Woods. Both are good names."

"I hear tell that Jim Newman is setting up a spread in northern Hockley County close to an area called Casa Amarillas. He's always been a friend of the Varnells and McGees. You can probably get on," Jasper offered.

"Sounds promising. I remember him from Hill County," Tom agreed in between bites.

The birddogs started barking. Before anyone could get up, they heard a voice hollering from outside, "Tom P Varnell! We know you're in there. We've come to arrest you. Come on outside and give yourself up."

Tom and Jasper rose from the table at the same time. Kerchiefs, being used as napkins, were hastily yanked from the neckline of their shirts. They fluttered down to the table and settled haphazardly atop plates full of their half-eaten meal. Jasper headed to the wall rack where his shotgun hung. Tom quickly pulled his pistol and bullets out of his saddlebags. Lina did not need the instructions soon to come from her husband.

"Take the children into the bedroom. Shut the door and get down by the bed away from the window. Do it now!" Jasper spoke rapidly.

Tom commanded, "I'll handle this. Let me do the talking."

Passing by him, Lina put her hand on Tom's cheek briefly, saying nothing but telling him everything as their Varnell eyes met. Then she herded her children away from the present danger.

Jasper briskly loaded his shotgun and headed for the kitchen saying, "I'll go to the back door. I don't intend to let these men into my house. You do what you need to do."

Cracking the front door open while keeping his body out of sight, Tom peeked out at the posse, observing only three men, still on their horses close to the hitchrack. He finished loading his gun. It was obvious the posse had been on the road for awhile, as the horses were lathered up. Tom was a bit relieved at the small number but not any less concerned. He recognized all three men.

"Hey, Deputy Green, you're just in time to enjoy some of Lina's homemade biscuits. Plenty of water in the trough for your horses. You boys are gonna have a long trip back to Hillsboro," Tom offered, conversationally.

"Now, Tom P, this ain't no social call. You got to come on out so we can take you back to stand trial. My orders are: dead or alive," countered Jacob Green.

"Hate to disappoint you, but I'm not going anywhere. I know all of you – Jacob, Jack, Delbert. You grew up with me. What happened on the Land farm was self-defense. I'd go back with you if I had a chance at getting a fair trial in Hillsboro," Tom argued, thankful for the silence in the rest of the house.

"Not my problem, Varnell. My job's to take you in. Time's a-wastin'," Green retorted. "Come on out now. Don't make us come in after you."

"I've already told you, deputy. I'm not coming out. I got plenty of fire power with me if that's what it takes," Tom responded. "All of you have met my sister and her family. I know you'll think twice before putting these innocent children in any more danger. I suggest you just ride away."

"Varnell, you're the one putting people in danger with your stalling," barked Green angrily.

The men sat uneasily in their saddles waiting for Tom to make the next move. None came. Silence. Nervously, Jack moved his horse a little closer to Green's. He peered at the cracked front door where a stillness prevailed. Darkness would be coming soon as the late afternoon waned.

"You know Varnell is one of the best shootists in Hill County, Jacob. He can pick us off one at a time if he wants to do it. I didn't sign on to get myself kilt. You're not payin' me enough."

"I didn't expect you to go all yellowbelly on me, Jack. Varnell's only one man," Green exclaimed.

Jack spit back, "He's one man who learned to shoot with either hand before he was old enough for his first shave. `Sides, we have no idea how many other folk might be inside that house."

Delbert spoke up, "I'm with Jack on this one. We left Hillsboro with two more men than what we have now. When they turned back, I knew then we should probably all turn back. Personally, I don't care enough about taking Varnell to risk making my children orphans or my wife a widow."

Green glared at the other two. The landscape cooled as the shadows lengthened, but he could feel nervous sweat trickling down his back. He lifted one shoulder, then the other. His actions didn't alleviate the itch where his wool shirt met his bare skin. They still had not heard another sound from the house. The deputy knew in that moment he'd lost to Varnell without so much as a shot being fired.

Angrily, Green muttered, "I don't know how I'm gonna face Bell when I get back."

"I rather doubt the sheriff intended for us to do something so risky as rushing in on a man who has his guns aimed at us. Besides, we can decide on the way back what we want to tell Bell," Jack answered. No one said anything for a few moments.

"All right. I give up." With that, Green, not wanting to afford Varnell the satisfaction of a spoken victory, turned his horse around. The other two followed suit as they left the McGee ranch.

Tom could hear the horses leave out. Straightening up from his crouch at the front door, he put away his pistol and touched his brow. His face was dripping with sweat.

Returning to the front room, Jasper spoke up, "I can't have

you here, Tom P. I have to think of my children. You need to get on out."

"I agree. I'll leave now," Tom replied. "We're lucky this bunch didn't have the stomach for a fight. I was waiting for darkness to get all of you out so that I could face them alone. I was surprised when they left. I'll get my things and slip away. Tell Lina and the boys I hope to see them again some day." Tom headed out the door.

Saddling up Midnight and quickly repacking the sorrel, Tom made ready to leave. Before he reached the barn door, Gus rushed in.

"Uncle Tom P, why'd those men want to take you?" he asked breathlessly.

"Gus, some things happened back home, and I had to leave. I'll be able to explain everything when all this blows over," Tom P promised as he reached out to tousle Gus's hair.

"Sure wish I could go with you," Gus lamented.

"Some day, I hope we'll ride together. I've got big plans for us when you get a little older. Right now, I need to go it alone. Listen to your ma and pa," Tom responded.

Lina arrived with some hastily packed food. "Tom P, I wish you didn't have to leave. I just hope you understand Jasper's position."

"I do. No hard feelings. I'm just glad all of you are safe," Tom replied. "Sis, you have a fine family. They are a credit to both you and Jasper."

Tom took the time to give his older sister a hug to let her know better than words that he loved her. Wordless emotion passed between the two. Stepping back, Lina took his hands and looked down at his long tapering fingers.

"I saw your fiddle case on the supply horse. I hope you have time to write some songs wherever you go. I always hear music when I think of you. Be safe and let me know when you can that you are all right."

"I will," responded Tom, pulling his hands away from his sister. He left the barn on foot but quickly mounted, once outside. He waved at Lina and Gus before disappearing into the early evening.

"Goodbye, Uncle Tom P.," Gus called. His mother walked up beside her son. Looking into the gathering darkness, they listened as the rider and two horses retreated into the west.

CHAPTER TWELVE

2 December 1884

Dusk deepened to raspberry darkness on the Texas landscape as Tom P headed west from his sister's homestead. The close call with the posse had solidified Tom's conviction that he needed to leave his native state. He hoped to find an environment where he could start anew. New Mexico beckoned.

Tom did not travel as openly as he had when he first left Hillsboro. He knew that Deputy Green might return, find him gone, and decide to pursue. So he adopted a cautious attitude and kept human interaction along his route to a minimum. The solitude of the trail heading through western Texas fit Tom's mood. Moving away from his family was not his desire, but he knew it was the only way he could protect them.

Adopting his new identity as Charles Crawford, Tom traveled through small West Texas settlements. He let his dark curly hair grow long and kept the luxuriant mustache he'd started during his months of hiding out in Hill County. He reached Centralia in two days, traveling west-southwest from the McGee ranch. Tom stayed only long enough to get a few supplies, including an extra warm wool blanket for his bedroll. He also purchased a Winchester rifle for added protection.

The landscape of West Texas was both beautiful and stark. At times the wind on the winter desert cut through him with such force, it took Tom's breath away. Even so, he enjoyed the ever-changing rosy reds, oranges, and yellows of the spectacular sunsets as the afternoon sun lowered in the western sky.

Following the route of the Butterfield Stage Line, Tom traveled through Castle Gap at King Mountain. He slipped over to the other side of the Pecos River at Horse Head Crossing. Once across, Tom changed his direction, heading north along the Goodnight-Loving Cattle Trail to the town of Pecos City. Jasper had told Tom that the territory to El Paso was the playground of disgruntled Apaches and desperate bandits. Trusting his luck with the cavalry from Fort Davis or its outpost, Camp Rice, was not an option. So Tom chanced the train at Pecos City. After watching from a distance, he decided the depot was safe enough to purchase a ticket on the Texas & Pacific.

In El Paso Tom hooked up with a wagon train heading north to Albuquerque along the Camino Real, which followed the Rio Grande. He hired on as a guard and scout. Tom kept his reasons for traveling simple when asked, saying he was headed for mining country in central New Mexico to do some prospecting. He rode ahead of the slow-moving caravan, returning only to report or for evening camp.

Several federal marshals joined the wagon train after they entered New Mexico Territory. Wary at first, Tom relaxed when he heard the lawmen were on the lookout for cattle rustlers known to roam the southern quadrant between Socorro and the Mexican border. Evenings were filled with stories of notorious desperados caught, including John Kinney, who had led a gang called the Rio Grande Posse but was now serving a term in the Kansas State Penitentiary.

Three weeks later the wagon train arrived in Socorro, where Tom P bid his fellow travelers farewell. He took his pay and got a room that included the use of a bath at the Socorro Hotel. Finding a Chinese laundry, Tom left all his dirty, travel-stained clothes to be washed and ironed. Then he parted with 75 cents to get a haircut and a shave. Being really clean again after so long on the trail was a just reward.

The discovery of gold, silver, and other precious metals, along with the completion of the Atchison, Topeka & Santa Fe Railroad in 1880, caused Socorro, a once quiet farming village of about 500, to more than double its population. The town became even livelier as miners and other prospectors arrived.

With many newcomers milling about, Tom blended in with the others. He heard talk in the saloons of men who had accumulated fortunes in the minefields almost overnight. Not everyone was thrilled with some of the new arrivals, particularly the gamblers, drifters, and cowboys. A group led by Candelario Garcia, a probate judge, did not want American Anglos in the area. An opposing group guided by Gustav Billing prevailed, as more citizens wanted the economic opportunities new businesses offered rather than isolation.

Tom joined some poker games and managed to add a small amount to the stake his mother had provided. One drunk tried to pick a fight after losing a hand, but Tom quickly picked up his meager winnings and left. He could not afford to get into a scuffle that might bring him to the attention of the local sheriff.

Staying in Socorro a week before heading out to complete the final leg of his trip, Tom followed alongside the Socorro Transfer, the local stagecoach, as it made its way west on a Wednesday morning. The steep grade slowed the stagecoach down. As he ascended onto the high desert, Tom pulled out his black woolen long-coat for warmth.

Tom noted the sparse vegetation. The cholla and cedar shrubs were sprinkled among the yellowed grass tufts. As he rode along, he saw the mountains rise up to the south. Winter was a serious business here as the elevation was much higher than Tom's native land back in Hill County. In the distance he saw antelope running.

Against the lemon-yellow morning light, the buildings of Magdalena could be viewed in various stages of completion and surrounded by a sea of tents, all indications of a small town in the middle of a boom. Tom heard in Socorro that many prospectors had headed to the Kelly silver mine area, south of Magdalena, in hopes of making a big strike.

Tom stopped in town at Charles Ilfeld's Co. to get some dry pinto beans, beef jerky, Arbuckle coffee, and raw sugar to add to his other supplies. Afterwards, he slipped into Keegan's Saloon to get a flask of stout whiskey to ward off the cold and the damp. Sitting at the bar, Tom pulled out the travel-stained, much-creased map George Walker had drawn for him. A burly, broad shouldered man with powerful arms and a three-day-old beard walked down the bar toward his newly arrived customer.

"Staying long, cowboy?" the bartender asked.

"Don't rightly know. How'd you know I'm a cowpoke?" replied Tom.

"Pretty easy. Most of my customers are either cowboys or miners. Your Stetson, red bandana, and high top boots pretty much give you away," replied the friendly bartender.

Tom extended his hand, "I'm Charles Crawford."

"Walt Conner, at your service. You sound like some Texans who came through here earlier this month. I imagine we'll get a whole lot more once that railroad gets completed next year. I suspect this area will become a shipping point for cattle being raised west of Magdalena."

"Say, Walt, I have a map here. I'm looking for a cave that's marked." Tom pointed to an "X" on the map.

Conner studied it for a few moments. He reached under the bar and pulled out a yellow stub of a pencil.

"I reckon I can help you out. It's about three miles to the southwest from here. I'll add a few more landmarks."

"Thanks," replied Tom finishing his whiskey. He paid for the drink plus the bottle to take with him before heading outside. Looking out over the crowd milling about, Tom noted few of the feminine persuasion. Probably just as well.

Tom quickly turned around to head for his horse tied to the saloon hitchrack. As he did, he collided with a young woman who was obviously in a hurry. Just in time, he caught her by the waist before the collision knocked her off the wooden sidewalk.

"Pardon me, ma'am," Tom said, removing his hands as soon as he was sure she had her balance.

"What is wrong with you?" the irate woman complained. "Can't you watch where you're going?"

This speech took Tom by surprise as his charm rarely failed him. Even so, Tom appreciated that here was a mighty handsome woman.

"Certainly my mistake," Tom replied. "How can I make it up to you?"

"Well, you can get out of my way to start with," she firmly ordered.

"As you wish," Tom grinned. She was not impressed. Sweeping past Tom, the lady continued on her way without another word or glance. Tom decided he was losing his touch, especially since he'd not even gotten her name.

Tom looked after the swiftly departing female. Dark hair piled on her head revealed a slender neck that went with a pleasing figure. Her purposeful walk in her sensible black lace-up boots was an indication of independence he decided.

Smiling, Tom mounted his horse to head out of town in the direction that Walt had indicated to him. The lady's fiery gray eyes flecked with green kept creeping into his mind as he rode along. He tried reminding himself that he had no time for women. The improved map made locating the cave easy. As George Walker had promised, a natural spring in the cave provided a steady supply of water. Tom decided this was as good a place as any to wait out those who would like to find his whereabouts.

Tom tethered the horses close by the entrance. His Winchester rifle was kept loaded and within easy reach for emergencies. After months of living outdoors, Tom was glad to have the extra protection provided by the cavern.

A week was spent resting, during which Tom rarely left his new abode. As time passed, he adjusted to the solitude and loneliness of a hermit's life. He woke up one morning to see snow on the ground outside. Tom brought the two horses into the cave and brushed them down so they would dry off quickly.

Slowly time drifted by. Tom went into Magdalena every week or ten days for supplies. He kept to himself in town, only occasionally spending afternoons in Keegan's Saloon or going by the stockyards. He rarely engaged in conversation, since he did not want to be asked the inevitable questions. With the influx of new citizens, few paid attention to one additional cowboy. He liked to watch the crowds of people, hoping he would see that woman again. He didn't, but she managed to stay on his mind.

The trek in and back from Magdalena offered open country of the type Tom soon came to enjoy. He liked to watch the wildlife and one time saw a mountain lion in the distance. Often the peaks of the mountains were lost in the clouds for days at a time. To keep warm Tom started campfires using piñon juniper that gave off a sweet aroma.

During the daytime, Tom often filled the silence with music. More than once, he mentally thanked his mother for grabbing his fiddle for him to take when he left Texas. Tom associated the fiddle and his love for music with his mother. After all, she was the one who had taught him to play when he was only a child. The music eased somewhat the homesickness he felt for his mother and the Varnell ranch. When not fiddling, Tom roamed the territory outside the isolated cave, seeing the Black Range and even the Tularosa Mountains in the distance on clear days.

One bright, crystal clear morning in early spring, Tom saw a horse and buggy pulled over to the side of the little-traveled dirt road that led to town. Curious, he headed his horse over to see who had entered territory he considered his domain. No one was near the buggy. Shielding his eyes from the sun and dust the wind was stirring up, Tom looked all around and finally spied someone walking in the red dirt among the piñon junipers. He could see that it was a woman who appeared to be putting something into a basket she carried. Tom got off Midnight and walked toward her.

"Morning, ma'am," Tom called out, hoping not to startle her. The figure jerked around. Tom quickly added, "It's okay. You needn't be afraid."

"You!" exclaimed the woman.

"Come on. I'm not so bad, at least not when you get to know me," offered Tom, looking into gray eyes flecked with green.

"I just don't appreciate you creeping up on me. That's all," retorted the woman, looking away from Tom toward her buggy.

"My apologies again. I can't seem to get on your good side," Tom replied. "How about we start over?"

Tom turned with his back to the woman. Whirling back around, he bowed low, sweeping off his Stetson, then spoke, "Hello! I'm Charles Crawford. I'm mighty pleased to meet you."

The woman didn't say anything for several seconds as the wind whipped around them. Just as Tom thought she was going to turn away, she laughed.

"Hello, Charles Crawford. I am Lillian Fairfield. I don't ordinarily talk to strangers."

"In a way we're not strangers, are we?" quipped Tom. "I would be honored if you let me call you Lilly."

Lillian frowned, looking at Tom for a moment. Then she surprised him by saying, "If you wish. I am curious as to what you're doing out here."

"Well, Miss Lilly, I'm doing a bit of prospecting. May I ask the same question in return?"

"I'm collecting certain roots and plants for medicines. Today, I needed some piñon nuts for an antiseptic," Lillian answered. As Tom started to speak again, Lillian hurriedly added, "I can't stay and chat any longer. I need to get back to town."

Tom walked Lillian back to her buggy. "My sister, Ade.., uh, my sister is an herbalist as well." Tom quickly covered his near indiscretion with a question. "Do you have a regular medical practice in town?"

"A small one. My husband left me only the house when he was killed in a mining accident. I'm certainly not qualified to do all a doctor can, but I can set a broken bone or give medicine to break a fever," she answered. "I use the local plants that natives have used for ages, like agave for aches and pains, manzanita for headaches, and barberry for cleaning wounds. So I often go out to collect."

Arriving at the buggy, Tom helped Lillian up to the seat. He doffed his hat in salute as she left. He was pleased to find out Lilly was not married and hoped he would see her again. Tom quickly forgot his pledge to avoid any more feminine relationships. Gray eyes flecked with green took care of that. He headed back to the cave, whistling the melody from a song he suddenly realized he was mentally composing. Overhead, a bald eagle soared making good use of the wind currents. Tom paused as he watched the bird's flight pattern.

As spring progressed Lillian often went out Tom's way looking for medicinal plants. He enjoyed walking beside her and listening as she chatted about Magdalena. She had been living there since the town was small. The boom was fairly recent to her reckoning. As accommodations were scarce right now, she rented out a couple of bedrooms. Rosalinda, a local Mexican woman, cooked and cleaned for Lillian, so she could keep up with her developing medical practice.

The constant wind often caused Tom and Lilly to have to put their heads together to be heard. Evenings, Tom took the time to shake out his clothes in hopes of ridding them of the accumulated daily dust.

Tom came to look forward to Lilly's trips out from town. Before long he was aiding in her hunt for certain plants. One day as he was about to help her back into the buggy, Lilly stopped.

"Charles, when's the last time you had a home-cooked meal?"

"It's been a long time," Tom answered.

"Next time you're in town, come on by my place. I need to thank you for all your help, anyway," Lillian offered, ascending onto the seat of her buggy.

"I'm heading that way tomorrow. Is that too soon?" Tom replied. "I don't know where you live, Lilly."

"My house is on Second Street. Ask anyone. They'll know which one. I'll see you tomorrow evening," smiled Lillian. With that, she grabbed the reins, snapping them to get her horse headed back to town.

After a delicious supper of roast beef, red beans, peppers, and tortillas, along with canned peaches for dessert, Tom asked Lillian to go for a walk. The twilight enveloped them as they strolled along Second Street toward Main. For once the wind was little more than a breeze.

"Can I ask a personal question, Lilly?" asked Tom.

"Not sure. Ask. I might answer," returned Lillian.

"Why haven't you remarried?" Tom asked. "You're a fine-looking woman, and I would think a lot of men here would be more than willing,"

Lillian didn't answer right away. As they strolled, the silence deepened. Finally, she stopped and turned to Tom.

"I'm not looking to get married again, Charles. In fact, I've made it a practice to keep my distance from the male population," she answered. "Except against my better judgment, I let you be a friend. I've been collecting medicinal herbs and roots for some time now, and all of sudden you turned up."

Tom grinned, "I'm mighty grateful for that."

"Don't misunderstand what I am saying. Having my independence has suited me just fine," Lillian said. Then she changed the subject. "Why are you such a loner? One would think you have something to hide."

Startled, Tom covered by pulling her arm through his to continue their walk. "Maybe I like the solitary life."

"I really don't believe that. You just don't seem the type," Lillian said. They strolled on in silence.

"Well, this got mighty serious," laughed Tom. "I have one last thing to say. I've always appreciated strong women. I was raised by one. I'm glad you didn't shut me out."

They arrived back at Lillian's adobe home all too soon as far as Tom was concerned. He bid Lilly goodbye and thanked her again for such a fine home-cooked supper.

Some days later an extraordinary event occurred as Tom sat in his cave on a makeshift seat he had constructed from wood and stone. He had his fiddle out and was practicing some runs and complicated finger work. Satisfied, he played the entire tune. As he finished, Tom was startled to hear clapping. He turned quickly toward the entrance, upset with himself for being so into his music he had not kept a vigilant watch. Lilly stood there with a huge smile. Tom relaxed.

Dressed in a serviceable yellow cotton dress with no discernible waistline, Lilly had obviously been out in the wind. Several tendrils of her dark hair had escaped their bondage from the matronly chignon secured at her neckline. Eschewing a bonnet most of the time, Lilly's face was tan, framing her sparkling eyes. Tom took mental note of just how pretty she looked.

"All these weeks, and you didn't mention you played the fiddle," she admonished.

Tom grinned sheepishly, "I told you I'm not much of a talker."

"But your music is wonderful," Lillian exclaimed.

Tom put down the fiddle and joined Lillian close to the entrance, glad he had put on a clean shirt that morning.

"What brings you all the way up here?"

"I didn't see you outside down on the ridge like I usually do." Lillian paused, then continued, "I guess I got a little concerned. That's all."

Tom felt something loosen inside. He walked over and took her hand to pull her farther into the cave.

"Come inside my mansion, mademoiselle. I'm fresh out of champagne and caviar, but I have a nice vintage cup of cool mountain water I can offer you," Tom quipped.

Lillian laughed again. His spartan furnishings showed a bachelor's lack of a decorative inclination. She looked around wondering if she had some items she could loan to make the space more comfortable. Tom watched her intently.

Grinning, Tom did something he had been meaning to do for a long time. He kissed her. Lillian stiffened for a few seconds, then Tom felt her relax.

Finally, she pulled back, flustered, "Charles, I..."

"Don't say another word," Tom interrupted, pulling Lilly close as his arms encircled her.

"But," Lillian started again.

"No more buts, Lilly." Tom kissed her one more time. He reached up to pull the pins holding her hair. Both of them knew that in this moment they wanted to be together.

CHAPTER THIRTEEN

2 July 1885

Thunderheads to the west promised more rain would arrive soon. The summer heat shimmered, creating misty mirages in the distance along the high desert landscape. Absorbed with his own thoughts, Tom P paid little attention to the ephemeral apparitions as he rode into Magdalena to see Lillian mid-morning. He tied both horses to the hitchrack and entered the cool, shadowed parlor that served as the waiting room for her patients who came for medical attention. Lilly looked up from her examination.

"Is there anything wrong?" she asked, looking at Tom's stern face. "You don't normally come into town this time of day."

"Lilly, we need to talk."

"All right. I'm just about through with my last patient."

After she finished tending a young miner who had suffered a deep cut on his arm, Lillian shut the front door and pulled down the shade, a signal to anyone passing by that she was closed. Turning back, she said, "This sounds serious. Are you all right?"

Tom stood nervously at the narrow window, not wanting to face Lilly. "I'm fine. I guess it's my conscience that's bothering me. When I arrived in Magdalena, I never intended to become involved with anyone, but then I met you. You're my problem," he began but stopped, unable to continue. He finally turned his tense face toward her.

Lilly stared at Tom for a long moment. Not sure where he was going with his opening remarks, she was irritated and felt compelled to speak, "If you're referring to how close we've become, I'm a grown woman. I fully understand the situation. I figured out a long time ago that you're probably not the marrying type, and I'm fine with that." Her gray eyes flashed.

Tom spoke quickly, "Lilly, the truth is I can't get married. If I could, you would surely be the one I'd want, but I've lied to you since the day we met. I need to come clean and hope that you will understand."

Lillian breathed deeply; then she spoke in a calm but quiet voice, "Go on."

"My name is not Charles Crawford. I was involved in a shooting in Texas. I had to leave before the law caught up with me." Tom stopped to see how she would respond to his revelation.

"Funny thing," Lillian commented. "I never thought you looked like a Charles."

Tom exclaimed, "Did you hear what I said, Lilly? I killed a man. I'm not who you think I am!"

"I think I do know who you are. Maybe not your name, but you are a good man. You can change your identity but not the man you are," Lillian stated firmly. "We've been seeing each other for months now. I've had the opportunity to get your full measure. You are kind, considerate, attentive, and an amazing musician. If you want to tell me about your past, I'll listen. But it's not necessary."

Tom gazed at Lilly for a long moment. He crossed the room and put his arms around her. Her tense shoulders matched his own. He held her as the wooden clock on the mantle ticked the minutes away. Slowly, they both relaxed in the familiar embrace.

Tom pulled back and looked directly into Lilly's gray eyes. "Thanks for not asking questions. I hope, some day, I will be able to tell you everything. Unfortunately, I need to leave Magdalena. My money's run out. I have to find a job."

"I'm sure there's plenty of jobs around here," Lillian countered.

"Can't do that. I have to be somewhere safe from the law," Tom replied. "I stayed longer than I intended because of you, Lilly, but I don't regret a single moment we've spent together."

After a couple of minutes of silence, Lillian stated simply, "I don't want you to go."

Tom sighed. He pulled her close again. "I wasn't sure how you would feel. I'm pleased to know you will miss me. If you'll let me, I will come back when I can."

Lillian replied wearily after a few moments, "Of course, you can come back."

"You are an amazing woman, Lillian Fairfield!" Tom exclaimed, kissing her, committing to memory the herbal meadowed fragrance that clung to her dark hair.

Lillian pulled back to catch her breath and then quipped, "Just one thing. Can I at least know your true name?"

"Well, it's Tom P. That's enough for now," he laughed and kissed the top of her head. "I'll be riding back to Texas to a ranch where I'm pretty sure I can find work. I'm leaving today."

"Today!" Lillian exclaimed, taken aback.

"I thought it best. I knew this would be difficult, at least for me," Tom stated. "I will miss you, Lilly. I have to leave now, or I'll change my mind."

Not trusting himself any longer, Tom headed for the front door. Lillian remained rooted to the spot of their last warm embrace. Tom turned back to look at her. "One thing for sure. I will return. Lilly, you're the kind of woman a man finds hard to leave or even to get off his mind. I will not forget our time together."

Walking to the door, Lilly watched Tom mount Midnight and grab the reins of the supply horse. She raised her hand in a farewell gesture.

"Goodbye, Tom P.," Lilly called. Then she whispered, "That's enough for now."

Tom's dark melancholy mood stayed with him as he traveled the dirt road east into Socorro. Seemed like he was always having to leave loved ones behind: his mother, his sister and her family, and now Lilly. He longed for a new life where goodbyes never had to happen. Not when they came with these kinds of feelings.

When Tom arrived in Socorro, he took the time to consult with some cowboys in the Last Chance Saloon about the best route to take back to Texas. He then headed almost due east, crossing the Pecos River at Fort Sumner in Lincoln County. Tom did not tarry at the outpost recently made famous by Billy the Kid. Continuing east, he found the trail up onto the Llano Estacado where as far as the eye could see were grassy plains. Tom was amazed at the flatness and vastness of the treeless prairie landscape. He knew immediately why this land was so perfect for cattle raising. Much of the grass was ten inches high and stretched to the distant horizon.

Crossing into Texas felt good. Tom had missed his home state, even if he couldn't go all the way back to Hill County or even to his sister Lina's place. Maybe some day.

Tom stopped at outlying ranches to ask the way. The area was sparsely settled except for occasional ranchers and cowboys. Tom found the Newman ranch close to the unusual land formation some called Casa Amarillas or Yellow Houses. From a distance the small cliffs did resemble the outline of buildings.

Riding up to the main ranch house, Tom tied both Midnight and his supply horse to the hitchrack. Even travel-weary and dusty, Tom P's appearance was striking. A middle-aged lady, wearing a plain, blue-flowered dress and a full-bibbed white apron, came to the front door when he knocked.

"Can I help you?" she asked, wiping her hands on a small blue kitchen towel.

"I hope so. I'm looking for Jim Newman," Tom replied, holding his hat in his hand.

"He's down by the corral behind the house," she replied.

"Thank you, ma'am," Tom said, while backing off the porch. He headed in the direction she indicated. The lady continued to watch Tom until he rounded the corner and was no longer in sight.

"Jim Newman, it's good to see you," Tom called as he rode right up to the corral and dismounted again.

Jim turned to the trail dusty cowboy, "Do I know you?"

"Yep. In another lifetime," quipped Tom laughing. "Remember Hillsboro?"

"Well, I'll be! Tom P Varnell. What are you doing in this part of Texas? Welcome!" Jim reached out to shake Tom's hand.

"Jim, to tell you the truth, I'm looking for a job. Hoping you might need an extra cowhand or someone to break horses," Tom responded.

"Why certainly. I know your abilities. Not too many can handle a horse better than you. I knew your father, Isaac, too. I heard something about your troubles back in Hill County. No need to talk about it here. Not too interested in your past anyhow. Just what you're willing to do now. I have to warn you though. Some of these range ponies we use here can be a bit ornery, but I can put you to work right away if that's what you truly want," offered Jim.

"Thanks, I'm much obliged. Actually, I just rode in from New Mexico. By the way, I'm going by the moniker of Bob

Woods. I like to arouse as little attention as possible," Tom said.

"No problem. It's possible some of the 'pokes will know who you are, for my family is not the only one out here from Hill County, but they'll mind their own business. I'll see to it," Jim answered. "Go ahead and put your gear into the bunkhouse. Your horses can go into the north pasture. It'll be time for supper as soon as you're settled."

Jim and Tom entered the large dining area set aside for the ranch hands and cowboys. Long tables and benches were crowded with men digging into the beef stew and sourdough biscuits the cook, Big Red, was dishing out.

"Men, we have a new hand," announced Newman, pausing for everyone to get quiet. "This is Bob Woods, freshly from New Mexico."

With that, Tom sat down and grabbed a blue tin bowl of stew. Talk resumed among the men. The easy atmosphere calmed Tom's tattered nerves. Here, he felt, was a safe place he could stay. Soon he joined in the conversation.

Tom had forgotten the rigid discipline of ranch life but was reintroduced to it when Big Red started ringing the metal triangle before dawn the next day. He wanted to turn over and go back to sleep and dream of gray eyes flecked with green, but he willed himself awake and was only a little behind a couple of others heading for a breakfast of sourdough biscuits, sausage gravy, and scrambled eggs. Afterwards, Tom watched the men rope and saddle their horses for the workday.

Once the cowboys were mounted, they crowded around the foreman, John Shellman, a tall, raw-boned, clean-shaven man who gave out the daily assignments for the men working the large ranch. The men scattered in ones, twos, and threes to get busy. Today, they were mostly heading out to look for mavericks in the brush and gullies in anticipation of an upcoming roundup. A few men were assigned to mending corral fences. Tom waited, leaning against the fence surrounding the remuda. He didn't have long to wait before the foreman headed his way.

"Jim told me we had a new hire who's ace high in the saddle. Missed you at supper last night. I was still out on the range. Let's get your personal mounts picked out, Bob," Shellman spoke. "Choose five or six. Not a lot of good ones left, but you shouldn't have much trouble." The men headed over to the pasture where the extra horse stock was kept.

"I'll try to do a bang-up job for you," replied Tom.

Watching the spare remuda, Tom took his time studying the horses. His first choice was a reddish brown gelding with a light-colored mane and the easiest gait for distance riding. He managed to spy what looked like a decent cutting horse as well. After that he selected four other likely candidates, having sized up the remainder of the herd. He knew after watching them that he would have to reach an 'understanding' with each horse he chose.

"I'll get the jingler here to move your choices over to the working remuda. Just so we're straight with one another, I don't care what your past is or if you're Jim's best friend. But I do expect you to carry your weight around here. Are we square with one another?" Shellman asked in a straight forward manner.

"Perfectly," Tom responded, gaining immediate respect for his new boss.

"Good. Once you get mounted, head out. I'm assigning you to a partner for a while until you get used to the place. With so few landmarks, it's easy to get lost out here until you get the lay of the land. You'll find Jake in the southern pasture. Just head down the path over by the barn. Work with him for the rest of the week."

Shellman turned and walked away. Tom grabbed a lariat,

tied a sliding loop at one end, and then headed back into the spare remuda. He walked quietly over to the reddish brown gelding, dragging the rope along the ground at arm's length behind him. When he got close enough, he swung the lariat with a side arm motion, outward and up. As the rope landed neatly over the horse's head, it was easy to jerk it snug with just a twitch of the wrist. Tom took the time to get 'acquainted' with the horse by rubbing his forehead and talking to him before walking the horse over to the barn where his tack was located.

As weeks passed by, Tom adjusted to being a hired hand on a ranch rather than running one. The thirty dollars a month was small but appreciated. He enjoyed the easy camaraderie he shared with the other working cowboys. He'd seen a couple eye him speculatively but no one asked personal questions. He did share one evening that he had a sweetheart he missed in New Mexico. Some of the men also talked about their ladies, at least those who said they had one.

Tom's easy-going manner and non-complaining attitude contributed to his popularity. He loved to joke with Big Red and even slipped the cook a pint of whiskey now and again. It paid off when Tom would see extra tidbits, like dried fruit or pecans and walnuts on his plate. He'd just turn around and share them with the others when Big Red wasn't looking.

Early one dusty, dun-colored morning, Tom sensed tension in the air when he arrived at the remuda to get his horse saddled. Next to the small corral, John Shellman was talking to Jesse Hawkins, one of the ranch hands. Tom wasn't surprised that Shellman was taking Hawkins to task as he was a shirker who rarely finished his work and often talked others into helping him. It was obvious that Shellman had had enough. Tom arrived at the end of the verbal confrontation.

"You're nothing but a deadbeat, Hawkins. The jig is up.

Fetch your gear and clear out," Shellman demanded.

"But, boss. You've been fed bad information. I pull me own weight 'round here. You can't just fire me," whined Hawkins, his shifty dark eyes darting around as other ranch hands arrived to back up John if he needed any help escorting Hawkins away.

"Enough. I've let slide your laziness, but no more. Now, skedaddle. Go!" Shellman yelled at the cowboy.

Hawkins started to plead again, but the scowl on Shellman's face made any further argument futile. He turned to head away from the corral, bumping into Tom. Hawkins stopped.

"Just who you staring at? You're nothing but a damn killer yourself," he snarled, then spit in the dirt for emphasis.

Tom stiffened. "What the hell are you talking about?"

"You know very well," Hawkins spat at him. "You belong in jail or better yet, hanged."

Tom took a threatening step toward Hawkins who quickly backed away. He turned to walk rapidly toward the bunkhouse. Tom watched angrily with half a mind to follow Hawkins.

"Men, get your mounts saddled. We have work to do. We don't have any more time to spend on that hard case," admonished Shellman, knowing only his command could avert an even more hostile situation.

Tom took a deep breath to alleviate the dark, boiling rage threatening to take control. Jake Johnson grabbed Tom's arm, pulling him toward the corral. Initially resisting, Tom managed to cool off enough to see reason.

That night after the evening meal, the men engaged in a game of mumbletypeg. Every man used his own pocketknife. Holding the tip between his thumb and index finger, each participant flipped the knife down into the dirt. The object was to get it to stick straight down with enough of the blade showing to put two fingers between the soil and handle. The men enjoyed competing or betting on their favorite contestant. No one gave another thought to Hawkins.

After the fall roundup, Tom sought out Jim Newman. "I haven't properly thanked you for giving me a job here," started Tom.

"No need. Shellman keeps me up-to-date. I'm glad you're here. I've heard the men like your company, too," Newman replied.

"I appreciate that, Jim. I've a favor to ask. I have a sweetheart in New Mexico. I haven't seen her in a long time. I'm asking for some time off to make a trip. I won't stay long," Tom explained.

"We have some lag time now. Sure, go ahead. Your job will be waiting for you when you get back. I like my cowboys happy," Jim answered, grinning.

"Thanks! You won't regret it," Tom replied. Laughing, he headed out the door to get his travel gear ready for the trip west. He decided to leave his supply horse in order to travel more rapidly. He told the other cowboys he'd see them in a couple of weeks. He endured some good-natured ribbing about what waited for him at the end of his anticipated journey. In the misty mauve morning before the sun had put in an appearance, Tom P headed out, riding Midnight.

CHAPTER FOURTEEN

14 October 1885

Tom P managed to make the return trip across the misty mountains and vast deserts of New Mexico in less time than he had expected. Stopping in the bustling community of Socorro once again, Tom went into Stern's Jewelry where he bought Lilly a delicate silver pendant necklace that he could now afford. Tom got a close shave and a much-needed haircut before returning to the Windsor Hotel to pull out clean dark pants and his only long-sleeved white shirt in anticipation of finishing his journey to Magdalena. Tom tucked Lilly's present for easy retrieval in the small pocket on the front of his black vest, which completed his attire for the next day.

Leaving Socorro on Thursday, Tom started his sojourn as the faint light of the pre-dawn framed the charcoal gray mountains to the west. Going toward the brightening horizon, he felt his own excitement increasing with each passing mile. Tom met no one on the westward trail in the early morning light and felt comfort in being the only traveler. Although autumn had arrived with a decided chill in the air, the hardy piñon junipers and cedar in the distance retained their cloak of greenery.

As Tom ascended to the higher elevation, his spirits lifted. He breathed deeply the cooler alpine air. This day he would be seeing his sweetheart. Tom imagined the surprised and pleased look on Lilly's face when he walked into her parlor. Daydreaming of feminine charms and favors granted, Tom paid little attention to the miles and familiar scenery that seemed to float past.

Upon arrival in Magdalena, Tom stopped in at Keegan's Saloon to warm up with a whiskey. He called out to Walt Conner but paid little attention to the other men standing around. He did not see the signal that passed between two men standing at opposite ends of the bar. Soon these men left. A few minutes later, Tom finished his drink, paid up, and left the saloon as well.

Tom stopped a short distance from Lilly's house. He looked around but saw nothing out of the ordinary. As a caution, he pulled his Winchester out of its scabbard attached to the saddle and carefully checked to see that it was loaded. Satisfied, he shoved the rifle back into its leather encasement. Covering the remaining distance, Tom brought Midnight to a halt at the hitchrack.

The front door was shut, and the shade was down. Tom was a little puzzled but decided that maybe Lilly was taking her dinner break, even though it wasn't quite noon yet. He hoped she hadn't gone to look for medicinal plants. As Tom dismounted, he was so intent on finding Lilly that he did not notice the tall, rugged man who stepped away from the far side of the Fairfield house where he had been staying out of sight.

"Tom P Varnell," barked the man sporting a black Stetson and wearing a badge on the front of his long-sleeved white shirt. "I'm here to arrest you. No use resistin'. We have you surrounded."

With no time to think, Tom whirled around, grabbing the Winchester, but found the rifle to be stuck in the scabbard as he tried to pull it out. Reaching for the reins, he stepped into the stirrup to remount Midnight. Tom did not quite make it onto the saddle before two men who materialized from the opposite direction of the lawman yanked him off.

Tom leaped up from the hard ground where he had fallen with both fists flying as he fought those who had jumped him. He managed to slug one lawman square in the jaw. The man howled as he landed in the dirt. Just then two more men arrived to grab Tom from behind, trying to pin his arms and keep his hands from seeing any more action. Tom P broke the grip and turned once again to place a boot in the stirrup of the saddle on Midnight, his only means of escape.

"I wouldn't try that if I were you," warned the man with the badge, aiming his Colt .45 directly at Tom, who heard the deadly click of the hammer being pulled back for action. "Just stand down and put your hands up easy-like. I'm not allowin' no more resistance."

Tom hesitated just long enough to allow the other two men to recover themselves, wrestle him to the ground, and slap on handcuffs. Unheeding of the lawman's warning, Tom struggled briefly as he felt the cold steel biting into the flesh of his wrists. In those storm-filled seconds, Tom knew his freedom was gone.

"Enough," barked the sheriff at the captive.

Tom gave up the fight as he was pulled up and the Colt was stuck hard into his ribs. He stood heaving, trying to control his ragged breath. Tom glared at the six men who had ambushed him. He was even angrier with himself for not sensing the eminent danger in his anticipation of seeing Lilly.

"Well, Tom P, it's been a long time," greeted Sheriff Tom Bell, who motioned to Sheriff Russell from Socorro that he could pull his gun away from his quarry. "I'm here with your one-way ticket back to Hillsboro and our cozy little jailhouse."

Instead of acknowledging the sheriff, Tom turned to the short, stocky deputy holding him, "Say, could you hand me my hat?"

"Stop right there, McKinney!" Bell barked at the deputy who was about to let go in order to do the captive's bidding.

"Varnell, I'm aware of your tricks, but no more."

Sheriff Bell, instead, retrieved the now dirt-encrusted Stetson. He didn't bother to dust it off before putting it on Tom's head. He said, "Are you ready to come quietly, or do we need to rough you up a bit more first? If necessary, I can put a rope collar around your neck right now for the trip home!"

Tom, feeling the dust from his hat float down around his face and neck, stared at the lawmen. His mind was racing, but instead of a plausible escape plan all his scattered thoughts led to no such foreseeable event. Tom took a deep breath, finally accepting his fate.

"All right. You got the drop on me. I won't fight no more," Tom announced wearily.

Bell turned Tom around to check for other weapons, which gave Tom the opportunity to eye Lilly's house. He was baffled that all the loud shouting and commotion had not caused her to come outside. He had to know.

"Sheriff Bell, would you answer a question for me?" Tom queried. "How'd you boys track me here?"

Bell looked at Tom P for a moment. "I don't see no reason not to answer your question. I'll admit you've been mighty tough to corner, but I knew if I waited long enough and offered a little incentive, someone would eventually come forward with the right kind of information to nab you."

"Are you trying to tell me that the woman who lives in that house alerted you that I'd be coming back to see her?" asked a shocked and angry Tom, looking at Lilly's house once again.

"No. Actually, it's your own big mouth that led us here," Bell responded.

Tom turned back to his captor. "You're not making any sense."

"Maybe this will clear it up, Varnell. You remember a 'poke named Hawkins who worked on the Newman ranch in Texas, same as you?" Bell asked.

"Yep. He was a lazy bastard. What's he got to do with any of this?" Tom P asked in return.

"When he left his job on the Newman ranch, Hawkins went over to Brigman's ranch close by, looking for a job as a rider. While there, he asked Jim Brigman if'n there was still a reward for your capture as he might have some important information," Bell responded.

"That son-of-a-bitch," whispered Tom, feeling his face flush in anger.

Bell continued, "So Brigman, who also has a farm in Hill County, had a rider go to the closest telegraph office in Colorado City. The message to my office said he thought you were at the Newman ranch working under the name of Bob Woods. I didn't know whether to believe him or not since we've had false leads before that didn't pan out. So I sent Deputy McKinney, here, out to the Panhandle to find out for sure and to watch your movements if you be there. McKinney reported that you were, indeed, on the Newman ranch."

Tom let the information sink in. Still not satisfied, he asked, "So why didn't you arrest me in Texas? You went to a lot of trouble to set up a trap here in New Mexico."

Deputy Bill McKinney, rubbing his sore jaw, answered for the sheriff, "Tom P, I stayed with the Newmans and observed your movements for quite awhile from a distance. It was obvious to me that you were among friends willing to protect you. I wired Sheriff Bell it might not be a good idea to try to take you there. Hawkins agreed and then remembered your stories about having a sweetheart in New Mexico. It took him some time to recall her name was Lilly something or other and that she lived in Magdalena. He was sure you'd go back to see her sooner or later."

"Damn it," Tom exclaimed.

"I guess it only takes one good cowpoke. Right, Varnell?" Bell stated. "Once McKinney sent me a telegram that you'd left the ranch, we knew exactly where you'd be headed. We were able to arrive ahead of you, traveling by train. I got Socorro County Sheriff Russell here and his men to help me figure out when you might be arrivin'. He was in Keegan's Saloon earlier. We waited for you here. Any more questions?"

Tom eyed the New Mexico sheriff in his blue denim pants and chambray shirt but didn't say anything to him. "Guess not. Can I at least see Lilly before we leave? I've got to explain."

"Can't do that Varnell. I warned her to stay out of sight. I doubt she wants to have anything to do with you anymore. Besides, I can't trust you. We'll be taking you over to the jail here, then we'll catch the train in the morning," Bell replied, starting to pull Tom down the street.

"Wait! My horse! My belongings!" exclaimed Tom, trying to buy some time.

The sheriff stopped, obviously considering what to do next. "All right. McKinney, grab his stuff. We'll arrange to take the horse back, but you'll have to foot the bill. Reckon your momma can pay for it if'n you can't."

Tom glanced at Lilly's house. He thought he saw a curtain move. When the group reached the end of Second Street, Tom looked back one last time. Lilly was standing at the spot where he had been jumped. From a distance it looked like she was holding something. Suddenly remembering, Tom reached inside his vest pocket with his free hand. The necklace was gone. He must have lost it in the scuffle when he was fighting with the lawmen. Tom wanted to call to her. He even opened his mouth but what could he say? Bell was right. She probably wanted nothing more to do with him. The sheriff jerked Tom around the corner of the livery stable.

The Magdalena jail was a small adobe building with a tin

roof. Inside were two dark cells that could hold two men each. For the moment Tom was the only forced occupant. Bell bid Sheriff Russell goodbye and left to check the train schedule.

The next morning Sheriff Bell arrived early to pick up his captive. "Tom, you and I are not only traveling together, I am going to handcuff you to myself," Bell said.

Bell pulled out a set of cuffs. He had McKinney put one cuff on Tom and then the other on the sheriff's own wrist.

"It's just about time for us to catch the eastbound train to Socorro. Your doings here are over." Bell pulled Tom P in the direction of the train depot. Tom looked around in hopes of one last glimpse of Lilly, but she was nowhere to be seen. Just as well, he mused to himself. Hadn't he known from the beginning that his capture would bring to an end their relationship? He just hoped she would understand and forgive him some day. The lawmen and captive boarded the train, which stopped at Water Canyon to pick up passengers before heading into Socorro.

The rail trip south to El Paso passed without incident. Tom spent most of his time napping, although being handcuffed to the sheriff was problematic and his privacy was gone. The three men had to disembark at El Paso to switch to an eastbound train.

Bell spied Macy's Boarding House, which had a public restaurant on the ground floor close to the train station. "Come on boys. Let's get some home cookin'," he announced.

Tom Bell, Bill McKinney, and Tom P walked the short distance down the dusty, wind-swept street. The owner turned out to be an elderly widow who led them to an unoccupied table covered with a red and white checked oilcloth tablecloth. Bustling about serving other customers first, she finally came back to get their order.

"Today, we got cowboy beef stew or frijoles along with

cornbread. What can I bring you?"

After listening to their choices, Macy took a wet cloth and wiped off their tablecloth. She turned to Deputy McKinney and pointed at Tom P. "My goodness, Mr. Officer. I feel so sorry for that nice looking young feller you got handcuffed to that Indian. I've seen me lots of mean looking hombres, but I do believe that Indian is the meanest looking one I ever saw."

For the first time since he had been cornered, Tom cracked a smile. His eyes twinkled as Tom winked at Macy. She smiled back. Bell jerked his arm, causing Tom to lose his balance and almost tip over his chair. McKinney was so amused he failed to correct the lady's impression.

A few minutes later, Macy bustled back with their meals. Tom noticed an extra helping on his plate. He grinned back at her again. At that moment William Poage, a detective from Waco, arrived.

"Hey, Sheriff Bell. I heard you were here with your captive. Care if I join you?"

"Of course not," Bell answered. "Are you traveling back to central Texas? You can help guard Varnell."

The widow's eyes widened as she looked between Poage and Bell and back to Tom. Macy quickly left for the kitchen saying, "Oh, my lord!"

"Be glad to travel with you," replied William Poage. "Did I miss a joke or something?" No one replied, but they all laughed.

Back on the train, heading east, William Poage managed to get a seat across from Tom P. As the arid, desert landscape sped past, Poage engaged Tom in conversation as they watched the tumbleweeds, pushed by the dusty winds, skip across the Texas landscape.

"Guess you never thought you'd get caught this far from Hill County," Poage stated.

"I'm more surprised I didn't get caught before now. I'm relieved in a way, even if it was a low-down skunk who turned me in for a little cash and a whole lot of revenge for something I had no part of," Tom answered.

"McKinney filled me in on what happened. Why are you relieved?" Poage asked.

"It's like this. I've lived on the run for almost two years now. I've spent many more days than I care to remember sweating in dirt dugouts, like I did in Hill County, or freezing while traveling along the desolate prairies of West Texas in wintertime. I've also had some mighty bad nightmares about my capture or death, only to wake up wondering where I was or how I came to be there. I was sure that every tin-starred lawman I came across was gunning for me, especially after I found out how widespread the news stories about the Land killing had become," answered Tom. "That's why I thought often of just turning myself in. Just to get it over with." Tom surprised himself at his own lengthy answer.

"So why didn't you?" When Tom looked puzzled, Poage added, "Turn yourself in?"

Tom considered the question for a couple of moments. "Two reasons, I reckon. I really didn't want to give up my freedom, especially since the chances of a fair trial were slim in my estimation. 'Sides that, I knew I'd never allow myself to be taken without a fight, and I'd probably get myself killed."

"So here you are," Poage summed up.

"Yep. Mother can stop worrying that I'll be shot dead," Tom replied.

"Would you two shut up," complained Bell, yanking on Tom's handcuff. "I'm trying to get some shut-eye." With that, the group fell silent. Soon all were snoring, except for McKinney who had been assigned to guard duty.

The trip to Hill County from New Mexico took four days. They passed through Fort Worth before turning south, heading for Hillsboro. Tom both dreaded his homecoming and yearned to see his mother as soon as possible. They arrived late at night with no fanfare. Bell quickly disembarked with his cuffed captive, heading for the county jail that was located only a couple of blocks from the train depot. As the three-story stone building loomed, Tom swallowed hard to hold down his feeling that he'd never be free again. With his charge safely under lock and key, the sheriff ordered the deputy to keep a sharp eye on Varnell. Then Bell departed to mingle with the newly arrived backslappers just outside the jailhouse.

Tom P was grateful for once that gossip traveled fast when early the next morning his mother appeared. She insisted to the deputy she needed to see Tom right away.

"Mother! You're a sight for sore eyes," Tom reacted when she was ushered into the small space next to his barred abode.

"Tom P!" Docia exclaimed, putting her arms through the bars to touch her beloved son the best she could.

"Sorry, Mrs. Varnell, but you'll have to stand back. We don't allow no touching," admonished the guard. Docia glared at him but pulled her arms out from between the bars.

"Tom P, you don't know how relieved I am the sheriff didn't take it upon himself to kill you," she told him.

"I'm sorry, Mother, that I've caused you such worry," replied Tom.

"Sh-h-h! No need," Docia retorted. "I've already contacted your attorneys. They'll be around to see you some time today."

"I'm wary of what the future's gonna bring, Mother," Tom replied. "I don't feel quite as hopeful as you do. Hiring lawyers is going to be an expensive endeavor."

"You listen to me, Tom P. You're a Varnell. We don't live by regrets. You know the charge of murder against you is bogus, and so do I. You have to believe in your innocence, or you will convince no one else," Docia stated vehemently. "I've been putting money to the side for some time in anticipation that it might be needed for this. I can afford the best, and that is what you are going to get!"

"Of course, you're right! Thanks does not seem to be enough," Tom replied. "Tell me how the ranch is doing?"

The two visited for as long as the guard let them. Docia told Tom she'd be back the next day with clean clothes and some bed linen to make him more comfortable. Docia told him that she wanted to hear all about his time away from Hillsboro. As Tom watched her leave, he wished he had half the conviction his mother had. Tom lay down contemplating the strong and willful women in his life – his mother, his sister Adeline, and until recently, Lilly.

CHAPTER FIFTEEN

7 November 1885

Tom P lay on the narrow bed. The thin, lumpy, stained mattress of no discernable color provided little comfort and was in much need of mending. Twin sets of bunk beds on opposite sides with a small aisle in between made up the space afforded to those forced to stay at the county-funded accommodations. Thick bars made up two sides. Two rock walls full of etched crude drawings and scribblings from previous occupants completed the rectangular space that Tom shared with three other men. Similar cells held altogether sixteen inmates when full. Saturday nights usually found the place overcrowded with merrymakers not content to keep their fists or six-guns to themselves while enjoying a drink or two at the local saloons.

As a man used to spending most of his time outdoors, Tom alternated between being angry and being depressed with his enforced confinement, though outwardly those feelings were not all that likely to be revealed. The only visitors allowed were his mother and his attorneys. With little to occupy his time, Tom spent hours on end reliving the events of the past three years that had brought him to this sorry state of existence.

The daily routine for the prisoners was monotonous and predictable. Each day the residents of the jail were allowed to exercise for a while in an area called the runaround, which was really the corridor outside the cells. Afterwards, they were locked up for the remainder of the day. Going outdoors was not allowed. Meals were fixed by the deputy's wife and eaten by the men inside the jail cells.

Tom often cracked jokes or made fun of the jailors, causing laughter among the inmates. He could mimic every guard's walk and even their mannerisms when they spoke. Tom was surprised by how often the other men turned to him for conversation. What the men did not see was Tom's increasing anxiety over his own situation.

"Hey, Varnell, your lawyer's here," called the jailor one morning. He stepped aside in the runaround to let Samuel Upshaw pass by.

Tom rose quickly and went over to the barred cell door. To his keeper he said, "Can't we have a little privacy?"

"Nope. Sheriff don't trust you, Varnell." The jailor remained but stood to the side.

Tom let out an expletive before turning back to Samuel Upshaw. "Any news, Captain? I am anxious to get out of here."

"No, Tom P," Upshaw answered. "You have to be patient. Sometimes the judicial wheels are mighty slow to turn."

"But you've managed to get a habeas corpus hearing, right?" Tom queried, gripping the round metal bars.

"Not yet," replied Upshaw. "The truth is District Judge Hall is dragging his feet. He says that other legal matters have to be settled first. With the judge living in Cleburne, he's not available to the court every day."

"What legal matters could the judge possibly be talkin' about?" challenged Tom.

"Really they're just procedural. When you were on the run, the court assigned a case number when they indicted you for murder. They recently quashed that case and dismissed it," Upshaw explained.

"Why would they do that?" asked Tom.

"Because they no longer want your name linked on paper with another defendant who has since been acquitted," Upshaw replied.

"George Walker!" Tom exclaimed, finally understanding what Upshaw was saying.

"The court re-indicted you for murder as well as renewed the lesser crime against you of assault with intent, but I don't think that case will be pushed forward until the murder case is resolved and maybe not at all," shared Upshaw.

"Sounds like they're determined to send me to prison," sighed Tom.

"It does. One charge against you I'm working to get dropped is for the rape of Ella Land," announced Upshaw.

"Rape! They can't be serious. No rape took place. Ella was more than willing," Tom stated heatedly, slamming his hands against the bars.

"I have evidence that the indictment was made by an illegal grand jury. I still have to go through the right channels to get it quashed, and that takes time," Upshaw stated, trying to calm down his volatile client.

"This is bull," grumbled Tom, starting to pace between the bunk beds. His cellmates stayed on their beds to give him room to walk.

"Like I said, it's legal maneuvering. Don't despair. Hopefully, it won't be much longer, and I can get that hearing to set bail."

"All right. But I need you to do something to get me moved out of here pronto," Tom continued.

"What do you mean?"

"It's like this. Rumors are circulating that some no-accounts want to organize a lynching. The *Waco Daily Examiner* and other papers keep stirrin' people up with editorials against me. I don't think this jail's gonna be safe for long," Tom explained.

"I'll talk to Sheriff Bell, but he may not be too receptive," Upshaw promised.

Thursday, November 12th, started out like all other days since Tom arrived almost a month previously. After breakfast, the jailor came back to let a few prisoners out for their exercise time. Generally, the men did not cause much trouble, so only one of the four guards stayed with them in the runaround. An inmate called Tom over to the side.

"Hey, Varnell, lookie here," George Hubbard whispered excitedly.

Tom walked over to the spot where the iron grate connected to the prison wall. Hubbard pushed, and the grate easily pulled away. Tom's eyes widened.

"Wanna make a break for it?" Hubbard offered. "I'm goin'. They've already got me down as a horse thief. Don't wanna serve no fourteen years at Huntsville."

Tom looked around quickly and noticed the jailor was on the other side of the runaround where the cells blocked his view. With the other three jailors occupied with playing cards in the front room as usual, the possible escape was inviting. Tom had little time to make up his mind or consider the consequences of leaving. He focused on his simmering anger at the disheartening news that his lawyer had failed to get him a hearing for bail or even moved to a different, safer location.

"I'm going, too," Jesse Graffinreid added. "I'm facing twenty years for takin' a horse I didn't even take."

Tom made his decision. "Homer, if you're not going, keep junior over there occupied for awhile, okay?"

"Anything for you, Tom P. Good luck!" Homer replied. He and a couple of other prisoners headed to the other side. Arriving, they stood blocking the jailor's view as best they could while engaging him in conversation.

Tom, Jesse, and George slipped out. A fourth prisoner, Tilton Moore, also escaped before the grate was put back into place. The men quietly climbed up to the second tier and entered the living quarters of the deputy in charge of the jail. Tom grabbed some wool blankets off unmade beds in an unoccupied area and quickly fashioned ropes that they all used to lower themselves out the second floor window.

Dropping to the ground, the escapees hid behind the two-story building. The jail was situated at the corner of Covington and Franklin streets across from the Hill County Courthouse and had a vacant field behind it. The men quickly dashed across the open expanse and into the grove of trees not far away.

About an hour later when a jailor discovered that some prisoners were missing, he sent a runner to get the sheriff. Bell arrived quickly, swearing expletives with every booted step he took. He could not understand how four men whose sole purpose was to keep an eye on the jailed inmates could have been blind to the jailbreak for so long. His frustration exploded when he learned Varnell was among those missing and once again on the loose.

"Damn it, I oughta shoot the whole lot of you!" yelled Bell. He turned around and left the premises. On the front stoop of the jailhouse, he started firing off his pistol. It helped to release some of the frustration he felt. The townspeople came running to see what all the commotion was about. Bell immediately organized and deputized several men to head up search parties. He not only sent groups to different areas of Hill County, he also gave out lists of known friends of Varnell, such as Ed Bryant and George Walker, for searchers and seekers of information to keep an eye on.

As word got out, John Decker, newsman for the *Hillsboro*

Mirror, stopped by to see the beleaguered sheriff, who proceeded to fill Decker in on the details. Normally, Bell despised these hack writers, but the sheriff needed help this time in getting word out quickly to the county citizens so they could be on their own vigilance for the fugitives.

"Put in there I'm offering a reward of $250 for Varnell's capture anywhere in Texas," Bell added.

"What about the other escapees, sheriff?" asked the news reporter, pencil poised above his notebook.

"I don't give a damn about any of the others. They won't be hard to track down," Bell exclaimed, tipping his chair back. "It's Varnell I want, even if we have to kill that son-of-a-bitch to bring him in!" To emphasize his point, Bell slammed the chair back down on all four legs.

At that very moment the door to Bell's office opened, and the penitentiary contractor, George Oglesby, walked in. "Evening, sheriff. Someone said you had a jail break."

"I'm `fraid so. Those men you're supposed to haul off today to Huntsville have managed to light out," Bell answered.

"Sounds like you need my bloodhounds," Oglesby responded. "I could bring `em up from Waco. Be glad to fetch `em."

"Go git `em. How long you reckon it'll take? One of the escapees is Tom P Varnell. That bastard is on the loose again," replied Bell.

"I'll take off right now to catch the twelve o'clock train to Waco. My bloodhounds are the best in the business. They'll catch Varnell. You can count on it," responded Oglesby, turning to leave.

Suddenly, the door jerked open, and Deputy McKinney rushed in. "Sheriff, you're gonna want to come outside."

Bell got up quickly and grabbed his Stetson before heading through the front door. Decker and Oglesby followed. Standing on the street near the jail was a boy about ten years old. Excited onlookers encircled him.

"What's this commotion all about?" demanded Bell seeing the gathering crowd.

"Sheriff, this boy seen the escapees," called a by-stander.

"Indeed!" exclaimed Bell towering over the youngster. "Exactly what did you see, boy?"

The youngster opened his mouth to speak but nothing came out. His eyes widened as he looked at the encroaching crowd and then back around to the big angry man wearing the badge who was yelling at him.

Finally, the sheriff knelt down so he could look at the youngster at eye level. "It's all right, boy. Calm down and tell me, first, what's your name?"

"Jake Smithson, sir. I ain't done nothing wrong," the boy whimpered.

"Of course, you didn't. Just tell us what you saw," coaxed Bell.

"I's comin' into town on our farm horse when two men jumped out from behind a tree. They took my horse. They really skeered me," replied the boy visibly shivering.

"What road were you on?" asked Bell quickly.

"Road to Itaskie, 'bout three miles out," replied Jake.

"Good. Thanks, boy. You came to the right place. Did those outlaws hurt you?" queried the sheriff.

"Nope. Just told me to get down 'cause they intended to borrow my horse. One even said he'd see I got it back. Asked where our farm was located. Don't know as I should rightly believe him though," Jake answered; then looking up at the sheriff, added, "But he did speak kind of kindly to me."

"Can you describe that outlaw?" encouraged Bell.

"Sure can. He had dark curly hair, a mustache, and big blue eyes," Jake replied.

"Go on home now, Jake. I got a man here with a buggy

who'll take you. Tell your ma and pa not to worry. I'll get that horse back to you," Bell spoke determinedly. With that the sheriff signaled his deputies and left quickly for the Itaska road.

On the following Tuesday after the jailbreak, Sheriff Bell sat at his desk. He was in a foul mood. Despite his best efforts, no one had come close to locating, much less nabbing, Tom P or his cohorts on the dodge. While the *Hillsboro Mirror* had given Bell a pass so far as blame was concerned, the sheriff also knew well that the voting public might be less forgiving come election time. The local news articles stated daily that Varnell's capture was eminent, but Bell wasn't so sure.

Deputy McKinney entered and threw a newspaper down on his desk, saying, "Thought you might be interested in this right here."

Sheriff Bell picked up the paper. It was the *Dallas Morning News.* McKinney pointed out a headline.

Bell scanned quickly, then looked up at his deputy.

"It says here that Dr. F. M Pitts was waylaid on his way home late at night by Varnell and the other two escapees. It even relates the supposed conversation between Varnell and the good doctor."

"That's right. But what's worse is the paper makes Varnell out as some kind of nice guy," responded McKinney.

Bell looked at the article again, reading slowly. "So it says that the doctor was scared when he realized it was the desperado but that Varnell stopped the others from hurting the doctor, saying that he was only out late doing his job and that they should let him pass unharmed. It's plain that the other convicts are looking to Varnell as their leader. That doctor was lucky I guess. But who would think Varnell was a nice guy after what he done?"

"You got a point. I guess the doctor was curious after he calmed down as he asked Varnell what he wanted him to tell those who were searching for him."

"That's pretty cocky to tell the doctor that it was all right to tell us exactly where they had their late night conversation because, according to Varnell's words, no one could catch him as he would be fifty miles from that location of Mt. Calm by the time the law showed up to investigate."

"Quite a boast," retorted Bell. "Damn it! Why can't we catch 'im?"

McKinney didn't dare try to answer the question as he knew Bell was in no mood to hear his theories. He knew that since Tom P and his mother owned that horse ranch that getting fast horses would not be a problem.

Instead, he replied, "They even tell how Varnell left money on the table of a farmhouse where he and the others took some food. Signing a note with his name is like taunting us that we can't get the drop on 'im."

"How in the hell did the paper get this story?" wondered Bell out loud. "I thought we kept it quiet."

"Well somebody told 'em," replied McKinney stating the obvious. "Now, you'll get questioned by others about this."

"Damn it!" Bell exclaimed when he finished. "They made him into some kind of folk hero. Ain't that great!" Throwing the paper into the trash, he slammed out the front door.

Docia Varnell entered Samuel Upshaw's office five days after her son broke out of the Hill County Jail. The smell of fine leather and cigar smoke greeted her senses. The lawyer took her hand and invited her to sit down across from his rich mahogany desk.

"Captain Upshaw, I'll get straight to the point as I know you're a busy man. My son made a mistake when he chose to leave with those two yahoos. I've come to enlist your help," Docia pleaded, sitting on the edge of her chair with her back ramrod straight. She nervously clutched her small black purse.

"Mrs. Varnell, I don't think I can help your son any longer. Breaking out of jail was an ill-considered thing to do. I was making progress in getting Judge Hall to listen to me, and Tom P goes and blows it all apart. I'm ready to give up on him for a client. I just can't imagine what he was thinking!" Upshaw spoke vehemently. He laced his fingers together in frustration but did look at Docia Varnell with a bit of compassion.

"I agree, Captain, that my son in a moment of aberration chose a course detrimental to his case. He knows it now as well and is remorseful. Confinement robbed Tom of his senses. That's why I'm here. Please accept his apologies." Docia reached out to grasp the front edge of Upshaw's desk.

"Well, I don't know what I can do now for you or for him," Upshaw replied, leaning back in his chair.

"Help him turn himself in. That's what Tom P wants to do, but he doesn't want to get killed or hurt in the process. Too many would like nothing better than to spill my son's blood. Can you help us?" Docia pleaded.

"You're saying he wants to surrender? Why now? They've not been able to catch him. The bloodhounds have been called off, much to Oglesby's embarrassment. Soon enough, Tom could slip out of Hill County and disappear forever," Upshaw retorted.

"What you say is true, but Tom P was actually relieved when he was caught in New Mexico. He doesn't like being on the run. He now wants to stand trial and get this trouble behind him. He wants to follow your advice," Docia stated vehemently.

"You plead his case eloquently. I hope I can do as good a job in court, but it won't be easy. Your son has done much to hurt his cause and his chance for real freedom," Upshaw admonished. The lawyer looked out his office window. He mulled over his knowledge that this would indeed be a tough case to win. Tom's two years on the run after the Land shooting and then his jailbreak served only to solidify the minds of those who believed him guilty of rape and murder. Ultimately, his belief in his client's innocence, based on self-defense not murder, won out.

"All right, Mrs. Varnell, I will get with Bell and work out the terms for Tom's surrender if you are sure this is what he wants to see happen."

"I'm very sure. Thank you, Captain Upshaw. I will never forget your kindness," Docia replied, visibly showing her relief with her smile.

"It may take a couple of days. I'll be in touch."

Captain Upshaw stood up. Docia did as well, shaking his hand. He walked her to the front door of his office. Waving, he proceeded down the street, heading for the sheriff's office.

CHAPTER SIXTEEN

19 November 1885

Since it was early on a Thursday morning, the Hillsboro Courthouse Square was fairly quiet. Sheriff Tom Bell left his office at eight o'clock to make the rounds. Listening to the rhythmic clink of his booted spurs, Bell remembered the tense meeting he'd had with Varnell's attorney, Upshaw. Bell had agreed to the terms of surrender, even though it rankled that he had not, with all his resources, been able himself to track down Hillsboro's most notorious fugitive. He was especially incensed when Samuel Upshaw told him that Varnell had never left the county.

Leaning up against the courthouse wall, Bell rolled a cigarette using tobacco from his draw-string bag of Bull Durham. Striking a match on the rough stone of the courthouse wall, he cupped his hands to shield the flame from the morning breeze as he brought it up to light. Bell inhaled slowly the acrid smoke, which calmed his nerves that had been raw for a week, ever since Varnell had escaped incarceration. He'd captured fairly easily the other escapees.

Pushing off from the wall, Bell rounded the southeast corner of the courthouse, noticing a slow-moving covered wagon heading toward town along the Bynum road. Bell stopped and waited on the courthouse steps, dropping the half-smoked cigarette to the ground, stamping it with his boot to put out the slow-burning tobacco.

The wagon came to a halt forty feet from where the law-man stood. Sheriff Bell used his thumb and forefinger to remove a tobacco fleck from his tongue. He kept his eyes on the new arrival. Repositioning his Stetson, he checked his holstered Colt .45. A couple of minutes later a lone man jumped out the back, rounded the wheels, then stopped to stare at the sheriff. Tom P Varnell had a road-weary look about him but was smiling.

The escapee paused long enough to make sure Bell had fol-lowed the agreement that no other officials be around to draw a crowd. Spotting none, Tom ambled over to the courthouse.

"Howdy, sheriff," greeted the fugitive.

"Varnell," Bell nodded his head. "Let's head on over to the jail. Won't be there long."

Tom looked at Bell in surprise. "Why? I gave my promise I wouldn't try to run off again. I keep my promises, sheriff."

"No need temptin' you, is there? I'm hauling you to Waco for safe keepin' `til we can get repairs done. Let's just say I'll sleep a lot better with you holed up in their new Pauly jail," replied Bell. "We'll catch the ten o'clock and be there `fore noon."

"That's a long way. Upshaw didn't mention my accom-modations would change. I'm not prepared for this," responded Tom. "What say you allow me to do a little lookin' for some new duds. You have my promise to be on my best behavior."

"We'll see once we get to Waco," Bell responded, not in the mood to make any promises. "Don't think for one second about askin' to visit Two Street."

"Why not? My treat, sheriff," quipped Tom. Bell glared at him before heading for the jail.

Tom sobered up quickly. "Sheriff, I know we have our dif-ferences, but you're a good lawman. And plenty fair. I `preciate that."

Tom Bell eyed Varnell again but made no more comments

as they entered the jail. The early morning pedestrians took little note of Tom's surrender. Samuel Upshaw, who had been waiting their arrival, stood up to greet his reinstated client.

The crowd in front of one of Waco's finer establishments, Mallory's Clothing Store, was growing by the minute as word spread rapidly that the notorious desperado, Tom P Varnell, was inside. Most were astonished to find out that the recently escaped fugitive, whose escapades had been followed across the state in numerous news accounts, had surrendered to authorities and was now walking side-by-side with the Hill County sheriff and his deputies.

A reporter for the *Waco Examiner* chronicled the event:

Varnell Surrenders

He Arrives in Waco With Sheriff Bell,
The Sensation He Created on The Streets
Was Very Great

Varnell stated that his intention when he broke jail in Hillsboro was to surrender himself. His hardships, he says, have been very severe since his escape. The man, that one would have selected from the crowd to be Varnell, would naturally have been a desperate appearing person, but Varnell is a young man of a most contrary description. He has a pleasant and manly face, good manners, and a prepossessing appearance.

On arriving here, he went to the county jail for registration, and then came uptown. He was on the street until 4 p.m. He was unusually gay for one with the charge that hangs over him, and his nerves are not in the least shaken. He expresses his confidence of an acquittal. He remarked

that he never would have given himself up, did he not judge
his chances of acquittal to be sure. He was escorted to the
jail by his party, and followed by a crowd of the curious.

Tom's stay in the Waco jail lasted only a couple of weeks before he was given his habeas corpus hearing for bail. Arriving to transport Tom back to Hillsboro, Sheriff Bell once again linked himself to Tom Varnell with metal. They left on the early morning train on December 5th.

"Well, sheriff," commented Tom, eyeing the handcuffs, "I'm hopin' this is the last time we keep such close company."

"I wouldn't get your confidence up too high," retorted Bell. "The prosecution's pretty bent on keepin' you in the lockup 'til your trial."

Tom settled down in his train seat, watching the late fall landscape flow past his vision. He was struck by the irony that his mode of transportation nowadays, while modern, was mostly connected to an event from his past he'd give just about anything to forget. Today, he would come face-to-face with his main accuser, Emma Land, who'd married that Beasley fella. Tom made it a practice to despise few people, but she was a likely choice if ever there was one.

As the train pulled into the Hillsboro depot, Tom suddenly remembered something. "Say, sheriff, did you ever collect that reward for me from the governor?"

"Yep," Bell answered with a grimace.

"Why the face? Didn't he pay all of it?" asked Tom.

"That's not it. Yeah, I received the $500 reward but nothin' more, and my expenses were considerable," admitted Bell. "If I'd been able to nab you here in Hill County, the reward would've been a nice bonus. You've been a real costly son-of-a-bitch."

The sheriff scowled. Tom grinned. Suddenly, they both laughed out loud. The train lurched to a stop. Bell stood up, recovering his professional demeanor.

"Come on, Varnell. You know the way," he commanded gruffly.

The district courtroom was packed to capacity with spectators when Tom walked in from the side door to join his attorneys, Colonel J. M. Anderson and Major Pearre from Waco, along with Captain Upshaw and Tom Ivy, Esq., from Hillsboro. Bell had conceded to removing Tom's handcuffs but stayed close until he was seated. Tom presented an outward confidence but felt a knot forming in the pit of his stomach. He watched the state's counsel, Honorable M. M. Crane from Cleburne and Colonel V. H. Ivy, the Hill County Attorney. They were busy scribbling notes.

Samuel Upshaw leaned over to Tom, "We won't be calling you to the stand. It's standard procedure. The prosecution will be tryin' to show just cause as to why you should not be granted bail. Then it's up to the judge to decide."

"I just hope he listens to our side," declared Tom.

"All rise," barked the bailiff at that moment, "for the Honorable District Judge, J. M. Hall."

The judge entered the courtroom and quickly ascended to the bench. He had lost an arm in the Civil War, but the flowing sleeves on his judge's robes along with his regal walk mostly hid this fact. The judge's steady and knowing eyes looked unblinkingly at Tom before he turned to the prosecution, signaling it was time to begin.

After some preliminary testimony, the prosecution called their main witness, Emma Land Beasley, who sat down in the witness box after being duly sworn. Dressed in a dark brown traveling suit, Emma's blond hair was pulled into a severe bun at her neckline. She folded her hands onto her lap and looked down demurely until the district attorney asked his first question.

Tom blinked, wondering if this was the same woman he'd had words with back on that fateful night.

"State for the court your name and relation to the deceased, Mr. Jonah Land," prompted Crane.

"I am Emma Land Beasley. Jonah Land was my father," answered the witness clearly.

"Now, Mrs. Beasley, were you present when your father died?" asked Crane.

"Yes, I was there. I witnessed his death."

"Is the person who killed your father present in the courtroom?" Crane pressed.

"Yes, he is," Emma answered, lifting her hand to point at the defendant. "His name is Tom P Varnell. He murdered my father after he raped my sister, Miss Ella Land."

The courtroom erupted in excited noise as Tom jumped up yelling, "She's lyin'!"

Judge Hall pounded the gavel several times. With pandemonium threatening, he announced sternly, "Order in the court. Any more outbursts from the audience, and I will clear this courtroom of all spectators."

A silence fell upon the room as the judge turned to the defense's table. "You will remind your client that he is to remain quiet during testimony or be held in contempt."

"Yes, Your Honor," replied Tom Ivy, after standing.

Tom leaned over to Samuel Upshaw, whispering furiously, "But she's lying."

"We'll have our turn. Now do what the judge says, or he'll call a halt to this and not in our favor," Upshaw admonished in a low but emphatic tone.

The district attorney stood up. "Now Mrs. Beasley, let's proceed. Did your sister witness the death of your father?"

"No, she didn't. She ran into the safety of the house after I pulled Varnell off her."

"If Mr. Varnell were to be freed on bond, do you have any fears for your safety?" asked Crane.

"Absolutely. He's a cold-blooded killer. I fear he will come after me for speakin' the truth," Emma spoke vehemently, then added, "My sister is frightened as well."

Upshaw rose while at the same time placing a hand on Tom's shoulder to keep him seated. "I object, Your Honor. Witness is coloring her statements with unproven pejorative observations. Defendant has had no interaction with witness since the alleged event occurred."

"Objection overruled," announced the judge with no explanation. "Mr. Crane, you may continue."

"Thank you, Your Honor. Mrs. Beasley, would you tell the court why your sister is unable to testify today?" queried Crane.

"Objection," cried Tom Ivy.

"Sustained," replied the judge quickly.

"Let me rephrase. Mrs. Beasley, is your sister here today?"

"Yes. She's here but unable to testify."

"Is she currently living at home with her family?"

"No. She is an inmate at the State Asylum for the Deaf and Dumb in Austin."

"How long has she had her affliction?"

"Since the day that man," Emma pointed at Tom, "murdered our father."

Upshaw rose quickly. "Objection, Your Honor."

"Overruled. Sit down, Captain," ordered Judge Hall.

Sitting back down, Samuel Upshaw stared at the judge in disbelief. Even as the hearing was turned over to Varnell's defense team, Upshaw felt a strong sense of foreboding take up residence in his logical mind.

Major Pearre stood up, calling George Walker to the stand. George nodded at Tom as he passed by on his way to testify. Tom allowed his mind to wander just a bit during the early questioning but soon forced himself back to the proceedings determining his immediate future.

"Now, Mr. Walker, is it correct that you were acquitted for your alleged role in the killing of Mr. Land?" asked Pearre.

"Objection. The question has no bearing on the hearing," stated Crane.

"Sustained," ruled Hall.

Pearre looked at Crane, then back at Hall. He continued, "All right. Mr. Walker, tell the court if you were present at the death of Mr. Land."

"Yes, I was there."

"Did you witness Tom Varnell being attacked in any manner by Mr. Land?"

"Yes. He was. Land had something in his left hand that he used to strike at Tom P. I mean Mr. Varnell. It was wooden and wider at one end. I couldn't tell exactly, but it looked like the handle of an axe."

"Did Mr. Varnell get your gun before or after he was struck by Mr. Land?"

"After. When Mr. Varnell turned back holding my gun, Mr. Land was already comin' back at him. That's when Varnell fired. Self-defense, if you ask me."

"Objection!" called Crane.

"Sustained," Hall ruled immediately.

"Were you present when Emma Land arrived to find her sister with Mr. Varnell?"

"Yes. I heard murmurin' from the two. Miss Ella seemed concerned with what her father would do if he found 'em."

"Objection!" Crane intervened.

"I'll rephrase it. What are the words you heard Miss Ella say?"

"Miss Ella said, 'I'm afraid father will kill me if he finds this out.'"

"Thank you, Mr. Walker. No further questions."

The judge retired to his chambers following the last few witnesses. Tom moved around his seat restlessly. His lawyers said very little. The crowd talked quietly. After about thirty minutes, the judge returned. The court was brought back to order as Sheriff Tom Bell arrived through the side door.

"After considering the strength and weight of the testimony plus the evidence of the defendant's actions since the death of Mr. Land, it is my decision that Tom P Varnell will be remanded back to jail until a jury of his peers decides his fate. Bail is denied. This hearing is hereby adjourned."

The judge did not wait for the bailiff to close the session out. He quickly stepped down from the bench and was out the door as the spectators sat in stunned silence. Few if any expected this outcome after having heard George Walker's testimony. Upshaw quickly put a hand on Tom's shoulder again.

"Tom P, we can appeal his decision. It's obvious there is some prejudice here. Stay calm and let me do my job."

"You're asking me to be calm when it may be weeks or months before I can get out of that hellhole called a jail?" growled Tom.

"Yes, sir. That is exactly what I'm asking," Upshaw urged.

Tom Bell walked rapidly over to Varnell. "Come on, Tom P. I have to get you back to the jail. I'm counting on your promise to behave yourself."

Tom stood up quickly, almost knocking over his chair. "All right, sheriff. Get me out of here!"

CHAPTER SEVENTEEN

30 March 1886

Tom P paced along the narrow confined area of his cell in the Tarrant County Jail, situated just north of the courthouse on West Belknap Street. He was waiting for Sheriff Bell to arrive to take him back to Hillsboro. Tom knew that Bell usually sent deputies to pick up prisoners housed elsewhere but that he did not trust anyone else to deal with Tom.

The Knights of Labor had delayed Tom's trip back to his home county, making his scheduled return unpredictable even though the jail repairs were complete. Tom knew little about nor understood the labor strike except that the work stoppage included the Texas & Missouri Railroad as well as other railroads across the United States. Fort Worth was especially affected by the actions of the trainmen. Tom hoped the problems of others would not prevent him from getting his own life back on track. No one seemed to be able to find out when the strike would end, although some trains did move goods and people on a very erratic schedule.

Picking up his precious few letters from home, Tom decided to pass the time rereading them. He put them in date order, sat on his bunk, and opened the first one he'd received.

Dec. 30, 1885

Dear Tom,

I wish so much that I could have accompanied you to Fort Worth when the sheriff decided to take you there for what he called safekeeping. The weather was so dreary the day you left. The constant rain matched my mood, knowing you were being taken so far away. That extra set of clothes surely helped since I have a feeling you got soaked walking uptown from the depot.

I hope you had a good Christmas. I thought about you often through the day. I was glad to read in your letter that they gave extra rations. Let me know if you received the package I mailed.

Your sister, Rosa, came out to the ranch with her family to help celebrate with me. We played some holiday music but all agreed it wasn't the same without you here to show us how a real fiddle player does it.

Your appeal for bail will be heard soon. I'm praying for good news. I will be coming to see you in January. Let me know what you need for me to bring for your comfort.

Your loving,
Mother

Jan. 28, 1886

Dear Tom,

Our visit was all too short. My stay at the Lindell Hotel was comfortable, and I appreciate its near location to where you are being forced to stay. Fort Worth is much too large for my tastes though. The train depot was confusing with all the different routes coming together at one place. I managed with the help of a conductor to board the right train home.

I have some bad news to impart. I got a telegraph message from Capt. Upshaw who went to Galveston to argue in your favor at the Court of Appeals for bail. They upheld the original ruling. So Capt. Upshaw will be coming back empty handed for us.

Do not despair as I am sure he will formulate a new plan. He is a most clever lawyer. Do not worry about the expense. Your freedom is worth the money spent. I still have savings set aside.

I will plan to come to see you again as soon as I can. Your sister, Rosa, sends her regards.

Your loving,
Mother

Feb. 10, 1886

Dear Tom,

I've sent extra warm socks as the weather has turned quite cold. I hope they gave you my package.

I was frantic for a while when I heard that the jail where you are staying had been quarantined because of the outbreak of small pox in Fort Worth. The newspaper reported that several prisoners got the disease but that the rest received vaccinations. I was so worried that I went to see Sheriff Bell. He was able to assure me that you were fine as he has been in touch with the jail officials there where you are. That was a relief since I was prevented from going to see you personally as travel has been re-

stricted due to the outbreak.

Sheriff Bell also told me that he will be going to Fort Worth to bring you back in March when they finish repairing the jail here. I look forward to being able to see you more often.

Your loving,
Mother

March 1, 1886

Dear Tom,

So happy to hear that the quarantine has been lifted, and you are still well. I made plans to come see you, but Sheriff Bell said he would be fetching you very soon. So I will wait to visit you here.

I received a letter from your sister, Lina, yesterday. I thought her stories might brighten your day. So I enclosed her letter for your enjoyment.

I am also enclosing a newspaper clipping I thought you might find interesting about Sheriff Bell's brother-in-law as I know you have met him. This has caused the sheriff untold embarrassment.

The ranch is doing fine, and I have plenty of help. No need for you to worry.

Your loving,
Mother

Tom picked up his sister's lengthy letter before reading the newspaper clipping.

Feb. 20, 1886

Dear Mother,

Hope this letter finds you safe and well. Jasper is better at writing letters than I am, but I will try.

Thanks for the update on Tom P. I'm hoping for good news soon for him. Please give him our love when you next see him. I try my best to control the anger I feel at the court for not allowing Tom out on bail. I hope his strength has helped both of you cope with this setback. I'm sure he appreciates your unwavering belief in his innocence. You and I both know Tom would never kill a man unless provoked beyond endurance. I pray for justice every day.

We are doing fine here although the winter has turned out to be quite cold most days. I'm hoping for an early spring. Belle is a big help around the house as the boys spend their time helping their father or going on cattle drives. Gus is almost as good in the saddle as Tom P. He's even picked up the fiddle and can now play a tune or two.

We had a bit of a fright about a week ago. You know how Jasper loves to recite all that poetry he writes. I told him I didn't have time to listen as I had chores to get done. The next thing I know, I heard him outside standing on the seat of our wagon, gesturing as he quoted stanzas. I just shook my head and went back to work only to be jerked back when I heard a yelp! Seems Jasper put his hands behind his back for a moment forgetting that he was holding his lit pipe. Sure enough his coattails caught on fire, and he had to jump off and race for the water trough. It was a good thing it was not frozen over. By the time I got out there, he had successfully put the fire out.

He took one look at me, picked up his poetry, and without a word wandered off reciting again like nothing had happened. I have to admit I laughed all afternoon.

I just wish I could get Jasper out the door on Sundays early enough to arrive at church before the preaching gets started. I can tell him to get dressed, come back thirty minutes later, and he'll still be reading a book. When we do finally arrive, he seems to enjoy walking down the aisle greeting folks. Even if the service has already started, he goes right up to Rev. Rawls and shakes his hand. The preacher usually cracks, 'Well with Brother McGee here, we can get started.' That bit of sarcasm and even the laughter from the congregation does not seem to bother Jasper. He just smiles at everybody like he's in on the joke.

As you can see, life is never dull with Jasper and the children. I look forward to your next letter.

Your daughter,
Lina

Tom laughed out loud again as he had each and every time he'd read his sister's letter. Then he sobered up thinking about his family. He would have given up long ago without their support. He turned to the enclosed newspaper clipping from the *Hillsboro Reflector*. He still found the story within to be unbelievable.

Excitement on Train

Hillsboro, Jan. 31 — Four deputy sheriffs of Hill County — Bill McKinney, Mont Frear, Mart Brigman and Frank Bawls — while under the influence of whisky, last night went to the Missouri Pacific depot to await the ar-

rival of the south bound passenger train, due here at 11:45
p.m. While they were waiting at the depot they pulled out
their bottle and asked the agents to take a drink. One of
the agents drank but the other, Mr. Ed Burgess, politely
declined, whereupon one of them placed his hands upon his
pistol and told him he must, but still he declined. When the
train arrived the deputies boarded it and started for Waco.
When they got below West Station they began to shoot
out window lights and to disarm passengers, shooting out
nineteen lights and breaking two doors. Conductor Buckley
endeavored to quiet them, whereupon one of them gave him
a very severe blow which disabled him, and another con-
ductor had to be put in his place.

"Varnell, get your stuff together. The sheriff's here to take
you back," called the jailor. Tom quickly put his letters into his
valise, deciding it would be smart not to question the sheriff
about the activities of his relatives or the other deputies. The
jailor unlocked the barred door to let him out.

In the perpetual semi-darkness of his stuffy jail cell, Tom
lay staring at the bottom of the bed above him. A coughing fit
hit him. This had become a common event. He had been ill for
some time. His mother had insisted the sheriff allow a doctor
to check him out. His diagnosis was that the close confinement
with no opportunity for fresh air was causing a downward spiral
in Tom's health.

The murder trial had been postponed three times over a period of fifteen months since Tom had returned from Fort Worth.
He had been confined to the Hillsboro jail that entire time. A
firm date for the proceedings still had not been established, but a
positive bit of news had been the dropping of the charge of rape
concerning Ella Land. The Grand Jury had lodged this against

Tom back in 1883, shortly after the death of Jonah Land. Tom's attorneys had gotten the charge quashed after threatening action due to the indictment having been made by an illegally conducted session of the Grand Jury. Judge Hall finally ordered the charge dropped.

"Varnell, it's time to get you to court for yet another bail hearing," called the jailor.

Tom got up to follow him out. When they arrived at the courthouse, Tom went over to sit at the defense table beside Capt. Upshaw.

"How'd you manage to get another hearing?" Tom asked.

"It wasn't easy. I had to insist that your health was in peril, which it is. The judge finally gave in, but I don't think he'll be very sympathetic. I do have several physicians lined up to testify, though. Maybe we'll make some headway," answered Upshaw.

"What day is it anyhow? It's so hard to keep up with the calendar," asked Tom, coughing again. He noticed his mother sitting in the visitor's gallery behind them. She smiled at him encouragingly. Tom nodded before turning back around.

"Tom P, it's June 14th. By the way, I tracked down George Walker who didn't show up for the last trial date. He's had his own troubles to sort out. Seems he was arrested in Waco for burglary and attempted murder. He's since then been cleared of the charges and should be able to testify for you when we finally go to trial," answered Samuel Upshaw.

"George works in a rough part of Waco. I've told him he should find another line of work than barkeeping, but he insists it's the life he likes," commented Tom.

"I guess you're happy Bell lost the election last fall for sheriff."

"Not really. To be sure, Bell and I have our differences, but he did his job without showing any malice toward me. I appreciate that. I guess that trouble his deputies caused on the train hurt his chances at being re-elected," answered Tom.

"That and your escape didn't help either," added Upshaw. "People at the time wondered why the sheriff wasn't able to track you down."

"Speaking of elections, congratulations on being elected State Senator. Your association with me hasn't hurt you none," grinned Tom.

"Well, you know your mother still has lots of respect and influence in this community. Her endorsement helped a lot," quipped Upshaw.

The two men's attention was turned back to the courtroom when the bailiff told everyone to rise. The hearing lasted several hours as Tom's defense team brought in expert medical testimony from several respected doctors in the community. All noted that Tom was showing signs of consumption, a deadly disease, brought on and aggravated by his confinement in jail.

Without any warning, Judge Hall interrupted the proceedings by slamming down his gavel.

"I have heard enough. Regardless of the prisoner's health, I have not been given any compelling nor legal reason to re-examine my previous ruling concerning bail, but I will make a concession," stated Judge Hall. "Bailiff, instruct Sheriff Cox to allow Varnell a cell on the bottom floor and the opportunity to go outside occasionally as will be consistent with his safekeeping. This hearing is adjourned." The judge stood up and abruptly left the stunned audience.

Upshaw turned to Tom, "This is not the end of this. I could have predicted his reaction. I now have good cause to appeal his decision. He did not conduct this hearing properly."

Tom sighed. He put his head down on his arms on the table. He no longer had the strength to contradict his attorney even though he was not hopeful.

A few days later, Captain Upshaw arrived early at the jail

asking to see Tom. He waved a newspaper at his client.

"This is exactly the reaction I was hoping for, Tom," he explained.

"What do you mean?"

"Read this from the *Hillsboro Reflector*," Upshaw instructed as he thrust the paper through the jail bars. Tom read:

The Trial of Tom P Varnell

June 16 – On Tuesday the trial of Tom P Varnell on habeas corpus was concluded. He had sued out that his jail confinement would endanger his life and that he needed outdoor exercise, plenty of fresh air and sunshine and that further confinement in jail would endanger his life.

The court rendered its decision in a most summarily and abrupt manner, not even waiting to hear the concluding argument of the counsel for the defense indicating that he did not desire to hear further arguments. This conduct upon the part of a District Judge so far as want of courtesy, propriety, and we might add, simple justice, is concerned, has no parallel so far as we know in the history of judicial conduct in Texas. Every man upon trial for his life or liberty should have an equal opportunity with any other person to have his case fully and thoroughly discussed according to the established rules of law and of courts. The unbecoming haste which characterized the court in its action on last Tuesday in rendering its decision in this case reminded one of the acts of a rural justice of the peace rather than coming up to what we might hope to expect from a District Judge.

Tom looked up at Upshaw. "What does this editorial have to do with anything?"

"It means, dear boy, that the judge has over-stepped. I have managed to get a hearing with the Court of Appeals. In fact, Judge Hurt will come here to hear it in a couple of weeks. I have a good feeling about this. I truly hope to get you out of here," Upshaw explained.

Tom peered out at the horizon. His mother had wanted him to ride in a buggy, but he had insisted, even as weak as he felt, on riding his horse, Midnight, and traveling alone. Eighteen months had passed since Tom had had the freedom of directing his own movements. Confinement had taken its toll for sure, but Tom breathed deeply the sweet morning air. He didn't even mind the oncoming heat of typical July weather that greeted him as he walked out of the Hillsboro jail. The sun on his face was like manna from heaven.

True to his word, Upshaw had been able to convince the judge of the Court of Appeals that his client deserved bail. Docia Varnell readily arranged for the $10,000 bail that was set. At last her son would be allowed to go home.

Tom knew his troubles were far from over, but for a brief period of time he could wrap himself in the cloak of his previous life as a stockman. The road home was all too inviting and familiar.

As Tom turned into the gate that led down to the ranch house, Queen appeared to greet him and to bark excitedly, alerting those waiting that Tom P had indeed returned home. His mother and sister, Rosa, along with Glory were on the porch waving as he arrived. Tom laughed and breathed deeply again. Dismounting, he tied Midnight to the hitchrack. He reached down to pat Queen on the head. The birddog's tail was wagging so hard Tom chuckled. He looked up at his family.

"Mother, Rosa, Glory! How good it is to see all of you!" greeted Tom. "Anyone know where my fiddle is?"

Tom grabbed each in as big a hug as he could muster given his weakened condition. Laughing, they went inside the house. Indeed, Tom P's fiddle was on the sideboard waiting for its owner to return home. Once again music filled the corners and rafters, replacing the gloom that had been so pervasive during Tom's incarceration.

CHAPTER EIGHTEEN

31 March 1888

Sitting at the kitchen table, Tom sipped his cup of Arbuckle's. Drinking in the normalcy of ranch life that he savored as much as the coffee, Tom watched Glory bustle around washing breakfast dishes at the wood-framed metal sink. After his mother finished getting dressed, the two of them would be leaving for Hillsboro where the long awaited murder trial was set to start.

More than five years had passed, leaving Tom with a sense of unreality. Hard edges of each riveting moment from that fateful night remained indelibly imprinted across his mind, while the aftermath had softened and blurred with the passage of time. So much had happened since that long ago evening in March of '83. His intense fear of capture, hurried flight to New Mexico, and ambushed arrest, which forced him back to face his accusers, colored the months that followed. Jail confinement had hammered home just how much freedom meant to Tom.

Immersing himself in the everyday life and work on the Varnell ranch during the year he'd been out on bond, Tom fashioned a normal routine that included caring for a herd of mares and colts. He enjoyed the sunlit days that improved his health considerably. He kept thoughts of the impending court battles facing him at the back of his mind. Friends stopped by often to pass the time. They offered mostly silent support for his pending case as they sensed that Tom had no wish to discuss his troubles.

Looking out the kitchen window at the hitched buggy, Tom, grateful his mother wasn't quite ready, sat, drank coffee, and contemplated. He thought about Lilly, whom he had not attempted to contact until after he was out of jail. His heart-felt letter came back marked 'Undeliverable.' While his practical self was not surprised, Tom still daydreamed of gray eyes flecked with green. Feeling somewhat defeated, he wished Lilly well wherever she might be. She deserved someone without the legal woes he was facing. Still…

"I'm ready," Docia announced, bustling into the kitchen. As she put on her gray dress bonnet, tying the strings, Tom shook his head, relegating his thoughts of Lilly back into the recesses. Docia walked over to Tom and placed her hand on his shoulder before he got up from the chair to reassure him she had confidence in the eventual positive outcome of his impending trial.

Tom glanced through the door to the parlor, seeing his fiddle resting on the mantle. He hoped to return a free man. He was ready for music to once again be the center of his world rather than wrestling with the legal system and those bent on seeing him convicted for murder.

As the district courtroom in Hillsboro filled up with excited spectators, Tom watched a brown spider busily weaving a web in the corner close to the ceiling where a wooden beam met the white wall. Out of reach of human interference, the spider continued her work even though the room rapidly reached capacity with friends, family, foes, and the curious. District Judge Hall entered, and the long-awaited trial began.

The spider's work seemed somehow appropriate, Tom mused to himself, and then he turned his attention back to the State's witnesses and District Attorney M. M. Crane, who was determined to weave a vivid picture of Tom as a cold, heartless predator of young innocent girls as well as being the murderer of an upstanding member of the community. On the witness stand was Robert Jones, a young farmer about 25 years old, who had been testifying for several minutes.

"Tell the court, Mr. Jones. Did you see the deceased, Mr. Land, shortly before he was shot?" asked Crane.

"Yes, sir," answered Robert Jones. "I went outside of the house where we were dancin'. Saw Mr. Land at a distance, walkin'."

"Did he have anything in his hands?"

"The only thing I seen was a lantern in his hand. Nothing else."

"Thank you, Mr. Jones," Crane stated. "Your witness, Captain Upshaw."

Samuel Upshaw stood up, picking up a notepad where he had been taking notes. He finished making a notation then turned to the witness.

"Mr. Jones, were you at the Land party very long?"

"I was there most of the evening."

"Did you see anyone drinking alcohol?"

"Yeah, but I didn't."

"Did you at any time see the defendant and Ella Land together?"

"I was standing in the area next to the dancin' room when Tom Varnell and Ella Land come by."

"Did you hear what was said between Mr. Varnell and Miss Land?"

"No, I didn't. I just saw 'em leave together."

"Did Miss Land appear to be under any duress?"

"I don't rightly know what you mean."

"Did she appear upset or like she was being forced to go outside?"

"I wasn't close enough to really tell, but I didn't see nothing out of the ordinary."

"Mr. Jones, did you witness the defendant shoot Mr. Land?"

"No, I didn't."

"So, you do not really know if Mr. Land had a weapon at that time, do you?"

"I'm just saying that I didn't before hand."

"Please answer the question," pressed Upshaw.

"I reckon … no," replied Robert hesitantly.

"Thank you, Mr. Jones. No more questions." Captain Upshaw walked back to the defense table and sat down. Crane stood up.

"Your Honor, the State calls to the stand Silas Barber."

As Barber was sworn in, Tom turned his attention back to the busy spider. A fly, unwittingly, flew too close to the sticky web and was now struggling to extricate himself. Futile, thought Tom, who without realizing it at first started composing a tune to illustrate the spider's activities. The fingers of his left hand 'worked' the fingerboard under the table where he sat. Finally, he turned back to the trial.

"Mr. Barber, how well did you know Jonah Land?" asked Crane.

"We were friends from the day he moved here from Wisconsin. Jonah and I were members of the same Masonic Lodge," replied Barber.

"Mr. Barber, were you present at the dance party at the Land farm?"

"No. I didn't arrive until after the shootin'," answered Silas.

"About what time?"

"After midnight."

"Did you stay until the next morning?"

"Yes, sir, I did."

"Did you notice anything at that time?" asked Crane.

"After dawn, I walked over to the area where Mr. Land died. On the ground I saw an article of clothing. I learned later from Miss Emma that it belonged to Miss Ella."

"What was this article of clothing?"

"A lady's undergarment."

"Mr. Barber, did you speak with either Emma or Ella Land?"

"Spoke with Miss Emma but not Miss Ella."

"Why not Miss Ella?"

"Miss Emma told me that Miss Ella was too upset to speak to anyone. Stayed in her room the whole time I was there. Poor little girl," Silas answered.

"No more questions," asserted District Attorney Crane, quickly.

Captain Upshaw remained seated a couple of minutes before rising. He looked at the witness.

"Mr. Barber, you said you went outside the next morning," stated Upshaw. "While you were outside, did you see any evidence that alcohol may have been consumed?"

"Saw a large number of bottles and flasks about the dance house."

"Did you see any weapons on the ground or anything that could be used as a weapon?"

"An axe was stickin' out of the ground at the place of the shootin'."

"One last set of questions. Even though you did not speak to Ella that night, you do know Miss Ella Land, do you not?"

"Yes. I know her."

"Would you please describe her physically?"

"Blonde headed and not all that tall, but she has the physique of a woman."

"I'm going to ask my client to stand up," stated Upshaw, who waited for Tom to rise up from his chair. "Now, Mr. Barber, I know you can obviously see the defendant, Mr. Varnell. Would you please compare Miss Ella's size with his?"

"Objection, Judge," called Crane. "I see no relevance."

"Judge, I will make the relevance clear later," Upshaw responded.

"I'll allow the question for now, but counsel for defense will need to show how this relates to the cause before the court and soon," announced Judge Hall.

"Thank you, Your Honor," responded Upshaw, turning back to the witness. "Mr. Barber, do you need me to repeat the question?"

"No, I don't. Not sure what you're after, but I'd say Miss Ella is not as tall as Varnell, but she's probably heavier."

"Thank you. No more questions," stated Upshaw.

Crane once again stood up. "State calls Mrs. Emma Land Beasley."

Tom studied Emma Beasley as she was being sworn in. She was dressed in a serviceable long, dark wool skirt with a buttoned-down white blouse with bell sleeves. Emma wore her hair parted down the center and drawn back behind the ears into a chignon at her neck and topped by a new straw hat. She adopted the same demure demeanor as she did for the bail hearing, with the exception of taking a brief moment to look directly at Tom. As their eyes met, Tom matched her icy cold blue-eyed stare with his own. She did not hold his intense gaze but turned back to the district attorney for questioning.

Emma's answers mirrored those she gave at the habeas corpus hearing when Tom sought bail, but without the histrionics. Crane had schooled her well. After establishing through Emma's testimony her view that her father was unarmed at the time of his death at the hands of Tom Varnell, the prosecution continued.

"Mrs. Beasley, you heard Mr. Barber testify that he found an axe the next morning after the fateful party. Can you explain how the axe got to where he found it?"

"I asked Babe Curry, who was at the dance, to put the axe in the ground so we could locate where my father went down after being shot, because we moved him to the house."

"It has been established that Ella Land is your younger sister. Would you tell the court what happened to her following the death of your father?"

"My sister, Ella, was so hurt and upset by what happened to her and the death of our father that she hasn't spoken since."

"Objection. Mrs. Beasley is not a doctor and cannot provide a valid diagnosis," exclaimed Upshaw, standing up.

Crane responded, "Your Honor, Ella Land is not physically able to testify. Her sister's observations are relevant to this case."

"I'll allow the testimony," announced Judge Hall.

"Your Honor," began Upshaw.

"I said that the objection was overruled. Continue, Mr. Crane," admonished Judge Hall.

"Mrs. Beasley, you may answer the question."

"Ella has been confined to the Deaf & Dumb Asylum in Austin since our father was murdered. I'm not sure she'll ever recover."

"Is it your belief that when your father walked up to where you were standing that night with Tom P Varnell, he was there simply to protect you and your sister from being outraged?"

"Objection!"

"Overruled!"

Emma sighed lifting her pink handkerchief to dab at her eyes. She then looked back at the district attorney. "Yes, it is my firm belief," she spoke in a lowered but steady, forceful tone.

"No further questions," ended Crane.

"Mrs. Beasley," Upshaw began quickly for the defense, "are you the oldest of Mr. Land's children?"

"Yes, I am."

"Do you feel protective of your sister, Ella?"

"Of course, I do. She's suffered mightily," Emma answered, dabbing her eyes again.

"So you would do anything or say anything to protect her, would you not?"

"Objection," Crane called out.

"Sustained," ruled Judge Hall.

"Mrs. Beasley, you testified that you already knew the defendant prior to the dance. Is it not true that you had romantic feelings for him and were jealous when you realized that he had gone outside with your sister and not you?"

"That's an outlandish and vile untruth," Emma answered, her face flushing.

Judge Hall spoke up, "Captain, I fail to see the relevance. Please refrain from this type of questioning."

"I'm sorry, Your Honor," Upshaw replied. "Mrs. Beasley, please describe the weather outside the night your father died."

"I recall it to have been cloudy but not raining."

"And you went in search of your sister and Tom P Varnell after midnight?"

"Yes."

"And you located them by hearing low voices?"

"Yes."

"Once you arrived where your sister and the defendant were lying on the ground, could you see exactly what they were doing?"

"No, but I could hear my sister struggling. When she saw me..."

"Yes, you've already stated that," interrupted Upshaw.

"My point is — could Ella simply have been making the noises of someone in the process of getting up from the ground?"

"Varnell was holding her down."

"Holding her down? Mr. Barber stated that Ella was heavier than Mr. Varnell. How could he forcibly hold her down?"

"But she asked me to get him off her as I stated before."

"Isn't it possible your sister made her accusation against the defendant because she did not want you to be angry with her for being with Mr. Varnell?"

"No! No! No! She was fightin' off Varnell."

"But could you really see this?"

"No, but I could..."

"So the answer is no. Thank you. Now let's go back to the subject of the weapon. Are you sure that your father did not have a weapon in his hand?"

"I am positively certain."

"How can you be so sure when you said that it was cloudy? When the shadows created by the lantern could have hidden the axe in your father's other hand? When your view could have been obstructed? When you were still in an embrace with Tom P Varnell after your sister fled? When you were already afraid of your father?"

"Objection, Your Honor. These questions are grossly speculative."

"Sustained. Counselor, you will refrain from badgering the witness," warned Judge Hall.

Emma answered anyway, "I don't know what you mean. My father did NOT have an axe in his hand, and he did NOT hit Mr. Varnell with nothing before he shot my father."

"The truth is Mrs. Beasley that in your anger over Ella going outside willingly with Tom P Varnell, you failed to see what really happened that night your father died. Isn't that true?"

"No, it isn't," cried Emma, who looked quickly at the district attorney. Crane started to rise from his chair.

"No more questions," announced Samuel Upshaw.

Judge Hall waited for a tearful Emma Beasley to leave the witness stand before he pounded the gavel. "We will adjourn until tomorrow morning, 9 a.m."

While waiting for the spectators to get up and leave the courtroom, Tom glanced at the ceiling. He could no longer see the fly as the spider had completed the cocoon, blocking out the light of day for her victim. The fly in its living tomb could only wait helplessly for the spider to complete its fate.

Scanning around, Tom noticed Emma Beasley was gone. Looking back at the witness stand, Tom spied Emma's pink handkerchief on the floor. Tom grabbed his Stetson.

"Mother, let's get out of here. I feel like I'm suffocating," exclaimed Tom.

CHAPTER NINETEEN

2 April 1888

George Walker found himself once again on the witness stand of a trial, but this time it was not due to one of his own troubles stemming from being a bartender in Waco on Two Street. He had not seen Tom P much since Tom had managed to get bail. George reckoned Tom had needed time to recover from the lung infection he'd gotten during the months of being the county's guest

Listening to the jawing among his patrons at the White Saloon had caused George to be aware that many believed Judge J. M. Hall intended to play a major role in securing a conviction against Tom. He overheard that Judge Hall and District Attorney Crane belonged to the same Masonic Lodge and traveled together to trials. George had not spoken to his friend about what he had heard, because he still hoped the high-powered lawyers Tom had retained would settle the case based on self-defense, which George thought was clear cut.

This morning the Hill County prosecution had rested its case against Tom P. Now, the defendant's attorneys, J. M. Anderson, Pearre & Boynton, S. C. Upshaw and Thomas Ivy had the chance to sway the all-male jury.

Captain S. C. Upshaw called Ed Bryant as the first witness, and he testified that he saw Jonah Land on that fateful night pass by him with a lit lantern in one hand and a short-handled axe in the other. Ed said Jonah Land was visibly agitated and added that Mr. Land told the witness that he was looking for Varnell and if he found him, Mr. Land would kill him. M. M. Crane for the prosecution threw doubt on Bryant's testimony by pointing out that Bryant had not testified to these facts at George Walker's trial or at Tom's habeas corpus hearing. Ed Bryant countered by stating that neither side had asked previously what he knew, even though he remembered telling some lawyer, whose name he couldn't remember, the information shortly after the killing. When pressed, Bryant admitted to being a friend to the defendant prior to the death of Mr. Land and still considered himself one.

Next, Joe Phillpot was put on the witness stand. He testified that he did not see the actual killing of Mr. Land but did find a .44 pistol on the trampled ground the next day near where the deadly altercation had taken place. He said the six-gun was new, unloaded, and had never been fired.

The county coroner, S. J. Hale, witnessed for the defense as well. He told the jury that while preparing Jonah Land's body, he found a large, opened knife in the deceased's coat pocket. He also stated that Mr. Land was a stout, chunky man of at least 175 pounds, much larger than the defendant.

Finally, George Walker was called. Colonel Pearre from Waco took over the questioning from Upshaw. Walker gave the now familiar, oft-repeated testimony about his own involvement, his gun that Tom had used, the shots fired, and the flight from the Land farm he'd taken with Varnell. He affirmed once again that Jonah Land had assaulted the defendant with what looked like a short handled axe.

"Mr. Walker, before Mr. Land arrived, was there a period of time when it was just you, Tom Varnell, and Emma Land Beasley standing outside after Ella Land ran into the house?"

continued Pearre.

"Yes, sir."

"Did Mrs. Beasley say or do anything to make you believe she was sweet on Mr. Varnell?"

"Yes, sir, she grabbed aholt of Tom's arm and said 'What does all this mean, after talking to me as you did tonight?' She even asked him to go back to the party with her. That's when Mr. Land came up. Only then did she try to move away from Tom," answered George.

"Mr. Walker, only you and Mrs. Beasley witnessed the defendant shoot Mr. Land. Knowing the facts, is it your belief that the defendant acted out of fear for his own life?"

"Objection," called Crane.

"Sustained," ruled the judge quickly.

"Mr. Walker, you did witness Mr. Land hit Tom Varnell with a blunt object. Correct?" Pearre asked.

"Yes, sir," replied George.

"Did his actions show intent to do bodily harm?"

"Yes sir. He raised the weapon so'd he could get some force with his left hand. Mr. Land was trying to hit Tom P again when he was shot."

"You have heard Mrs. Beasley testify that her father did not have a weapon. Yet you said he did. How can you account for the discrepancy?"

"I stood at a different angle than Mrs. Beasley and closer after she moved away from Tom P when her father walked up. Can only think that with the lantern not putting out much light, maybe Mrs. Beasley just didn't see what Mr. Land had in his left hand," George answered.

"Objection," called Crane.

"Sustained," replied Hall.

"No more questions. Your cross," finished Upshaw.

As District Attorney Crane pulled his papers together, Tom

turned in his uncomfortable wooden seat to look at his mother, who sat close behind the railing that separated the trial proceedings from the crowd of onlookers. Docia smiled reassuringly. The spectator gallery was packed to capacity, as it had been all week, with many willing to stand at the back just to watch. The air had quickly grown warm and stale as the room's temperature rose steadily. Tom glanced at the sea of fidgety, curious gawkers who seemed eager for what might happen next. Few, mused Tom, outside of friends and family, really cared about him. Newsmen were busy scribbling notes, he decided, that would be fashioned later into an exaggerated story in an effort to entice the public to buy their papers. Tom shrugged and turned back around. George's questioning by the prosecution was already in progress.

"Now Mr. Walker, the court is aware of your friendship with the defendant..."

"But I wouldn't lie to the court for him if'n that's what you're gettin' at," interrupted George heatedly.

"Let me ask the questions first before you jump in with answers. You've had your own problems with the law, haven't you?" asked Crane.

"Objection. Irrelevant to the proceedings before the court," Pearre called out.

"Your Honor, it speaks to his character of being a law-abiding citizen and provides the jury with information they need to weigh his testimony against that of others," argued Crane.

"Objection is overruled," stated Hall.

"Well, Mr. Walker?" prompted Crane.

"I won't deny I've had brushes with the law, but I've never been convicted of a crime," George answered.

"Let's get back to your friendship with your crony, Varnell. Tell the court if you saw the defendant shortly after your own court case for murder was tried in the winter of 1883 when Varnell was still a fugitive from justice."

"Yes, I did."

"Is that when you two came up with the additional testimony you have given here that you did not give previously?" asked Crane.

"Don't know what you're talkin' about. I've added a few details, but only `cause I remembered `em since my own trial," George answered. "I ain't lying about none of what I've said, though."

"So you do admit to embellishing your original story," shot back Crane. "No more questions. You may stand down."

George opened his mouth to protest but thought better of it when the judge dismissed him. Instead, George stepped out of the witness box. He looked straight at Tom but said nothing as he passed by and through the swinging gate.

"Call your next witness, Captain," ordered Judge Hall.

Tom pulled on Upshaw's sleeve, "Captain, let me testify."

Simon Upshaw turned to the judge, "Your Honor, defense requests five minutes to consult with my client."

"Granted," replied Judge Hall.

Samuel Upshaw turned back to Tom, talking in a low, earnest voice, "We've been through this already. I do not believe you will help your cause by testifying. The prosecution could ask detailed questions meant to embarrass you about events we do not want brought up in court, such as your being on the run for almost two years and escaping from jail once you were brought back."

"But the jury will think I'm guilty if I don't testify," replied Tom.

"They will be instructed not to infer that. Do you really want your sexual encounter and what happened between you and Ella Land discussed in detail?"

"They have the wrong impression of what really happened

between me and Ella. I could clear that up," Tom pleaded.

"We've already established the facts when we got the rape charges dropped. If they ask for salacious details of your tryst with a sixteen-year-old, the jurors may forget she was above the age of consent and concentrate on how her father felt and that she has been afflicted since. We've done the best we can do to establish reasonable doubt based on self-defense. Your testimony could harm your chances considerably," stated Upshaw. "Trust me."

Tom gave in but was not happy about it. Upshaw stood up and addressed the court, "Defense calls G. W. McNeese."

G. W. walked to the witness stand. A tall, lanky man in his mid-forties, McNeese had been a resident of Hill County since he was very young. He was respected by all who knew him as hard-working and honest. His testimony as a character witness who had knowledge right after Tom's flight was the defense's ace in the hole.

"Mr. McNeese, you own a farm in eastern Hill County, do you not?" began Upshaw.

"Yes, sir."

"Do you know the defendant, Tom Varnell?"

"Yes, sir, I do."

"Did you see him in the early morning of March 6, 1883?"

"Yes, sir. He arrived at my house around 3 a.m. George Walker was with him. Tom woke me up by knocking loudly at my back door."

"Describe the defendant as you saw him that night."

"Once I held up the lantern I could see that Tom Varnell had blood on his face, a bruise near his eye and on his chin," answered McNeese.

"Did Varnell complain about any physical symptoms?"

"Yes, sir. He said his shoulder was very sore having been hit by a blunt object."

"No more questions. Your witness," Upshaw stated.

Crane stood up. "How far do you live from the Land farm?"

"I'd say about five miles, maybe less," answered McNeese.

"Is it not true that you have no personal knowledge exactly how the defendant got his bruises or blood on his face?"

"That is correct."

"In fact, the defendant could have deliberately hurt himself between the Land farm and yours. Is that not right?"

"Objection. Calls for speculation."

"Just establishing that the witness did not see what caused the defendant's physical discomfort, judge," argued Crane.

Judge Hall turned to the witness, "Did you see or know for sure how Varnell, the defendant, received the wounds you saw?"

"No, Your Honor, I did not," confirmed McNeese.

"The witness may stand down," stated Crane.

"Wait right there! Defense requests a recross," called Upshaw. "Mr. McNeese, could the wounds you saw on Tom Varnell have been easily self-inflicted?"

"I don't believe so. Tom Varnell's face looked like it had been hit by a hard, blunt weapon."

"Thank you. No more questions for this witness," stated Upshaw. "Defense rests its case."

After the recess, both sides presented rousing, impassioned closing remarks fashioned to influence the hearts and minds of the jury made up almost entirely of townfolk. Then Judge Hall issued his instructions.

After going over the legal definitions of manslaughter, first and second degree murder, and self-defense, Judge Hall said, "Gentlemen, the court instructs you that every man has the right to protect his minor daughter from debauchery; and if the defendant was at the house of Jonah H. Land, and sought to have carnal intercourse with one of the minor daughters of said Land, and if the said Land was killed while he was endeavoring to see that no such carnal intercourse should occur between the defendant and his daughter, and if the defendant killed him because of such interference, and such killing was done with express malice, you will find defendant guilty of murder of the first degree. If such killing was done without express malice, then you will find defendant guilty of murder of the second degree."

The judge then dismissed the jury to deliberate and adjourned the court until a verdict could be reached. Tom turned to Upshaw noticing his attorney's lips were so compressed together that they were rimmed in white. Suddenly, Tom had a premonition of impending disaster.

Samuel Upshaw turned to Tom in a pre-emptive strike. "The judge's instructions stacked the deck against your cause. He made what happened between you and Ella Land a part of what should have been only a murder trial by adding it to the jury instructions. No matter what happens, please remain calm, and let me do my job. Do I have your word?"

Tom looked at the door through which the jury had left to deliberate and then back at Upshaw. "I'll try."

The two men got up to leave the courtroom. Tom stopped to shake George's hand. Tom's mother joined him as they left.

Judge J. M. Hall pounded the gavel and called the courtroom to order at 2 p.m. An electric calm prevailed as the jury filed back in and took their seats.

"Have you reached a unanimous decision?" asked the judge.

"Yes, we have, Your Honor," spoke G. W. Hughes, the jury foreman, passing the written verdict to the bailiff. The judge read it, nodded, then passed it to the district clerk, E. S. Crumley.

"Defendant, please rise," commanded the judge. "Mr. Crumley, you may read the verdict."

"We, the jury, find the defendant guilty of murder of the second degree and assess his punishment at confinement in the penitentiary for the time of nine years."

Tom felt the air in his throat constrict and his chest tighten. Samuel Upshaw placed his hand on Tom's shoulder and pushed him back down into his chair. The courtroom exploded in noise as excited newsmen sprinted for the door.

"What happens now?" asked Tom, oblivious to the chaos erupting behind him.

"We ask for a new trial, which the judge will most probably refuse. Then we will give notice that we will go to the Texas Court of Appeals. The law does not provide for bail during this time, Tom P. You will have to wait it out in the county accommodations."

"Can we win that?" asked Tom who was now facing more time in a confined space he had come to hate.

"I'll give it my best shot," promised Upshaw, gathering his papers.

As the two men stood there, a reporter rushed up. "Varnell, you must consider this a victory. Only nine years for killing that poor farmer is amazing. Most believe you are not only guilty but should have experienced the stretched hemp of the gallows. What say you?"

"Get out of here," growled Upshaw, "before I ask the sheriff to throw you out. We will give no more comments."

Samuel Upshaw signaled Sheriff Cox. Tom insisted on kissing his mother on the cheek before he turned to leave with the sheriff.

Upshaw gave Tom one last assurance. "There is much reversible error that happened in this trial. I'll get right on it. Your patience right now is the best thing you can do to help. Do you hear me?"

Tom looked at Upshaw but could do no more than nod. He had always believed that in the long run the truth would prevail but wasn't so sure now. Glancing up at the ceiling, Tom saw that the spider and her web were gone. Looking around, Tom noticed the judge and prosecuting attorney were gone as well. Turning, he allowed Sheriff Cox to lead him out without protest.

CHAPTER TWENTY

30 July 1888

While he lay on the top of the multi-colored quilt covering his bed at the Varnell ranch, Tom P winced as a crimson haze of pain washed over him. He tried to close his tired eyes but the pin pricks behind them felt like needles and only added to the discomfort of his throbbing headache. Shifting his sore, ill-used body slightly onto the right side to ease the pressure on his left shoulder, Tom glanced out the open window of his bedroom. The leaf-wilting July heat had already stolen into the shadowed room by mid-morning to create sweaty moisture, which gathered quickly along his bruised skin.

Tom was a prisoner again, not in the county calaboose, but on his mother's ranch because of a freak accident. While traveling back home from the eastern portion of Hill County, Tom had been riding on Midnight when the horse stumbled, tossing his rider unceremoniously onto the uneven ground near a ravine. Tom, after a glancing blow to his head, bounced on his left side along the rocky ground, causing a painful fracture to his upper arm. Battling nausea, Tom lay on the pebble-strewn hard earth for several minutes trying to catch the breath that had been knocked out of him, waiting for his head to clear enough to get up and fashion a temporary sling from his red kerchief. The arduous task had been finally accomplished. With his arm somewhat immobile, Tom limped slowly, leading Midnight to the closest farmhouse to ask for aid.

Tom arrived back at the ranch in James Welborn's buggy. Every bounce was agony and never had home looked more welcoming than when he finally arrived. Docia immediately sent for Dr. Joseph Woods. The country doctor wrapped the upper arm but told Tom to stay in bed until his fracture and the rest of his body mended.

Less than a month had passed since word had arrived from Austin that the Court of Appeals had reversed the verdict of the district court in Hillsboro, citing several errors. Tom concentrated his mind on the elation he felt when the telegram had arrived. It eased the pain somewhat.

Tom remembered the look of excitement on Captain Upshaw's face when he brought over the news to the county jail where Tom had been in residence since the guilty verdict was rendered in early April.

"Tom, great news! Your conviction was overturned for more than just technicalities. I'm sure Judge Hall is livid at the ruling. This bodes well if the district court decides to try you again, which, unfortunately, I think they will," Upshaw spoke as he handed over a copy of the appellate opinion for Tom to see.

After reading through it, Tom gave back the opinion saying, "Not sure what all this legal lingo means."

"It means that Judge Hurt and the appellate court took Judge Hall to task for his charge to the jury during your trial. Do you remember how angry I was after the judge gave his instructions right before the jury left to deliberate?" asked Upshaw. When Tom nodded, the lawyer continued, "Look again at this paragraph in the ruling. Better yet, let me read it out loud:

> *It is preposterous to assume or indulge the hypothesis*
> *that Varnell intended to provoke a combat, or produce the*

occasion, in order to obtain a pretext to kill deceased, or inflict serious bodily injury, or any injury, upon him, by having carnal knowledge of his daughter with her consent, at night, thirty or forty yards from the house and away from the deceased. The charge under discussion was wrong, was out of the case, was not supported by any evidence, and was very damaging to the appellant. The appellant's conduct with Miss Ella Land was most fearfully calculated to prejudice his case with the jury — not legally, but unlawfully — and hence the necessity of proper instructions bearing upon this matter. These were requested by counsel for appellant which should have been given."

"Which means?" puzzled Tom.

"It means that Judge Hall erred by instructing the jury that you planned to take Ella Land outside to have sex with her to produce an occasion that would give you the opportunity to kill Jonah Land when he arrived to defend her honor," explained the lawyer.

"But I thought you were also angry about what Judge Hall said concernin' Mr. Land having the right to do what he did because of what happened between Ella and me," mused Tom.

"I was, but the higher court even addressed this by saying that Land could not defend Ella's honor as it was already gone. Here it is:

If deceased attempted to kill or assaulted the accused because of what had occurred between his daughter and the accused, the attempt or assault was not to prevent, but to revenge, what had already occurred. And while the act of Varnell was morally wrong, he was guilty of no offense against the law of the State, and had not forfeited his life to the father of Ella Land; nor had he lost his right

to perfect self defense because of *this matter, if entitled to
it otherwise.*

It is clearly stating that while some might see your actions as breaking a moral code, you actually broke no law in having sex with Ella, and the evidence indicates that she consented to it. It's a huge victory. I bet they will be writing this case up for other lawyers to use in the future."

Tom took a deep breath. For the first time it seemed a judge was looking at the events from a legal standpoint outside of the emotions garnered from what had happened just prior to the deadly confrontation with Jonah Land.

"What happens next?" asked Tom.

"I get you out of here. Then we wait for the court to act," replied Upshaw.

Tom spent the rest of the summer taking it easy as his body slowly healed from his unfortunate fall. He didn't stray very far from the farmhouse when he was finally able to get up. His mother fussed over him as if he were a little boy, and he let her do it, as he was never more grateful to have someone who truly cared for him.

Tom P's fiddle lay unused on the mantle in the parlor during his recovery. Being unable to lift it to the proper position at his shoulder had irked Tom, but he appreciated the evenings when his sister Rosa came out, because she and Docia would perform duets for his pleasure. Fiddle playing was indeed a family affair.

By the early autumn, Tom was well again, but with the change in season came the news that the district court had decided to retry Tom once again. The new court date was set for November. As the trial docket approached, Tom's apprehension increased, even though his attorneys seemed confident.

Arriving at the courthouse early, Tom navigated through the crowd of early spectator arrivals to his attorneys' table. Samuel Upshaw was already there going over his notes. Glancing over at the prosecution, Tom noted that they had grim looks on their faces.

"What's up with them?" Tom asked.

"Seems their star witness and her husband are not going to be here," Upshaw replied. "Chances are the case will be continued to the spring. The judge has yet to deny any of their requests. Are you okay with that?"

"I guess so," Tom replied. "Just wonderin' when this nightmare is going to be over."

"Soon, I hope," said Samuel. "I do believe this time we will win the day. I've made sure that the word has spread concerning what the appellate court had to say about your case. It's time that news that supports your cause was presented to the people instead of the biased, one-sided reporting the newspapers have printed, although the *Hillsboro Mirror* did state that the ruling of the Court of Appeals was tantamount to an acquittal."

When Judge Hall entered the courtroom, M. M. Crane for the prosecution asked for a continuance as key witnesses were absent. The district judge quickly ruled in their favor and dismissed the prospective jurors.

"Tom P, it's time to pick up the pieces of your life if you haven't already. It will be March or April of next year before this case will come up for trial again. The court will have a tougher time painting you as the evil debaucher of a young innocent girl and as a cold-blooded murderer," announced Upshaw.

"Thanks for all you have done, Captain. I'm much obliged indeed," Tom replied, getting up to walk out into the bright sunshine of a crisp fall day.

Early spring brought Tom into Hillsboro to consult with

his attorney as his trial was once again looming. He had enjoyed one of the most carefree Christmases since his trouble began. The hoe-down held at his sister Rosa's house in town had drawn neighbors and friends. Many came just to hear Tom's newest songs he'd made up for the fiddle. His shoulder was still sore, but Tom ignored the pain as his music and the occasion were more important.

Rosa was tall and had the temperament that went with most red-heads. Adjusting to living in Hillsboro after marrying blacksmith John Sweeney, Rosa devoted herself to raising her children, Herbert who was nine and baby Ethry, not quite a year old yet. Her blue eyes flashing, Rosa also loved to play the fiddle. She and Tom P entertained with traditional Christmas songs and carols, individually and as duets.

The winter months had passed quickly – too quickly, for Tom was once again facing an all-too-uncertain future. He entered the law office, and the secretary quickly took Tom into Upshaw's office. When Tom entered, he saw the captain pacing by the high windows that overlooked the courthouse square instead of being seated at his desk.

Turning to Tom, he said, "I expected the prosecution to pull something, but not this. Tom P, sit down."

Tom, suddenly apprehensive, sat on the brown leather chair in front of Upshaw's desk. He waited for his agitated attorney to continue.

"I got word from a friend close to the prosecution that they will be asking the court to transfer your murder trial out of Hill County on a change of venue," Simon stated.

"Why would they let another court try this case?" asked Tom surprised.

"Well, I also got the wording they intend to use. This is what it says:

> *It being well known to the court that this case has*
> *been so often tried and so much discussed in Hill County*
> *both publicly and privately by the newspapers as well as*
> *individuals that no jury can be had to try said case. Be-*
> *cause the court is of the opinion that none but partisans*
> *of the state or the defendant could be found to try said*
> *case in Hill County. Wherefore the court is of the opinion*
> *that a trial fair and impartial to the State and the defen-*
> *dant cannot be had in Hill County, Texas."*

"They make it sound like this is something you are advocat-ing as well," responded Tom.

"They sure do, but I assure you that I was not invited to the conversation that cooked this up," spit out Upshaw.

"Can we stop them from transferring the case?" asked Tom.

"No, 'fraid not. Usually, only a defendant's attorneys re-quest a change of venue, not the State. This tells me that they are no longer sure of their chances here. Public opinion is on your side now. We will not have a say in this," Samuel replied, looking out the window again. Turning, he finally sat down. "My guess is that they will send it to Waxahachie in Ellis County. Judge Hall is friendly with Judge Rainey who presides over that court. I'll let you know as soon as I hear. The only good part of this is that your trial will be delayed until the fall or next year."

As predicted, a few months later the prosecution sued the district court in Hillsboro for a change of venue. Judge Hall, without hesitation, signed off on the order. What Tom had not anticipated was that he would have to submit to being taken over to Waxahachie in handcuffs and booked into the Ellis County Jail for yet another bail hearing. Upshaw secured the renewal of the $10,000 bond for Tom as quickly as was possible.

Tom's anger at the recent events turned into a devil-may-care attitude. He no longer kept a low-key existence, confining himself mostly to the Varnell ranch, as he had before the change of venue. Tom, instead, started hanging out in saloons with his friends. He was determined to live his life to the fullest, as it seemed his freedom was chronically endangered. No longer was he afraid to join in poker games or to bet on the horses at one of the private racetracks in the county.

One Saturday night, Tom joined a group in the back room of the Old Rock Saloon. The table was already crowded with Ed Holt, Charley Maron, Len Lynch, Joe Criner, and Ezell Lewellen.

Len called out, "Tom P, come join the fraternity."

Everyone greeted Tom. The laughter, liquor, and profanity flowed freely among the men. The five card stud game lasted several hours, late into the night.

"Damn it, Varnell. You've won all my money," complained Charley Maron.

"Charley, you left your poker face at home," quipped Tom, gathering his winnings.

Quickly standing up, Charley almost overturned the table. He glared at everyone and stomped out of the back room. The remaining men could hear him noisily leave the saloon.

"What a hothead. Whose turn is it to deal?" asked Tom, reaching for his glass of whiskey.

About ten minutes later, the door to the back room slammed open. Standing in the entrance was Sheriff Cox.

"All right. What's going on here?"

"Nothin', sheriff," answered Tom for the group. "We're just visitin' a bit. That damn Charley didn't come see you, did he?"

"Varnell, you've no business coming here, beings you're under indictment for murder. Now I'm going to have to arrest you again, along with your pals here," announced Cox.

"Damn it, Sheriff Cox, we weren't botherin' no one. Why don't you just leave and pretend you didn't come here?" suggested Tom.

"Nope. Not gonna to do that," answered Cox. "Deputies, search each man. Make sure they don't have weapons before you handcuff `em."

Tom rode home the next day on Midnight, having been booked in jail for the misdemeanor crimes of playing cards in public, gambling, and cursing. He had paid his bail and endured the admonishment of Upshaw, who had to go down to the jail to get Tom out.

"Tom P, I can't stress strongly enough that you need to stay out of the limelight of the law."

"I know, Captain. I'm just so tired of it all. Nothin' would've happened if Moran hadn't fetched the sheriff when he lost all his money. I'll be more careful. Thanks for comin' down," Tom answered.

Samuel studied Tom for a moment, hesitated, then decided to state what had been on his mind for a long time, "Tom P, I'm only going to say this once, and I say it out of concern for you and the respect I have for your dear mother. You, my friend, are your own worst enemy. Don't give the law any more ammunition to use against you. Everything you do can be brought up in court. I know you're thinking that since your case has been transferred, no one in Ellis County will know what goes on here, but I'm telling you that they will. Word travels. Do you understand?"

Tom cocked his head to the side and looked at his lawyer. "Captain, I'm just tryin' to live my life one day at a time, but I `preciate your advice."

Samuel Upshaw stood outside the jail on the sidewalk while Tom mounted Midnight. Tom waved before taking off in the direction of the Varnell ranch. Upshaw shook his head, then headed for his office.

Chapter Twenty-One

30 March 1890

The twelve jurors for the Tom Varnell trial sat around the oblong table at the Ellis County Courthouse in Waxahachie. The men had just voted again; and again, it stood eleven to one in favor of conviction for murder.

Willard Rutherford, the jury foreman, looked around the table at his fellow jurors. Saul Satterfield, Jesse Scott, Atticus Workman, Micah Wright, John Youngblood, Jared Carter, Thomas Curry, John Ray, Daniel Magee, Marion Milligan, and Sam Curry stared back. This had been the fourth vote without a unanimous outcome.

"It's time for whoever is holdin' out for an acquittal to speak up so we can knock some sense into ya," spoke Willard in frustration.

Silence greeted his demand at first. The round-faced, wooden clock on the wall ticked loudly in the suddenly quiet room. The twelve men looked at each other suspiciously. It seemed for a few strained minutes that no one was going to speak up. Finally, the calm voice of a short, thin, older man with a leathery face and blue eyes was heard.

"I reckon it IS time to speak up. I kept waiting for all of you to act rationally. The evidence given during this trial is clear to me. Varnell shot Old Man Land in self-defense. Hell, what else could he do? He was being beaten up with an axe handle. Lamentable as it was, I say he had to do it," declared Jared Carter firmly.

"But you have Land's daughter statin' that her father had no weapon. I'd say she has no reason to lie, whilst George Walker certainly might do so to protect his friend. Besides, Walker's had his own troubles with the law. He's not `xactly reliable," argued John Ray, placing his elbows on the table to lean toward the dissenting juror.

"I don't think he WAS lying. G. W. McNeese's testimony lends credence to Walker's," shot back Jared.

"Think about it, Carter," offered Sam Curry, standing up to pace around the small room. "Varnell's actions after the murder are just as damning. He fled the scene and had to be brought back from New Mexico for justice. After that, Varnell broke out of jail in Hillsboro. Those are not the actions of an innocent man. Hell, he wasn't even willing to testify in his own behalf!"

"Well, he did turn himself back in, didn't he?" replied Carter. "Varnell probably should have testified, but we shouldn't assume it means he's guilty. I'll agree if you're saying he made bad decisions, but that doesn't change what happened the night Land died, does it? Are we tryin' Varnell for murder or ever' little thing he's ever done?"

"Carter, there's more at stake here than whether or not Varnell shot Mr. Land in self-defense. I have a daughter. I'd kill any son-of-a-bitch who took her outside just to have his way with her," stated Satterfield vehemently, slamming his fists down on the table for emphasis. "AND I'd be justified in doing so."

"I agree," chimed in Milligan. "We can't let Varnell, who defiled that poor man's daughter, get away with it or with his murder, for that matter."

"I understand your anger, fellas, but you're losing sight of the true facts of this case. Ella Land was not raped, and she was above the age of consent when she agreed to go outside with Varnell at that party. Drinking alcohol impairs everyone's judgment. While it's sad she's suffered, this trial's not about her, anyway," replied Carter.

"I don't give a damn how old she was," declared Tom Curry, ignoring much of what Jared said. "Ella Land was not married. Varnell had no right to do what he did. I don't know if Land had a weapon or not. It don't make no difference to me. Varnell deserved a thrashing after what he done. I see him guilty even if Land did have a weapon, which I don't think was proven."

Several of the men nodded in agreement. Jared looked at each convinced face, knowing his statements had not made any difference at all. Before he could marshal another argument, a voice spoke up.

"Tell me something, Carter," sneered Youngblood. "What's the defense payin' you to give them an acquittal?"

"I take offense at your insinuation," growled Carter, finally losing his patience.

"All right, men. No need to have a brawl in here," admonished Willard. His words did not keep the irate jurors from glaring at Carter who stood his ground and was just as angry as they were.

"Let's take a break and send out for some lunch. Maybe on full stomachs, we can look at this more calmly," announced Willard, trying to defuse the tense atmosphere in the room.

Mostly in silence, the jurors ate their lunch of roast beef sandwiches and potato salad sent over from Rose's Café. Carter sat by the tall window and kept to himself.

After awhile, Rutherford stood and cleared his throat, then turned to Jared Carter. His tone of voice was pleasant, almost conversational, "We've all heard your arguments, Jared, and none of us are with you. If you'll just come over to our side, we can get this over, and all of us can go on home. I've plenty of work to do as I'm sure you do, too. We've all known from the beginning that Varnell's guilty. His story's been in all the papers for years now. He's lucky Judge Lynch didn't catch up with him. Varnell's a no count ne'er-do-well. He deserves a lengthy stint in the state prison. What say you?"

Jared felt the hardness of the wooden chair he sat upon, but it wasn't nearly as rock solid as the totally convinced countenances of his fellow jurors. He glanced back out the window at the busy street where people were going about their normal daily business with little or no thought to the drama inside the room where he sat. Jared felt the strong, inviting pull of the easy road to take. Just agree with the rest of these resolute men. Why not? He looked back at the eleven pairs of expectant eyes, waiting for him to come over to their side of the fence.

"I have to make my decision on facts, not emotion, gentlemen," replied Jared Carter, taking a deep breath before continuing. "I cannot in good conscience send a man to prison if the evidence doesn't support that action, even if the man's character is questionable. Who's the real Tom P Varnell? The young man who sits out there expecting justice based on the evidence of self-defense or a cold-blooded killer the news accounts paint him to be? What I believe is that we can only convict if there is proof beyond a reasonable doubt supportive of that decision. Well, I have my doubts, gentlemen, and nothing any of you have said has convinced me otherwise."

"You son-of-a-bitch," growled Milligan. "Your brand of justice will do nothing but see a guilty man go free."

The deliberations continued the rest of the afternoon. Not threats, arguments, pleadings, nor any other tactic used by the other men changed Carter's mind. Finally, a message was sent to District Judge Rainey that a verdict could not be reached. The case was held over to the next term to be retried once again.

On a Tuesday afternoon in February, Tom P and Zack Taylor walked across the courthouse square of Hillsboro on their way to the Old Rock Saloon. Ten months had passed since the jury in Waxahachie had failed to reach a verdict.

"Not to be too nosey, Tom P, but what's happenin' with your court case?" asked Zack.

"It's comin' up for trial again at the end of next month," answered Tom, not willing to say too much about it.

"Maybe this time a little good luck will come your way," commented Zack, letting the subject drop. "Say, have you seen Bailey's new roan mare? She's a beaut."

"I've heard that. I'll stop by and take a gander. I don't need any mares right now, but I enjoy seeing good horseflesh anytime," answered Tom in a congenial tone.

Neither man was particularly paying attention when they rounded the corner of the courthouse. City Marshal James Wood was coming from the opposite direction at the same time. To ward off a near collision, Tom quickly side-stepped and raised his arms, causing his vest to skew open revealing the Colt .45 he had put there.

Instead of being grateful Tom had prevented the collision, Wood barked, "Varnell, you know you're not supposed to go onto a public street armed. You'll have to hand over your weapon and pay a fine as well."

"Come on, marshal. Even you can understand that I've a need for protection against those who'd take the law into their own hands," Tom argued. "I've had threats against my life almost daily."

Not replying, Marshal Wood reached toward Tom's vest in an effort to take the pistol from Tom, who in return grabbed the marshal's arm to stop him. Tom wasn't quick enough since Wood managed to get the pistol and toss it to City Attorney Ivy, who was standing close by.

"Damn it," yelled Tom, shoving the marshal away from himself.

Wood shoved back, and the two quickly embroiled themselves in a fisticuff scuffle with both trying to get the best of the other. Wood tripped, pulling Tom down on top of him. Taking advantage and in a full rage, Tom straddled the lawman, putting his fists to steady use as he defended himself.

Wood finally managed to pull his own pistol out of his holster. Seeing this, Tom reached for the pistol to prevent Wood from using it on him. The two rolled on the ground, each trying to get control of the weapon. Bystanders watched, but no one interfered with the struggle between the two men, which continued unabated. The crowd grew steadily.

Marshal Wood rolled away from Tom and staggered to his feet. Tom came up with him and wrapped his arms around Wood from behind, still striving to get the marshal's gun away from him. Wrenching away, Wood turned and fired at Tom twice in quick succession. One bullet missed Tom entirely, but the other grazed his left shoulder. He went down on one knee checking his wound. All the fight within left Tom. Marshal Wood pulled Tom up and took him to jail to book him. Later that night, Tom posted bond and traveled home.

The next morning Tom sat facing his mother at the breakfast table. He sipped his Arbuckle's, waiting for her to let loose. He didn't have to wait long.

"Tom P, what were you thinking pickin' a fight with the city marshal?" Docia asked, puzzled.

"Mother, I can't tell you how much the lawmen in Hillsboro have gone out of their way to taunt and harass me. I guess it was all too much when he grabbed my pistol. After that, I felt like I was in a life-or-death struggle with him. You saw the wound when I got home," answered Tom.

"Of course, they're keepin' a close watch on you. They'd

like nothing better than for you to do what you did yesterday," Docia announced. "You're lucky he didn't shoot you dead and call it self-defense." Both of their eyes locked on each other for a moment on that thought.

"I'm just tired of it all," Tom finally stated. "Maybe I'll leave this part of Texas when my trial's over, that is, if I can finally get a fair trial."

"I hate to hear you talk like that, Tom," softened Docia. "Many might like to see you leave, but I'm certainly not one of them. I need you here. I'm only saying that perhaps it might be better not to play into their hands by going into town with a pistol."

"All right. I'm sorry I keep bringing you grief, Mother," Tom admitted.

Docia walked over to her seated son and checked the bandage on his shoulder. She retrieved a pan of warm water to clean around the wound. Tom winced when she got too close to the broken skin where the bullet had traveled.

Finished, Docia stated, "I know how hard it is to walk away from a fight, especially when you really didn't start it. Your father certainly would never have backed away from standing up for himself, and you're a lot like him. I'm afraid, Tom P, we're living in new times where men can no longer settle disputes with their fists. That's all."

Tom put his good arm around his mother. "I really can't change who I am, Mother. I'm proud to be my father's son. But I will try my best to avoid any more confrontations with the local lawmen."

The second murder trial took place in Waxahachie in March, 1891. After five days of fierce battle by the prosecution, led once again by M. M. Crane, the case was winding down. He was not the district attorney for Ellis County, but his offered services had been readily accepted. M. B. Templeton, G. C. Croce, and R. M. Clark of Waxahachie assisted Crane. Captain Upshaw, as usual, led Tom's legal team, which also included William Croft of Corsicana and T. P. Whipple of Waxahachie along with C. B. Pearre of Waco and Tom Ivy of Hillsboro.

As with the previous trials, the Ellis County courtroom was packed to capacity by those wanting to watch the now-familiar witnesses recite for each side their conflicting versions of the events of March 1883. A sensation erupted when the prosecution announced that Emma Land Beasley and her husband, Arch, would not be testifying, as they were currently living in Missouri. Crane requested that jurors from the previous, unsuccessful trial be allowed to recount her testimony as they heard it. Captain Upshaw vigorously objected to this as outrageous hearsay, but District Judge Rainey ruled in favor of the prosecution. The trial continued until it was time for each side's summation.

M. M. Crane stood up and faced the jury. "Gentlemen, it is time for you to rectify a wrong committed eight long years ago. As proven in this trial, Tom P Varnell did knowingly and with malice murder Jonah Land following the outrage Varnell committed upon that poor man's daughter, Ella Land, who has spent many years in recovery in an asylum in Austin due to the shock to her system.

"You have heard and must believe the testimony given previously by Emma Land Beasley that, in fact, her father did not have a weapon of any kind that cold, dark night. Mr. Land's ghost, his widow, and his children cry out for justice. You have it within your power to grant that request. Search your conscience and bring back the only just verdict – guilty of murder."

Crane sat down while Upshaw slowly stood up to face the jury made up of mostly farmers with a few businessmen sprinkled in the group. "Gentlemen, Tom P Varnell is better advertised in Texas than some of her candidates for governor. This kind of notoriety perpetuated by newspapers has many believing that he should have been convicted and hung years ago without the benefit of a trial of his peers. Thank goodness we live in a civilized society in Texas today.

"As my esteemed colleague, Mr. Crane, has pointed out, you have listened to the testimony, but he must have been listening to a different trial than the one being held here. The evidence has clearly shown that Tom P Varnell in a desperate struggle to save his own life killed Jonah Land. This was never Mr. Varnell's design or his desire. It has been shown that the drinking of alcohol was allowed at this party at Mr. Land's, and my client did go outside, but with a willing partner, Miss Ella Land. He should not be convicted of murder because of his impaired judgment that brought about his involvement with her.

"I am asking you to think with your rational minds and not with an emotional view of this. Do not judge Tom P Varnell by any yardstick that measures his actions following the unfortunate death of Mr. Land. If you do as I ask, the only verdict worthy of your consideration is not guilty due to self-defense. That is what I ask of you today, and in doing so you can go home with a clear conscience that you did not send an innocent man to prison."

Judge Rainey addressed the jury, giving them their instructions. At the end, he ordered, "If you find the defendant Tom P Varnell guilty of murder in the second degree, you should assess punishment at confinement in the penitentiary for a term not less than five years. If from the evidence, you believe that Jonah Land had an axe or any weapon with which he was trying to kill Varnell, return the verdict of not guilty. You may now leave to deliberate. Return when you have reached a unanimous verdict."

CHAPTER TWENTY-TWO

27 March 1891

"All rise," called out the bailiff. District Judge Anson Rainey quickly took the bench and called the court to order. The jury filed back in and took their seats. S. H. Mason, the jury foreman, answered in the affirmative that a verdict had been reached.

Tom P was ordered to stand. He looked at the jury and knew what the piece of paper had on it before the district clerk read it. Feeling his knees weaken, Tom reached out and put his hand on the defense table. Standing as straight as he could, Tom faced the jury.

"We, the jury, find the Defendant guilty of murder in the second degree and assess the punishment at twelve years in the penitentiary," read the clerk.

Tom had been on the receiving end of this kind of bad news once already. It was like reliving the same nightmare over and over. He let his attorneys buzz around him, but Tom chose to give no reaction at all to the announcement of his conviction. Words and phrases like 'appeal,' 'reversible error,' and 'court action' floated around him like falling rain as Tom stoically stood staring at nothing.

Without protest Tom allowed Sheriff Meredith to put handcuffs on him to walk him the block and a half to the Ellis County Jail. Two days later, Docia arrived, insisting on seeing

Tom. At first, the jailor was reluctant, but Docia drew herself up to her full height, even though it was only 5'1" in all.

"Young man, you have no business keeping a mother from her son. If you don't let me see Tom Varnell immediately, I will take my case of your cruelty to Sheriff Meredith. Do you hear me?" admonished Docia, glaring at the guard.

"Uh…Yes, ma'am, I surely do. Just followin' the prison's regulations, but beings you're his mother and come all the way from Hillsboro, I reckon it's okay for ya to see him for a few minutes," answered the jailor, going to the wall to get the key to unlock the door into the runaround that surrounded the cells.

Docia could not recall ever seeing a jail quite like the one at Waxahachie. The cells were arranged on two floors, one above the other. Each cell was shaped like a wedge or a piece of pie in a circle around a central rotating vertical axle. To get to the stationery vestibule or runaround, the wide end of the wedge was rotated with a hand crank. Only one cell could be opened at a time.

"Mrs. Varnell, we have the finest facility anywhere around. It was built by the Pauly Jail Company out of St. Louis. We have all the safeguards to ensure no one can break out of this here jail," informed the jailor, who suddenly stopped, then looked flustered.

Docia stared at the guard, frowned, but said nothing. He turned back to the cell. "Varnell, your mother's here."

Tom lay on the narrow bunk with his back to the outside. He had heard the rotating barred wall being cranked around to his cell. He sat up on his bed but did not have the emotional energy to get up to greet his mother.

"Never mind, young man. I'll talk to my son. Just leave me be," instructed Docia. She stood looking at her son. She understood Tom only too well.

"Tom P, I'm sure you have no wish to say much, and that's

all right. I'm just as devastated as you are about the verdict. I want you to know your lawyers feel confident that they will get a reversal. Mr. Pearre told me that you wouldn't talk to him. It takes time, and patience is something that may be in short supply for you right now. I'll come to see you often and, hopefully, we will hear from the Court of Appeals as quickly as before. Hold on, Son," Docia talked calmly, willing him strength.

"Mother, I no longer believe in the courts. Too many are determined to see me serve time. You best be believin' it, too," Tom answered, resigned to his fate. "Save your money, Mother. You need it."

"I know how you feel, but we can't give up hope," urged Docia. "You placed your trust in me when you signed over your half of the ranch. I will not betray that trust. You know you would do the same thing. So stop worrying about the money."

"Well, I am. Go home, Mother. My freedom is lost to me," Tom spoke angrily. "No sense in throwing money away on a lost cause."

Docia waited a few minutes, not knowing really what to say to cheer up her son. She hoped Tom would get past his anger and depression of the moment.

"Tom P... Son! I will never stop believing in you or your innocence. We will continue to fight this. I'll be back soon," Docia promised before the jailor returned to escort her out.

The months stretched out endlessly. Tom remained in the Ellis County Jail because bail, while an appeal was in process, was not obtainable. He could not understand the delay in the disposition of his case, and neither could his lawyers. With few chances to go outside, Tom's health slowly deteriorated once again, although his natural optimism eventually revived his spirits somewhat after a few weeks.

In December his attorney's impatience spilled over to publishing an editorial in the *Hillsboro Mirror*:

The Varnell Appeal

> *Dec. 14. – In the last canvass for governor, the pres-*
> *ent executive had much to say with reference to the speedy*
> *and just execution of the laws. Last March a year ago T.*
> *P. Varnell charged with the murder of Jonah Land in Hill*
> *county, which case has been carried by the state on change*
> *of venue to Ellis county, was tried and convicted, the jury*
> *assessed his punishment at twelve years confinement in the*
> *penitentiary. The defendant's counsel appealed at once and*
> *for sixteen months his case has been before said court, while*
> *he has been wearing out his health in a most miserable cell*
> *within the walls of the Waxahachie jail. If the defendant*
> *be guilty and no errors have been committed by trial court,*
> *then why allow this man to live in a place for so great a*
> *length of time which is but little better than h___ upon*
> *earth? And if his case should have been reversed, why this*
> *delay? There is some reason not mixed up with fairness*
> *and justice, in our humble opinion, which has caused this*
> *delay. If so, what is it? If such be the fact, can it be that*
> *lives and liberties of our people are to be made subservant*
> *to political trickery? I don't know who will try this man's*
> *case eventually, but in the name of all that is right, proper,*
> *and just, let the facts in the case, as contained in the record*
> *and the law, govern you in your action. I write this because*
> *I have a right to do so, having been of counsel in his case*
> *from the beginning. S. C. Upshaw*

The editorial received no reaction from the highest court
in Texas. Two years passed in frustration for Tom and his legal
team. Mr. Pearre reported to Tom that the appeals court had

been divided into two courts and that his case was now before the Texas Criminal Court of Appeals formed in 1892. On the next visit, Pearre explained that two of the judges on Tom's case had recused themselves and that was causing more delay.

Docia visited often, bringing family news. Tom found it hard to believe that little Rosa Belle McGee at age sixteen had married some fella named John Marshall Templeton, and Gus was now twenty-two years old and regularly going on cattle drives, leaving his brothers to help Jasper on the ranch.

On April 22, 1893, both Samuel Upshaw and C. B. Pearre arrived at the jail in Waxahachie asking to see Tom P. Ushered into the vestibule outside of his cell, the two men found Tom sitting on the bunk. Seeing his lawyers, Tom stood up.

"Hey, Tom P. Good to see you," began Upshaw. "Yes, I do have news. It's not good but not without hope."

"The court upheld the conviction, didn't they?" spoke Tom.

"Yes, but Judge J. M. Hurt dissented against the other two judges who were specially appointed by the governor to decide your case. Hurt has spoken openly that the district court should not have allowed the jurors to recite Emma's testimony and that the district judge should have told the jury they had a third option of manslaughter to consider. His written dissenting opinion will go a long way to our getting a hearing at the Supreme Court of the United States," explained Samuel Upshaw.

"Both of you told me to trust the courts. Now look where it got me – twelve years at Rusk. I should have stayed gone back in '85 when I broke jail. For eight years I've waited for justice, most of it in jail. Now this!"

"Don't give up, Tom P. We're not. I'll get right onto the appeal," promised Upshaw.

"I can't take another two years in this hellhole. I just can't," retorted Tom.

"This appeal will surely be much quicker. I'll get back to you soon, hopefully with good news," Upshaw promised.

Tom waited for his attorneys and the guard to leave. He then pulled out the small block of wood he'd been carving with a penknife smuggled into him by George Walker. It was beginning to take shape. Other prisoners had watched Tom but had said nothing to him or to the jail staff.

The inmates milled about the runaround. Sheriff Meredith allowed the prisoners the freedom of the corridor outside the circular nest of cells twice a week.

Tom called John Stacy over to the side. "John, I'll be needing your help this evening."

"Sure Tom P. What's up?" replied Stacy.

"I'm blowin' out of here. Going to the pen was never something I cotton to," Tom replied.

"What do you need?" asked Stacy.

"If anyone asks if I've gone to bed, just say 'yes.' All right?" replied Tom.

"Good Luck, Varnell," offered Stacy as he nodded his head.

Tom went inside and pulled out the dummy he'd worked on for weeks. He'd made the torso from old newspapers rolled together. The 'head' was an old plaid wool shirt wadded into a ball. He placed his 'double' into his bed, covered it up with the bed blanket, putting the new hat his mother had brought him the previous week over the 'head.'

When the guard, posted in the runaround, was otherwise occupied, Tom climbed the cage to the back and leaped down to the first floor. He took out the wooden key he had carved and slipped it into the lock to the door that opened into the room where the guards stayed. Tom hoped they were all busy getting the jail secured for the night or otherwise occupied.

Hearing the key connect with the locking mechanism, Tom smiled at his answered prayer. Pushing the door open as quietly as he could, Tom's pleased reaction quickly turned into a whispered expletive. A single guard sat at the desk with a six-gun in his hand and his back to the door Tom was unlocking.

Tom rushed at the guard, who did not have time to see him before being knocked to the floor along with the chair that toppled over on top of him when he went down. The guard was still on the floor tangled with the chair legs when Tom sprinted out of the room and into the hallway. The guard retrieved his six-shooter but looking around saw no one.

Again Tom used his 'key' to get into the living quarters of Sheriff Meredith. The sheriff's wife and another lady were fixing supper when Tom passed through the kitchen. Mrs. Meredith turned from the stove only to be face to face with Tom.

"Oh my goodness. Who are you?"

"Tom P, ma'am. Just passin' through," grinned the prisoner, as he moved quickly out the door and into the jail yard.

Tom could hear screams behind him, as he sprinted across the yard and over the fence. He slid down to the Waxahachie Creek bottom. Tom knew he had very little time. He moved along the creek and then back up to Rogers Street. Staying in the shadows, he moved along to the town square. He ducked into the Edens Building and up the stairs to a room with Y.M.C.A. lettered in paint on the entry door. George Walker had assured Tom that the room was no longer in use.

Settling down in the dark, Tom spent his time listening intently. Before long, he heard several shots being fired, signaling an emergency to the townspeople. He didn't dare peek out the window but was trusting that the posse would head out of town in search for him. As the noises gradually died down, Tom dozed fitfully. He was exhausted from his efforts during his escape, as he had weakened physically during the two years of confinement. He found a jug of water, some bread, and a flask of whiskey placed behind a broken chair left in the room by his friend in anticipation of a successful jailbreak.

In the early hours of the morning the next day, Tom suddenly awakened. He had heard a noise. There it was again. He moved over behind the door and watched the doorknob turn slowly.

As the door opened, a voice called out, "Tom P, are you here?"

"Damn it, George, you scared the hell out of me!" hissed Tom. "And you almost got yourself knocked in the head."

"I was just trying to stay quiet," responded George Walker.

"What's going on out there?" asked Tom, pointing to the window across the room.

"The newspapers are all carrying the story. I brought you the *Dallas Morning News*. Here's the article dated today, May 13th, "Escape of Varnell." It gives the particulars of your exit. I was surprised to read that Sheriff Meredith added two guards recently, and you escaped anyway. He didn't believe his wife that it was you who had escaped and went to check your cell before raising the alarm. One paper said you out-generaled the sheriff," George responded excitedly.

"I'm just lucky that key I carved out of wood worked," stated Tom.

"Well, anyway, can't stay. I was able to get you a pistol, money, and some food. If someone sees me come out of an empty building, they'll probably be suspicious," George responded, handing Tom the envelope.

"You're a good friend. I won't forget this," replied Tom. "I have one last request. Can you bring a fast horse and leave him tied up down Waxahachie Creek about a mile to the south? I'm going to be slippin' out tonight when everyone gives up the hunt for the evening."

"I'll see to it. Better go," replied George. "Good luck, Tom P. Kinda surprised you didn't ask me to bring your fiddle, ol' boy, but this worked out like a charm."

Docia sat at the kitchen table, keeping a watch out the window. Word had gotten to her about Tom's escape from the Waxahachie jail. She wasn't surprised, but at the same time she was worried about his safety. Would this be the decision that would cost him his life? she wondered. Docia got up and paced around the room. Glory suggested that she lay down. Docia refused. The hours stretched out as the shadows lengthened across the yard. Then she heard Queen barking the arrival of company.

Docia was on the front porch when Tom Ivy rode up. She searched his face for an early sign of what news he had to bring.

"Mrs. Varnell, Tom P has been recaptured and returned to jail," Ivy quickly answered her unspoken question. "I have a copy of the news article from Waxahachie that explains everything. I thought you might like to read it."

Docia placed her hand on the porch post as if she needed the support. Quickly recovering, she took the paper.

"Won't you come in and have a cup of coffee?"

Tom Ivy dismounted and followed her into the kitchen. While he sipped, Docia summarized out loud as she read silently as if Tom Ivy had not read the article yet.

"They're saying that Tom's escape was one of the most daring events ever heard of in the news. It says that Tom made a dummy as a means of escape but stayed in downtown Waxahachie as he figured the posse would spread out and search away from that area. He watched the search parties organize to hunt for him. Makes you wonder what he saw from that window. How desperate he must have felt," lamented Docia.

Ivy interjected, "Yes, Tom spent the night evidently in the Edens Building on the town square. I wondered if somehow he managed to make contact with you or perhaps told you he was planning this desperate attempt at freedom ahead of time."

Docia looked at the lawyer thoughtfully but said nothing. She continued her summation neither confirming nor denying what she may have known.

"Seems telegrams were sent all over the state, but search parties could not find a trace of him. Well I guess not if he was holed up in that building."

"The paper states they think someone was helping him," observed Ivy. "If it wasn't you, Mrs. Varnell, I wonder who it could have been?"

"Tom has lots of friends, Mr. Ivy, who would be willing to risk their own lives to help my son. It could have been most any of them. We'll probably never know as Tom is not a person who would reveal this kind of information, especially if it meant that the person would get into trouble with the law. He'll take his fate solo on this."

Docia turned back to the news article. "They're pretty clear on how he was caught."

"Yes. According to the paper if Tom had not looked out the window just when that washerwoman was passing by, they might still be looking for him," stated Tom Ivy.

"Tom's luck has a tendency to run out on him all right," observed Docia turning back to the paper. "Sheriff Meredith had some thinking to do since no one wanted to go up the narrow stairs to confront Tom. I could have told them that even though he had the ability to take several of those men out before they could have captured him, Tom would not shoot someone down in cold blood. Their fear of him comes from all the exaggerations found in newspaper stories. They don't know the real

Tom Varnell."

"That's true. Wonder if anyone will really think about the fact he gave himself up without harming anyone —saying that he'd had enough trouble—that'd he'd have gone ahead and escaped if he could have but not if it meant harming others," mused Tom.

"My son is no cold blooded killer, Mr. Ivy," announced Docia again.

Tom nodded his head in agreement. He stood up to leave, placing his hand on Docia's back in a show of sympathy.

Docia put down the paper. She breathed a sigh of relief. "Mr. Ivy, thank you for bringing me this account. My son is safe. I was afraid he'd do something desperate, and he did."

"Mrs. Varnell, there's something else I need for you to know, and it pains me to tell you," spoke Tom Ivy. "Tom P's actions will not go unpunished. We will not be able to make any more appeals on his conviction. He will now have to serve his time at Rusk."

"I'm sure Tom realized what might happen. He gave himself up without bringing more trouble upon himself. I do have a question. Is there a chance that the two years he spent in the Ellis County Jail waitin' on the appeal will be applied to the time set out by his conviction?" Docia asked.

"Unfortunately, no," replied Tom Ivy.

"Well, then, I will look forward to the day he will be a free man. Tell all of Tom's attorneys that I appreciate all that you have done for him."

"Mrs. Varnell, it was a privilege to be on your son's legal team. I wish the news could have been better. The scales of justice don't always balance out. I will be available if you need any more legal help. Good day!" Tom Ivy reached for Mrs. Varnell's hand, then turned to leave.

CHAPTER TWENTY-THREE

19 June 1893

The early morning sunlight sifted through the high unwashed windows into the cellblock area. Dust motes drifted through the rays, hazily zigzagging to the floor. Tom and most of the rest of the prisoners were already awake, as they knew breakfast would be arriving soon, starting their predictable daily routine. Summer weather had already caused the cells to warm up rapidly with the coming of daylight. Tom lay quietly on the bunk listening to the good-natured joking among the men.

"Hey, Varnell," one of the prisoner's called out. "You gonna need that homemade blanket and extra pillow when they come to get ya?"

"Reckon not, Hank. I'll see that you get it," replied Tom.

"Just so you know. The rest of us here think you got a raw deal. We hoped you'd make it when you hightailed it out of here."

"I guess if life were fair, most of us wouldn't be in this hellhole," replied Tom.

Seeing some movement, Tom P looked up to see his mother standing at the barred door to his cell. His first curious reaction was to wonder why the prison guards, who had been swarming the place since his return from his escape, had not announced her arrival.

"Good morning, Son," greeted a solemn Docia, dressed in a dark gray travel suit and black bonnet.

"Mother? You're here awfully early," responded Tom, getting up to walk over to the bars that separated them. "Must be a special occasion."

When Docia did not answer immediately, Tom realized why she was there. "They're taking me today, right?"

"Yes, Tom P, Sheriff Meredith asked me to come in and tell you what's to come," answered Docia, keeping her voice as even as possible.

"To come? Meaning?" asked Tom, puzzled at first.

"The prison contractor, George Reeves, will be here shortly to take you by train to Dallas and then on to Rusk Penitentiary. He's allowing me to be on the train to Dallas with you, and I've already made plans to go to Rusk as often as I can," responded Docia.

"Mother, I..."

"I just don't want you to have any more trouble," Docia rushed on. "Do as they say, Tom P. It'll be easier for you if you do."

"I'll try," answered Tom, sensing the strain his mother was under. "Would you see that the boys here get my things, especially Hank?"

The door to the hallway opened, interrupting their conversation. Sheriff Meredith entered, walking briskly past Docia to crank the mechanism, moving the one and only barred exit around to Tom's cell.

"Moving day, Varnell. Stand back while we open the door," ordered the sheriff.

Entering the cell, Meredith immediately put handcuffs on Tom. Most of the inmates from adjoining cells called out 'goodbyes' and 'good lucks' to Tom. Several banged on their bars to show their support for the popular, departing inmate. During all this, Tom said nothing. Neither did he resist when the cuffs were put on him. His mother stood quietly to the side.

Meredith did not waste any time once he had Tom cuffed, pulling him through the door and away from the noisy jailmates. Docia followed them out. A trusty darted into the cell and quickly gathered the inmate's possessions of a hairbrush, a wool blanket, a pillow, and other items of comfort Tom had been allowed to keep in the small cell, stuffing them into a tan canvas bag to give to Docia.

In the main jailor's office, George Reeves waited for his famous prisoner. A medium-sized man, Reeves had been hauling men from county jails to Rusk for several years. He had taken scared teenagers who'd never been away from home as well as hardened hombres who'd slit their own mothers' throats for an extra dollar. He had no sympathy for any of them.

Tom entered, but his mother was blocked and not allowed to witness what came next. Tom's eyes widened immediately, seeing what the contractor had in his hands, a chain neck collar. Tom, realizing he would be leaving in more than handcuffs, pushed the guards away with his cuffed wrists in a panic, wildly looking for any way out.

The struggle was intense but short as the guards anticipated his reaction and quickly grabbed him, wrenching his arms upward to force his acquiescence. Once the neck chain was secured, Tom stopped his struggle. His humiliation was complete. Looking around, Tom was glad his mother had not been allowed into the room.

Upon arriving in Dallas, Tom P and his mother said their good-byes, as she could travel no farther with them. Tom was determinedly stoic in front of Reeves, while tearful promises were made by Docia before she left. Since the contractor had to go to Fort Worth to pick up another prison-bound inmate, Tom was lodged at the Dallas County Jail overnight.

The next morning, Contractor Reeves was joined by Capt. W. J. McDonald, a Texas Ranger, who had arrived in Dallas to help guard the group of prisoners headed for Rusk on the eastbound train. This trip had several convicts, but McDonald decided to sit close to Tom.

"So, you're the son-of-a-bitch who caused such a stir in Waxahachie," spoke Ranger McDonald, a medium-sized man with a barbered mustache, wearing a Stetson along with a Colt .45 holstered and slung low on his hips. McDonald's reputation had been greatly enhanced by the media. He loved the attention and never bothered to correct the exaggerations.

One story had Ranger McDonald showing up in Dallas to prevent a prize fight. The mayor nervously met him at the train station asking where the others were. McDonald reportedly replied, "Hell, ain't I enough? There's only one prize fight." That quote morphed along with others into "One riot, one Ranger" by the press.

"Don't know what the hell you're talking about, Captain," responded Tom, who wasn't so impressed with his guard.

"We got us a smart mouth. You'd better lose it where you're going," retorted McDonald.

"Go to hell," growled Tom, turning to look out the train window.

As the summer landscape flowed past, Tom noticed his cuffs were loose. He had asked that they be taken off while the train was moving but was told that he'd just have to tough it out. Tom squeezed his right thumb inward toward his little finger and twisted carefully. He managed to slip out of the cuff. That small bit of freedom caused him to smile and relax a bit. It was his private secret for many miles. Watching the terrain change from rolling hills to piney woods was unlike anything Tom'd seen in central Texas. The foliage was lush, green, and thicker by the mile. He thought he glimpsed a swamp or two but wasn't sure.

For a few moments Tom forgot his predicament, enjoying the scenery after being in confinement for so long. When his head itched, he reached up to scratch. Dangling from his left hand was the empty right cuff. The movement caused Ranger McDonald to notice and immediately grab Tom's wrists, while Contractor Reeves rushed up the aisle to secure the cuffs on the prisoner again.

"Damn it, Varnell, were you going to make a break for it?" asked McDonald.

"Hell no. I just can't stand being so confined. That's all," answered Tom, more upset with himself than anyone else.

"Better be. Won't bother me to put a bullet hole through you. Save the state some money," threatened McDonald.

"Hell, don't get your back up. I'm not trying to go any-where," retorted Tom, turning back to the window.

Soon, another excitement took Ranger McDonald's atten-tion as a commotion erupted in the back of the passenger car. A convict was talking excitedly to Reeves, pointing at several others in handcuffs. A little later, Reeves came up the aisle to inform McDonald that the convict had 'peached' on others who were supposedly planning to make a break for it when they switched trains at Mineola.

"I've passed the word around. I don't think anyone will try for it now," finished Reeves. "I'm not sure the plot was real, as it was a sure way to get shot in the back, but I guess we'd better be extra cautious at the station."

The rest of the trip was uneventful. Soon enough the pris-on came into view. Tom was struck by the immense size of Rusk State Penitentiary when he arrived. The center of the four-story building was obviously where the administration office was locat-ed. Two wings on either side housed the cells for the inmates.

Like the other prisoners, Tom stopped in his tracks after getting off the train to take in the immensity of the compound. He'd been told the enclosure could hold over a thousand prisoners.

The process of incarceration began as soon as the men arrived. The convicts were lined up and taken into the first office at the gate, one at a time. All their possessions except the clothes on their backs were taken, but not catalogued. From there they were steered into the convict clerk's office one at a time. The chain neck collar was finally struck off. Tom reached up to feel the edges where the collar had scraped his neck raw during the trip.

For several minutes Tom answered questions that were recorded on his official prison record:

> No: 9438
> Name: Tom P Varnell
> Age: 28
> Hair: Dark
> Height: 5'8-1/4"
> Distinguishing Marks:
> > upper front tooth gold filled;
> > 2 gunshot scars on right shoulder;
> > 4 moles on back;
> > scar left forearm
> Weight: 135
> Complexion: Light
> Marital Status: No
> Habits: Intemperate (drinks alcohol)

Tom looked down at the record, realizing they had his age wrong by three years. He started to correct the clerk but changed his mind, deciding it really didn't matter. He finished answering questions about where he was born, education, and details of his conviction.

Coming out of the clerk's office, Tom was told to get back

in line. Once everyone was questioned, the men were informed they had to go everywhere in lock-step lines. They were placed one behind the other and instructed to put their right hand on the shoulder of the man in front. The men were then marched to a trusty tapping on a triangle with a small metal rod.

The next stop was the wash shed where Tom was commanded to remove his normal clothes, scrub down, and then put on prison issued blue-striped garb. The poorly made garments of cheap cloth immediately started Tom's skin to itch. He weathered through it all until they arrived at the barbershop, where he was informed that his mustache would be removed. Tom felt his body tense in preparation to resist. Finally getting ahold of himself, he submitted to losing the mustache he felt was a part of his identity, as he'd had one for at least the past ten years. His haircut was close to the scalp in a winding stairway pattern.

Freshly donned, shorn of hair, and travel trained, the newest inmates arrived outside the dining hall. Tom smelled the food inside, but the aroma wasn't especially inviting. His stomach churned from all the indignities he'd been forced to endure. A convict flunky led the men to their assigned benches. Four or five were expected to share each bench. The men stood as the regulations were given out to them.

"Dining is to be done in silence with only low whispers, and only if absolutely necessary. Extra helpings can be requested by holding the following up in the air: knife for bread; fork for meat; plate for vegetables; cup for water. Asking does not guarantee more will be given," barked the trusty.

Finally, the men were told to be seated. They received the normal fare: cornbread, cowpeas, fatty meat, and weak coffee. Most readily ate, as they had not had a meal since early morning. Tom looked at the food, knowing eventually he would have to eat, but today he just didn't have enough appetite nor could his stomach tolerate the poorly prepared meal. Others gladly took his portion.

After dinner, each man was given his work assignment. Tom was told he was staying inside the prison as his health was not good enough to be assigned to the wood cutting detail, the iron smelter, or one of the farms that leased convicts from the state. Tom suspected the real reason was not his ill health but his ability to escape, but he did not complain, as he soon heard plenty of horror stories of how convicts were treated outside the walls on work details.

The new inmates were finally herded to their nightly accommodations. Tom's cellmate was Randall George from Tarrant County. A large man with blond hair and brown eyes, Randall had been at Rusk for two years already. He had grown up on a farm with nine brothers and sisters but had gone into Fort Worth to look for work after his father's farm had failed to produce enough food for the large family. Randall ran afoul of the law when he got into a scuffle with a deputy outside a saloon in Hell's Half Acre, the local red light district. When the smoke cleared, the deputy was on the ground dead. The jury had little sympathy for his plea of self-defense other than to give him a life sentence. Randall guessed he was lucky he had not been hanged. Tom told Randall an abbreviated version of his own troubles. He had no wish to dwell on what had sealed his own fate.

"You got any family, Tom P?" asked a friendly Randall.

"Yes, but the only one who'll probably be able to come see me is my mother. Why?" asked Tom, sitting on his newly assigned bunk.

"Well, she can do a lot to help you if'n she has some money to spend on ya," responded Randall. "Your mother can have better food sent in on a regular basis or give you money so you can buy it at the 'commissary.'"

"Commissary?" puzzled Tom, warming up to his new roommate.

"It's the name for those who run a side business here. You can buy just about anything you want, even forbidden items, if'n ya know what I mean," explained Randall.

"Do the guards know about this business?" asked Tom.

"Yep. Probably get a cut of the profits. It's best you don't ask too many questions about how the commissary works," answered Randall. "By the way, you can fix up your part of the cell any way you want. As you can see, I don't have much. My family's done forgot I exist, I guess."

Tom didn't know what to say to Randall's revelation, so he changed the topic, asking about how convicts were treated.

"Some guards are okay, some ain't. But the one you don't want to rile up is Messenger Marian Ezell."

"Messenger?" queried Tom, knowing he needed to learn the prison lingo and pleased to have a talkative roommate.

"Yeah," laughed Randall, mirthlessly. "He claims he just brings messages from the assistant superintendent, Captain Douglas. You'll have a problem if'n he takes a dislike to you. He's a brutal one. I seen him use his steel-handled bat on a poor son-of-a-bitch who crossed him. Ezell has those Negroes with him handy-like to hold down a man. Then Ezell gets in fifty licks or so. I seen him do it again, right then, when he thought the feller hadn't learnt his lesson."

Randall fell quiet for a few moments. Tom decided to wait rather than ask another question. He didn't have to wait long.

"I have some more advice. If'n you do get crossways with Ezell, don't fight back. He really likes having an excuse to beat a con to death, and he has. Not that a beating is put down as the cause of death. No one challenges Ezell without consequences."

"Sounds like a hard one all right," acknowledged Tom. "Anybody try to escape around here?"

"Not often. Most don't succeed. Too hard. Those bloodhounds are trained daily and few men know this area well enough to get very far. You pay a big price for tryin'."

"How so?"

"If you don't lose your life, they bring you back for a solid beatin', then it's off to the blind slaughter-house with you," answered Randall. Tom looked at him quizzically. "You know, solitary. It's a separate building entirely and a real hellhole. You're kept in darkness with no air 'cept a couple of small holes in the door. No clothes, no bed, little food, and no visitors. And no one comes around to hear your complaints."

Tom swallowed hard at the idea of suffering through such an ordeal. Melancholy threatened to take possession of his immediate thoughts. Looking around, Tom felt the walls closing in on him. He got up to walk in the limited space between the beds, hoping to calm down.

"I will tell you somethin' no one's probably explained yet, Tom P, bein's I like you. I'm in for life, but you ain't. They have a system here. If'n you manage to stay out of trouble, you can earn time off for good behavior and get outta here early."

Tom looked at Randall with renewed interest. "How does that work?"

"You have to go a whole month with no bad conduct marks, which is pretty hard to do. They keep a tally. You get a day off for each month served; then it goes up from there after a year, I think. One more thing, if'n you try to escape, it wipes out all the days saved up."

"Thanks," replied Tom.

"Lights out," yelled a guard.

"One more thing, Tom. We can't talk after the guards put out the lights except for the ones located outside the cells in the hallway. Another useless rule."

Silence descended on the cellblock. Tom moved around getting ready for bed. He mentally went through all his options.

Lying down, Tom finally decided this time he'd play by the rules. He'd hate doing so, but he figured this was his best course of action. Mental exhaustion eventually helped Tom fall into a sound sleep.

CHAPTER TWENTY-FOUR

25 June 1893

Sunday was the one day of the week when the routine at Rusk changed. Tom P enjoyed the extra half-hour sleep his first Sunday morning at the prison brought. Although church services were mandatory, he didn't mind, as he'd always enjoyed gospel music, even though he did prefer playing on the fiddle to singing.

After the noon meal the men were allowed some time outdoors in the prison yard along the outside walls of the main building, since work was suspended on the Lord's Day. Tom hated the penitentiary, but at least he could get out in the sunshine, unlike the county and city jails where he had stayed during his trials and appeals.

Tom was walking along the prison yard with Randall that first Sunday since his arrival when he turned to ask, "Who are those men with round spots painted on their shirts? Even you have a spot on yours."

"Easy enough to answer. Men with black spots on their clothes are in for 15 to 99 years; red spots are for 99 to life. They're called red ball and black ball men. As ya noticed, I'm a red ball man," explained Randall.

"Varnell, it's time we had a little talk!" came a voice from the side.

Tom turned around to see a group of men, some sitting on a bench, some standing. Regardless, they were among the roughest looking sort that Tom had seen anywhere. He wasn't sure which one of the motley crew had been the source of the command. So Tom did not respond at first.

Randall whispered quickly, "They're going after you early, Tom P. It's the kangaroo court all new inmates have to go through. Secret's not to be too tough nor too weak."

"Someone call my name?" queried Tom, as he sauntered toward the group.

"You might say that. We're here to try you for crimes against humanity, Varnell," stated a tall, muscular man with a scar across his right eye that ran up to his hairline. Tom noted the red circle on the man's shirt. He sat on top of the back of a bench surrounded by his burly cohorts.

Tom stayed quiet for a moment but made eye contact with the obvious leader. Neither one broke the stare.

"Do say?" Tom finally quipped. "I take it you're the judge of this court? Am I allowed to proclaim my innocence, or do we go straight to the punishment phase?"

Tom grinned nonchalantly at the men, as he took the time to look at each member of the 'court.' He then walked over closer, planting his feet slightly apart, waiting for their next move.

"Word's already gotten here about you, Varnell," replied the scarred leader. "So I've put it to the boys here, and they've found you guilty. What say you?"

"Looks like a jury of my peers has spoken," answered Varnell, careful not to agree or disagree.

"Good. Glad you see it our way. As judge, I'm assessing you a fine of $5.00," announced the leader.

"$5.00! That's a lot, but I guess I'll have to pay. You'll need to wait `til my mother comes for a visit. Will that do?" Tom replied, looking directly at the convict judge again without flinching.

"Done! Court's adjourned," announced the judge, reaching his hand out. "I'm Sheldon James."

Tom shook the man's hand. He knew at that moment he had passed some unspoken test. He nodded at the rest of the men, then turned to leave.

"You did great," exclaimed Randall. "I've seen new men get taken down by that group, and the really weak ones are picked on all the time. I can also tell you they would have attacked you in a hallway if they had not accepted you."

"I've been in quite a few jails in the past few years, Randall. I'm not afraid of bullies. Most men know I'll fight if'n need be. That's usually all it takes to get 'em to leave me alone. Come on, let's get away from here," replied Tom, heading away from Sheldon James and his followers.

Early the next week, Tom was called off his work detail in the prison garden. Shown into the office of the assistant superintendent, Captain E. G. Douglas, Tom sat down. The guard had not told him the purpose of the visit, so Tom waited quietly. On the administrator's desk was a very familiar fiddle case.

"Varnell, your mother was here this morning. She'll be back tomorrow during regular visiting hours," announced Douglas, a short balding man with a full beard.

Tom nodded his head but did not speak. He couldn't quite figure out why his mother's visit would involve Captain Douglas who, according to the other inmates, had little to do with the men forced to stay at Rusk. Rumor had it Douglas was about to be replaced anyway.

"Let me answer your unstated question. First of all, your mother left a goodly amount of money with me for your comfort. We do have cells that are a bit more commodious if that is your desire. Your mother's willingness to defray some of the expenses of the state for your stay here will allow us to assign you to less strenuous work. Your mother's desire is that you regain your health that she says was seriously impaired during your two-year stay in the Waxahachie jail," stated Douglas.

"Captain, my mother's generosity is most welcomed. I am fine with my current accommodations but will accept the work inside the prison," stated Tom.

The assistant superintendent pushed the case toward the inmate. "She left this for you. Are you as good as Mrs. Varnell says you are?"

Tom looked at the fiddle case. It had been a long time since he last played.

"I'm a bit rusty, but I do love to work the strings," Tom answered.

"Good. I'm also assigning you to a group here we call the Old Alcalde Minstrels. They do entertainments a few times a year for the public. If you're good enough, they'll let you perform with them," stated Douglas.

Tom took the case, placed it on his lap, but left it closed. He didn't want to open it in front of Captain Douglas. He waited.

"One last thing. Your mother also paid for you to have a newspaper subscription with our permission. She left you a paper," noted Douglas who handed the copy over.

"Varnell, I can tell you're a polite sort, regardless of the reports I received. I don't expect to hear much about you from here on out," stated Douglas.

"You won't," responded Tom simply.

"You can leave now," Captain Douglas dismissed the prisoner.

Tom picked up the fiddle case and tucked the paper under his arm. At this moment he knew he would be able to withstand his time in the pen.

After supper that night, Tom lay down on his bunk to look

through the June 20th rear issue of the *Hillsboro Mirror*. He wasn't surprised to see a short article about himself there:

Travels to the Pen

> *George C. Reeves, state agent of the penitentiary stopped over in Dallas yesterday from 10 a.m. until 7:30 p.m. with Tom Varnell, whom he was taking to the penitentiary. A News reporter saw Varnell at the jail, but he refused to say anything, except that he had been convicted unjustly. He is about 5 feet 10 inches tall, has brown hair, a heavy brown moustache, rather sallow complexion and blue eyes. He is an intelligent and determined looking man. He gave as his reason for not talking that the papers had written too much about him already, and a great deal of which he said was not true.*

Tom spent the rest of the evening before lights out reading the entire paper. He was glad to have this connection to the outside world. He looked forward to his visit with his mother set for the next day.

The months passed into years, and Tom got used to the prison routine. He stayed out of trouble and kept his own tally of the days off he was accumulating. He spent his Sunday afternoons practicing on his fiddle. Tom's mother came at least once a month to see him. She made sure he had as many comforts as the prison staff allowed.

Tom still spent time in the infirmary, as from time to time his weakened lungs would cause shortness of breath necessitating bed rest. Tom came into contact with several of the men who worked outside on convict lease programs. Some came back in such poor health from being overworked and underfed that the doctor could do little to save them.

Tom also saw men who deliberately inflicted wounds on themselves to return to the main prison where life was easier. One young prisoner threw lime into his own eyes to get off a cotton plantation. Another cut his Achilles tendon so that he could no longer walk.

One of the most interesting inmates Tom met was Henry Tomlin who'd been at Rusk since 1889 for a rape for which he proclaimed his innocence. Tom saw Henry occasionally in the infirmary, but most of the time Henry was confined to solitary, as he refused from the beginning to work, proclaiming he owed the state nothing. The newspapers carried stories about Tomlin's refusal to work.

Henry was on a hospital bed one day when Tom entered to get a lung treatment. As he had to wait for Dr. Lacy, who was with another patient, Tom walked over to see the infamous inmate.

"How ya holdin' up?" inquired Tom.

"Good as can be expected, Tom P," answered Henry. "That damn Messenger is determined to make me heel, but I'm more stubborn than he is."

"Ezell is a tough one all right. I've made it my business to stay out of his way, but your stubbornness may get you killed," observed Tom.

"Maybe, but I won't go down without a fight," retorted Henry.

"Well, I haven't had a run-in with Ezell. Hope to keep it that way," stated Tom.

"Messenger's a mean son-of-a-bitch," replied Henry.

"Has Ezell done anything besides beat ya?" asked Tom.

"I've been on bread and water more times than I care to remember. Nothing Ezell does can break my will, and when I get out of here, I'm writin' a book. Someone needs to tell the truth about this place," replied Henry, vehemently.

Just then Dr. Lacy called Tom over to check his lungs. The best part of spending time in the infirmary was getting a bit of whiskey for medicinal purposes. Dr. Lacy was usually pretty easy to convince.

Lying on the infirmary bed with a hot mustard poultice on his chest, Tom pulled out his sister Lina's latest letter, which he kept in a tattered envelope:

December 15, 1899

Dear Tom P,

Hope this letter finds you well and bearing up. I think about you often. I wish I could go to east Texas to see you, but we are so busy here. I do hope when you are released that you will come to Sterling to see us.

Your cousin Rosa Belle has two children of her own now, Opal and Pearl, and is expected another soon. Jasper really likes her husband John Marshall Temple-ton. You'd like him, too, as he's a good horseman. Gus has his eye on a young lady named Cora Garrett. I expect a wedding soon. He asks often if I've heard from you.

I was out at the smokehouse today. I remembered that you were here just shortly before it was finished. I thought you might enjoy the story of the time I discovered your cousins, Dee and Ed, using it as a gaming parlor. They know how I feel about gambling and drinking. I found a card they must have dropped the last time they were there. Instead of confronting them with something I knew they would deny, I just waited. Sure enough, it wasn't long before I caught movement while looking out the window. They thought I was busy canning peaches and wouldn't see them and their friends sneak into the

*smokehouse. I waited for all of them to get in there. I,
then, put the crossbar up on the door so they could not
get out that way and found a stave off an old barrel. I
banged on the door and ran to the back where the only
window is located way up high. It wasn't long before
that window opened and out came each culprit. As
they dropped to the ground, I gave each one a couple of
whacks. The others, inside, couldn't see what I was doing. It didn't matter if they were mine or a neighbor's son.
I reckon they will never gamble in our smokehouse again.
Sometimes you just have to take action to get your point
across.*

　　*I'd better close for now. This letter is long enough.
Please write when you can!*

*Your loving sister,
Lina*

Smiling, Tom put the much-read letter back in the worn
envelope. He'd probably read it again this evening. He was glad
Gus had found a good woman. Tom knew he had one thing
many of the other inmates did not have, a family who believed
in him.

After supper a few months later, Tom noticed that Randall
seemed to be agitated about something. Tom waited, but Randall said nothing.

"We're been `mates for awhile, Randall. You have a prob-
lem?" queried Tom.

"I might as well tell ya," answered Randall. "They're ship-
pin' me out to the tree cuttin' crew. It's my death sentence."

"Is that where they make charcoal for the iron smelter?"
asked Tom.

"Yep. The men are overworked, the conditions are terrible, and there are lots of accidents," lamented Randall.

"What happened to pull you off your work detail here?" asked Tom.

"That damn Ezell," muttered Randall. "I've been able to avoid him until today. He came into the blacksmith shop to see about his horse we were re-shodding. He was plenty angry when he found out the job weren't done yet. He decided 'twere my fault. Made the mistake of arguing with 'im. He struck me across the face."

Tom moved off his bunk to take a look at Randall. He had not noticed the ugly red mark across the left side of Randall's cheek earlier.

"Damn," whispered Tom.

"He didn't stop there, even though he left the shop. Ezell sent one of his lackeys back to inform me of my new assignment," Randall growled angrily.

"When do you have to go?" asked Tom.

"Next Monday if'n I stay that long," answered Randall.

"Stay? Are you thinkin' of makin' a break for it?" asked Tom shocked.

"It's my only hope," mumbled Randall.

"Not saying it's the best thing for you to do, but here's a bit of money in case you need it. What a sorry business all this is," stated Tom, reaching into his pillow case for his small stash of cash.

"Tom P, you're the one person in my life who's shown me any kindness. I won't forget. I hope we meet again on the outside," responded Randall.

"Well, a good friend would talk you out of running," Tom replied.

The two men lapsed into an early, uneasy silence before the guard yelled for lights out. Tom figured Randall must truly be desperate.

Two days later Tom took note that Randall did not return to their cell after supper. About an hour later, a guard passed by taking a tally. Tom said nothing, knowing the guard would be back, and he was.

"Prisoner, state your name and number," barked the guard upon returning.

"Tom P Varnell, No. 9438."

"Where is Randall George?"

"Don't know. Didn't he get sent to cut trees?" asked Tom, hoping to buy a little time for his former cellmate, while mentally hoping Randall managed to get away. The guard left.

Tom heard the prison bell ringing a little later, alerting the surrounding community of an escape attempt. Less than an hour passed before the hounds were baying as they pursued the fleeing man.

Tom had difficulty sleeping that night as he thought about Randall. He dozed, but his own nightmares returned, centered around running from the law. All was quiet as the early morning fog brought an ethereal stillness to the compound.

Tom sought information, but the guards refused to say much. That evening at supper the news was passed around quietly that Randall George died as he was being recaptured along some swampland east of Rusk. Tom said a silent prayer for his friend who probably knew his fate before he even started his desperate escape attempt.

CHAPTER TWENTY-FIVE

19 January 1902

Tom P sat once again across from the Assistant Superintendent of Rusk Penitentiary. He knew this time why he was there. Tom glanced at his discharge papers sitting on the administrator's desk. Piled neatly on top were five one dollar silver coins. Tom had been told that each discharged inmate, no matter how long they served, received the same amount. Assistant Superintendent W. M. Lacy, whose brother was the prison's doctor, came back into his office, having taken some papers out to his secretary.

Lacy began with no greeting or preamble, "Tom P Varnell, it's my duty to formally discharge you from the custody of the State of Texas and Rusk Penitentiary. Due to your good conduct record, you reduced your stay here by three years, three months and three days from your twelve year sentence."

Tom took the papers and money handed to him. W. M. Lacy, a political appointee, was a short, round man with dark hair stuck close to his head with the aid of pomade and who obviously had not missed many meals in his lifetime. Tom and his fellow inmates had weathered through several changes of the main administrator without much impact on their lives. They rarely saw the assistant superintendent, as he tended to stay in his office rather than mix with the prisoners. Lacy reached across his desk to shake Tom's hand before continuing his prepared speech used on all departing inmates.

"I hope you have been reformed and will never trespass upon the rights of society again," preached Lacy. "You have paid your dues. Good-bye and good luck."

Tom looked at the administrator. Irritated by the sermonizing and abrupt dismissal, Tom still managed to force a smile onto his own face. He believed this fool had little understanding of the men he lorded over on a daily basis. Tom took his leave without speaking. He had nothing he wanted to say to his chief jailor.

Tom walked out the front gate of Rusk Penitentiary. He was informed along the way that no transportation would be provided for him. Tom didn't care. Once outside, he laughed and turned his face to the weak warmth of the winter sun. He was prepared to walk to the train station, wearing the sweet cloak of freedom.

"Tom P," called a familiar voice.

Turning, Tom spotted his mother waiting in a buggy. He walked over and threw his canvas bag onto the floorboard He placed his fiddle case on top of the bag and climbed in. Briefly hugging his mother, Tom picked up the reins. Each hoof beat seemed to say over and over again – "Going Home, Going Home, Going Home."

Docia studied her son as they made their way to the railroad station in the town of Rusk. She had noticed over the years a hardening in Tom P's countenance and personality. He still laughed on occasion but was quicker to get angry or take offense than when he was younger. Docia detected a renewed recklessness and could only blame prison life for the changes in her son. She reached out and put her arm through Tom's, as he guided the horses toward the stables close to the train station. He hugged her arm next to his side but kept his eyes on the road.

Arriving back at the Varnell ranch, Tom threw himself into the ranch work. He picked out a new saddle horse, as Midnight was no longer alive. Tom named the black stallion Hurricane but decided to call him `Cane for short. Docia offered immediately to sign over half of the ranch back to Tom. He declined, saying she had worked too hard on his behalf. He was content to share the burden for now. Maybe they could talk about it again when he had shouldered his share of the work for the still-thriving horse ranch.

A few days after returning home Tom received a large envelope in the mail. The return address indicated it was from the governor of Texas, Joseph D. Sayers.

"What is it, Tom P?" asked Docia.

"I don't know. Guess I'd better open it to find out," replied Tom, who carefully separated the flap from the rest of the envelope and pulled out an official looking document. He laid the paper on the kitchen table.

"Looks like a full pardon from the governor," Tom announced.

"Thank goodness. That means you get your citizenship rights back," exclaimed Docia. "I think we can thank State Senator S. C. Upshaw for this."

Tom put the pardon carefully back into the large envelope. He handed it to his mother.

"You'd better put this someplace safe for me. I'd probably just lose it," Tom explained. "Have you heard if they've dropped those other charges against me? I spoke to one fella in prison who got out only to be tried again for indictments still on the books. He was sent back to Rusk for another two years."

"I think the other charges have been dropped. The county has had enough of dragging you through the courts," answered Docia. "There is something I held off from telling you, but I see no reason not to do so now. Captain Upshaw tried very hard to get you a pardon in 1898. He even got the Prison Board to recommend your release, plus he presented the governor with a petition from the citizens here in Hill County. Governor Culberson nixed it. Not sure why, but Captain Upshaw told me it had more to do with politics than you. I'm sorry, Son."

"Mother, I've seen some hard things in prison. If not for you, life there would have been a lot rougher. Don't ever think I don't appreciate what you did for me. It's over. Done with," Tom replied. "Not much has changed around here. I even read in the newspaper that Tom Bell got re-elected sheriff. I suppose he's as good as any."

"What say we have a hoe-down this Saturday night? Maybe your sister, Rosa, can come out with her brood. I wrote you about it. It's been mighty tough for her since John, her husband, died from that fall out the window in downtown Hillsboro. The weather was bad that night. John worked late and decided to stay downtown rather than walk home. Rosa believes that he was sleepwalkin' when he fell out that second story window. It's been so tough since then. I think fiddle music would cheer everyone up," suggested Docia. "Bet you had time to write some great music." Tom grinned at his mother, confirming her suspicion.

Trying to rebuild the ranch's stock business, Tom traveled widely looking for good mares. On First Mondays, he usually went down to Waco to do some bargaining and swapping. While there he'd go down to the Reservation, not so much to sample the pleasures offered as to see George Walker. Tom'd not been out of prison long when he visited George's saloon the first time.

"Can a `poke get a decent whiskey in this joint?" hollered Tom, slamming the front door open.

George turned around to see who the loudmouthed customer was who'd entered so noisily. Seeing Tom P, he threw down the towel he was using to clean the bar and headed around the end of the counter to slap his good friend on the back.

"Well, I'll be, Tom P. Rumor had it that you'd gotten out of the pen early. Welcome," smiled George.

"You own this run-down tavern?" quipped Tom, looking around.

"Yep, but I can't seem to keep out the riffraff who darken the doorway," laughed George. "Seriously, it's great to see ya. Here, have a whiskey on me." George pulled out his best jug and poured Tom a tall one.

"Thanks," Tom spoke, taking a swig.

"Got girls upstairs if you're a-hankerin'," offered George grinning.

"Maybe later," answered Tom.

"You got someone waiting for you on the side already? No surprise," quipped George. "Never seen anyone gather the females any faster. You've been outta circulation for a mighty long time, but I guess it's like riding a hoss. You never forget how."

"Truth is, there is someone, but I haven't seen her for years. She's probably already married or has forgotten me," retorted Tom.

"What's her name?" asked a curious George who'd never known Tom to be sweet on a girl.

"Lilly. I did hear that she moved to the Oklahoma Territory. I hope to go up and see if I can find her before too long. I need to go when Mother doesn't need me on the ranch," Tom replied, then switched the subject. "Looks like you've made it good here."

"I've done all right. Had some legal trouble of my own but nothing I couldn't handle. It can get mighty rough around here, but I don't mind. I told you long ago I wouldn't be busting sod all my life. My family's disowned me, but I don't care. My girls and my bartender are my family now," replied George.

"You got your friends, too," replied Tom mildly.

"Yep," retorted George. "Let me pour you another one while we catch up. I want to hear about Rusk and more about this Lilly."

The two men spent several hours visiting and talking about the past and the future. Tom left saying he'd be back to see his old friend again soon.

Tom headed to Mangum in mid-July to visit his cousin, John Griffith, who was a lawyer there and to see if the rumored sighting of Lilly could be true. He took the train but had to make several changes to get over to the Oklahoma Territory town located close to the Texas Panhandle.

After supper, Tom and his cousin went to the Sundown Saloon. After buying them both a whiskey, John lifted his drink in salute.

"Plenty of opportunity in Oklahoma, Tom P. It's going to be a state soon. You should consider leaving your troubles behind in Texas and relocating."

"Sounds promising, cousin," replied Tom, "but my mother would never consider leaving Hill County. I'd better stick close by. I've left her alone to deal with too much already."

The saloon doors opened, and a noisy group entered. Dr. Silas Border bellied up to the bar ordering drinks for his group.

Observing the newcomers, Tom spoke to John quietly, "I know that man. His brother lives in Hill County."

Border spied Tom P sitting with John and, without a proper greeting, called across the room, "Well, if it ain't the jailbird from Texas. We don't need your kind!"

"Really? At least I'm not stealing from the poor like your brother in Texas," retorted Tom angrily.

"You son-of-a-bitch," growled Border, slamming down his drink to head toward Tom.

An altercation was barely avoided when Border's friends

hustled him out of the saloon. Tom downed his whiskey and stood up.

"Leave him be, Tom P.," warned John. "Border's a blow-hard. He's not worth your irritation. You've got time for one more before your train leaves."

Tom eyed the door but sat down at John's behest. He relaxed again after awhile. He listened to his cousin talk about Oklahoma's prospects for becoming a state soon. Tom finally told John he needed to catch the train.

"Why you goin' up to Hobart anyways?" asked John. "That prairie town sprung up from nowhere. I guess the Great Land Lottery in 1901 brought land-owning hopefuls, but it also attracted gamblers, con men, and outlaws."

"There's someone I've been told has moved there. I need to see if it's true. Plus, I'm checking a few things out. I got a lead on some good horses for sale. If it pans out, I'll ride one and herd the rest back to Texas. Better get going. Thanks for the refreshment."

Tom shook hands with John before he left. The evening air felt warm on Tom's flushed face. Feeling pretty good, he purchased his ticket for the local to Hobart. Standing on the platform at the end of the caboose as the train left the station, Tom pulled his .45 out. Laughing as he thought about Lilly, Tom shot off several rounds into the gathering darkness.

"What do ya think you're doin'?" demanded one of the train conductors, arriving to see Tom shoot off another round.

"Jist havin' a little fun. No harm done," countered Tom, putting his pistol away.

"Well, you need to go git in the passenger car. We can't have all this shootin'. Someone'll think we're bein' robbed," admonished the conductor.

"Oh, all right." Tom headed inside. He couldn't see any of the nighttime landscape, so he drifted off to sleep dreaming of someone from New Mexico.

A bit more sober when the trained pulled into the Hobart station, Tom disembarked. He marveled at the activity in the streets even though the hour was late. He moved carefully down the main street as it was quite muddy from a recent rain. He overheard someone call the main road 'Goo Goo Street,' and he had to agree.

Tom managed to procure a spot on the floor at the crowded Bolton Hotel. He didn't sleep very well and was up early the next morning. He inquired at the territory land office about Lilly. He was told to go to the Smithson farm, that she might be there. Tom went over to the stables to see about getting a saddle horse for the day. He was told one would be available after dinner.

Taking in the sights of the bustling town, Tom listened to bits of conversation between other pedestrians. The Kiowa Indians once occupied the area which was also used as a thoroughfare on the Chisolm Trail leading to the shipping yards in Kansas during the heyday of the cattle drives. He learned that Hobart was originally named Speed for a U. S. Attorney, but the name was changed to Hobart after the land rush, for Garrett Hobart, the vice-president under President Hardin. Tom wondered what had brought Lilly here. He had to admit the place was a lot like Magdalena, raw and bustling. No matter. Hopefully, he'd be seeing her soon.

Tom noticed a man who kept watching him as he walked around the main street through town. Tom ignored the Mexican, as he'd never seen him before. Pretty hungry at dinnertime, Tom stopped in at the Blue Point Restaurant. Sitting on a stool, Tom ordered the daily special of beef 'n biscuits. He went in early enough that only a few other diners were there.

The door to the restaurant opened, but Tom took no notice as he knew no one in Hobart. He wanted to finish his dinner quickly, so he could get the horse from the stables.

"You be the sorry son-of-a-beech who stole my saddle," yelled a man in the doorway.

Tom turned around on the stool. Before him was a short, swarthy man with a dark complexion who was obviously already tipsy from too much drink. His brown pants were dirt-stained, and the aroma wafting off him indicated one who hadn't seen soap and water in a good while. Tom noted the man was the same Mexican he'd seen on the street earlier.

"I don't know who the hell you are, but I've not stolen anything. You got the wrong man," answered Tom evenly.

"The hell I don't. I've been followin' you for some time. You know my name's Frenchy, and I know'd you took my property. I want it back," yelled the Mexican.

"Don't know too many Mexicans called Frenchy. In fact, I don't know any," snapped back Tom.

"You be makin' fun of my name?" snarled Frenchy.

Tom became increasingly irritated at this obviously inebriated local. "I done told ya. 'Tweren't me who stole your saddle. Now get lost so I can finish my meal in peace," Tom retorted, turning back to his dinner.

Frenchy quickly covered the distance from the door to where Tom sat. Reaching out, Frenchy knocked Tom off the stool while pulling out a stiletto. Before Tom hit the floor, he yanked out his pistol from his vest. Realizing his danger, Frenchy dropped the knife and grabbed Tom's six-gun with both hands.

The two men rolled on the floor. Each was fighting for control of the .44. One shot was fired. Missing both men, the bullet lodged in the ceiling. Tom and Frenchy continued to struggle when another shot was fired. When the smoke cleared, the man called Frenchy lay bloody and dying on the floor.

Shaken, Tom remained while an observer of the fight went for the town marshal. Tom had run once before, but not now. Witnesses assured the lawman when he arrived that Frenchy

Rauls was the aggressor, but the marshal said he had to arrest Tom anyway until everything could be investigated thoroughly. Not again, thought Tom!

"We don't have a jail here yet, Varnell. I'll be taking you to Mangum to await trial," ordered the marshal.

"I have a cousin who is a lawyer there. Would you get word to him when we arrive?" asked Tom P.

"Sure thing," answered the marshal. The two men headed for the door of the restaurant on their way to the train station. As Tom sat on the train back to Mangum, he thought more about his missed opportunity to see Lilly than his own immediate troubles. He came to the conclusion that without even seeing her, he had lost her again.

CHAPTER TWENTY-SIX

25 July 1903

Dicey Belle Wallace sat at the wooden table in her small farm kitchen surrounded by her brothers. A young woman in her late twenties, Dicey had reddish brown hair she kept pulled back and piled in a bun at the crown of her head. She loved to wear her plain shirtwaist cotton dresses in such as way as to show off her natural assets – a small waist and large bosom.

Married for several years, Dicey was the mother of two small boys. Her husband A. D. stood off to the side, not really wanting to be a part of the quarrelsome confrontation. A mild-mannered man, A.D. never much understood the family he'd become a part of through marriage. The anger in the room was palpable. Dicey's brothers pretty much ignored her husband anyway.

"You're an embarrassment to the family," yelled William, the oldest. "More than one person done told me they seen you talking to that convict."

"I surely don't know why all the fuss," retorted Dicey. "No harm in being friendly." She got up to move away from her brothers, making herself busy over at the nearby sink, hoping they would take the hint and leave.

"I can't believe you're that ignorant, Dicey," retorted John. "Varnell's reputation with women is well known. People talk.

You know that."

"You can't pick my friends. I've done nothing wrong," yelled Dicey, clinching her fists.

"You're a married woman with a family and responsibilities, Dicey. You don't want your reputation ruined, do you?" asked Sam, in a reasonable tone of voice.

"How can you cavort with our sworn enemy? Have you forgotten that Varnell killed our Aunt Minnie's father, Jonah Land? Varnell shoulda been kilt back then for what he done. He didn't even spend ten years in prison. Where's your family loyalty?" asserted Oscar angrily.

"All of you are acting all crazy over nothing. Just leave me be!" cried Dicey, looking to her husband for some support, but getting none. Why was he leaving her to deal with her brothers? A. D. didn't seem to have much backbone as far as Dicey was concerned.

"Well, if you're not going to heed our warnin', we'll just have to do somethin' about it," admonished William. "Not the first time you've gone against our advice."

Dicey heard the deadly serious tone in her brothers' voices. She looked at their angry, determined faces. She loved them but hated the way they were always ordering her around.

"I don't understand why y'all are so angry all of a sudden. Why?" Dicey asked.

"Mark Jolson told me that he overheard Varnell speak yore name at the Old Rock Saloon Saturday night. Varnell acted like you two have been friendly," answered Oscar.

Dicey blushed, then counterattacked, "That's not true. You didn't hear this yourselves, and now you're taking the word of a known drunk."

"That's the point, Dicey. It don't matter if it's true or not. People are talking. We're honor-bound to do something. Now, do you understand?" explained Sam.

Dicey gulped, trying to get enough oxygen. How had all of this gone so wrong?

"What do you mean to do?" she asked.

Instead of answering her, Oscar turned to Dicey's husband, "Keep her home tomorrow. No going to church. Varnell told Mark he'd be in Abbott on business. Think we have a bit of business of our own."

"You can't force me to stay home," shouted Dicey in a panic, wondering if there was any way to get word to Tom P.

"We can, and, if necessary, one of us'll stay with you while we clean up this mess," ordered William picking up his hat and heading for the door. "Sam, stay here. You know what to do."

Tom P sat on `Cane, gazing down the road toward Abbott. He looked around, realizing he'd spent more time moving down the road through his memories than paying attention to the passing landscape along the route to Abbott. His mother would be misput with him if he didn't get home by mid-afternoon.

Almost a year had passed since he'd killed Frenchy Rauls in Hobart. Tom's cousin, John Griffith, had taken care of his troubles there. Tom understood his arrest better when John explained to him that territorial marshals were paid according to the number of arrests and convictions they accomplished.

Tom had spent some time in the jail at Mangum. His trial was quick and the outcome not surprising even though witnesses swore that Tom acted in self-defense. Interestingly enough, once Tom's lawyer filed an appeal, bail was set. John told Tom to go back to Texas and not to worry as he saw no problem in getting the conviction overturned. Tom stated he wanted to go back to Hobart, but John warned him to stay away for now. Tom agreed but knew he would be back.

With encouraging letters from Griffith in Oklahoma Territory, Tom went back to his normal life. Putting the episode behind him, Tom had bought the acre lot in Rienzi the previous January. He'd probably go ahead and tell his mother about the property when he got home this afternoon. Once that appeal was dealt with, Tom intended to return to the Oklahoma Territory.

Looking at the sun, Tom figured it was about noon. Almost time for the churches to let out if the preachers weren't wrapped up in their sermons for the day. Arriving in Abbott, Tom guided `Cane down the main street. He stopped to talk to John Stone about a mare he knew John was interested in buying. They agreed to meet the next day at the Varnell ranch to complete the deal.

Hoping to beat the church crowd, Tom headed over to Mayo's Confectionary for a bite to eat. Dismounting, Tom pulled off his gloves and put them in the saddlebags and tied `Cane to the hitching post. He looked down the street at the First Methodist and Baptist Churches located across from each other. He could hear both congregations singing as though being louder than their counterpart across the road was of paramount importance.

Smiling, Tom started humming his own composition again, blocking out the competing congregational choirs. He'd finally worked out the melody. He'd need to jot it down when he could so he wouldn't forget the notes.

The Fergusons had originally moved to Limestone county before drifting on to Hill County where their farm was located, two miles north of Abbott. The family was known in the community as clannish and at times unfriendly. They didn't always answer the door when company came calling. Fiercely loyal to one another, they never forgave a slight nor a perceived insult.

William, John, and Oscar Ferguson all wore determined faces along with their regular farm clothes of wool plaid shirts and tan canvas pants held up by suspenders. The final decision had been made the night before. One of them would be saving the honor of their family. All three were packing a gun of some sort, be it a shotgun or a pistol. Sam had stayed at the Wallace farm to make sure Dicey didn't leave.

The only one with any real experience with a firearm outside of general farm use was Oscar. Although the youngest of the brothers, he was the self-appointed leader of this deadly errand. He had served in the military during the Spanish American War, coming home to a hero's welcome. Enjoying his status, Oscar accepted the invitation that came to join the local Masonic Lodge. He came home with a worldliness that commanded the respect of his brothers as well as others in the Hill County community.

Saddling up their horses, William, John, and Oscar headed into Abbott. They spoke to no one, but each took up a station around the small farming community, waiting for their quarry. The town was fairly quiet, as it was just past noon and the churches were still in session.

Entering Mayo's, Tom walked over to the counter and sat down on a stool. He ordered a sarsaparilla and some salt water taffy from Elvie Conover who was working the counter.

"Afternoon, Tom P," greeted the young clerk, a boy who'd just turned sixteen years old.

"Afternoon," returned Tom P reaching for his drink. "Anything new or exciting happening around here? I've been hearing about these new motorized vehicles. Have you seen one yet?"

"Yep, Henry Conover brought one of those horseless carriages through just the other day. Caused a sensation among the boys in town. I think he said it was called an Oldsmobile. Funny-lookin' thing. Won't ever replace horses for transportation though. Much too noisy, and I hear they break down kind of easy," replied Elvie.

"I agree. Don't like 'em myself," commented Tom. "Horses are much more dependable. Trains are available for long distance. I do think everyone's gonna have electricity one day, though."

"Of course. Being able to turn on a light by pulling a cord rather than lightin' a match is the way of the future. Hope we get it soon," replied Elvie.

"Looks like we're going to have a good cotton crop this year," remarked Tom. "I noticed the fields riding over from the ranch."

"Seems so," answered Elvie who looked up and noticed his boss, John Mayo, signaling. "I'll be right back, Tom P."

"Say, can I borrow that pencil?" asked Tom.

"Sure," answered Elvie, taking a small pencil out from behind his ear and handing it over.

Pulling out a piece of folded white paper from his vest pocket, Tom started making musical notations. He paused and put the green pencil down across the leaded hand-drawn score.

"Gray eyes flecked with green," Tom whispered. Then he once again wrapped his long fingers around the pencil and concluded his composition.

Elvie had put down the cloth he'd been using to clean tables and headed to the back of the store. He was curious as to why his boss had not come out to greet Tom and why Mayo would pull him off the counter. Mr. Mayo led Elvie outside.

"I want you to stack these crates."

"But, sir, we have a customer up front," protested Elvie, who much preferred being inside.

"Never mind about that. Just do as I say," retorted John Mayo irritably.

Elvie watched as Mayo walked around the side of the building. He knew not to argue with his boss. He needed this job. He started stacking crates.

Docia walked into the kitchen at the Varnell ranch. Tom hadn't returned yet, so she figured she'd get a bite to eat. Glory was standing at the sink, looking out the window. Her right hand was curled and resting on her heart. Her stillness alerted Docia.

"Glory, what's the matter?" inquired Docia, walking up to stand behind the older woman.

"I don't know, missus, but somethin' ain't right. It just ain't right. I feels it in my bones," replied Glory, who continued to stare out the window.

Docia looked at Glory, then through the window but saw nothing out of the ordinary. Suddenly she shivered, even though the temperature was quite warm.

No longer hungry, Docia poured two cups of coffee. She invited Glory to sit down for awhile. The two women sat quietly, sipping. Neither felt like talking. So they waited. For what they didn't know.

Oscar Ferguson, standing in the alley between buildings, had seen Tom P enter Mayo's Confectionary. He signaled to his brothers, who took up lookout stations on the sides of buildings in the business district and across from the candy store.

Seeing Mayo and Elvie out back of the building, Oscar checked his .38 Smith & Wesson to make sure it was fully loaded. He waved at his brothers, crossed the street, and walked to the doorway of Mayo's. Glancing around, he noted no other customers.

Tom P was sitting on the stool with his back to the doorway, finishing the musical notations he'd been working on. He felt the hair on the back of his neck rise, then heard the click of a gun being cocked. Tom turned. The first bullet slammed into his jaw, forcing his body back around toward the counter. Seconds later another bullet entered his back, exiting out his chest just above his heart.

Tom grabbed the counter but did not have enough grip to hold on. He sank to the floor. Ferguson walked over to Tom, not saying a word. He lifted the gun one more time, aimed at the top of Tom's head, and fired at close range. He quickly turned and walked away.

Tom, lying on his back, turned his face toward the doorway as the green pencil rolled away. He thought he could hear fiddle music. Was that his father waiting for him at the door?

Sheriff Tom Bell made his way the necessary ten miles east of Hillsboro. He dreaded the chore he would have to perform at his destination. Arriving, he turned his horse past the gate that led down to the Varnell ranch. Birds were twittering in the trees, and in the distance he could hear the hooves of horses running in the pasture. Everything seemed so quiet and ordinary. As he rode down to the porch following Princess, who was barking, he saw Docia Varnell standing with her arm around a post, watching him almost as if she were expecting his arrival. He dismounted, taking off his hat. In his hand Tom Bell held a folded deed and a sheet of hand-drawn, blood-stained fiddle music.

Tom P. Varnell, Died July 26, 1903, Aged 41 Years,
5 Mos. 13 Days

Abbreviated Bibliography

Books:

A Memorial and Biographical History of Johnson and Hill Counties, Texas. Chicago: The Lewis Publishing Company, 1892.

Abbott, Texas 1881-1981. Belton, Texas: Centex Press, Inc. 1981.

Coombes, Charles. *The Prairie Dog Lawyer.* Dallas: University Press, 1945.

Gournay, Luke. *Texas Boundaries: Evolution of the State's Counties.* Centennial Series of the Association of Former Students, Texas A & M University, No. 59. College Station, Texas.: Texas A & M University Press, 1995.

Hardin, John Wesley. *The Autobiography of John Wesley Hardin as Written By Himself.* Reprint. Norman, Okla. University of Oklahoma Press, 1983.

Heritage of Hill County, Texas, The. Clanton, Alabama: Heritage Publishing Consultants, Inc., 2006.

Hittson, Jack Homer. *The Brazos Broncbuster's Scrapbook.* Brazos Books, 1971.

Stoecklein, David R. *Cowboy Gear: A Photographic Portrayal of the Early Cowboys and Their Equipment.* Stoecklein Publishing, 1993.

Tomlin, Henry. *Life of Harry Tomlin.* [publisher unknown] c. 1900.

Court Records and Official Documents:

Arrest Warrant for T. P Varnell and George Walker. Case No. 1849. Hill County District Court. Hillsboro, Texas, March 9, 1883.

Conduct Register (Ledger). State Penitentiaries. Huntsville, Texas.

Hill County District Court Minutes. 1883 – 1889. Hillsboro, Texas.

Indictment. "Tom P. Varnell. Assault to Rape." Case No. 1846. Hill County District Court. Hillsboro, Texas. March 9, 1883.

Prison Ledger – Rusk. "Convict Record." Texas State Penitentiary. p. 110.

Probate. Isaac Alexander Varnell. Died January 1, 1876. Hill County Courthouse. Hillsboro, Texas.

Proclamation. Pardon of Tom P Varnell. Governor Joseph D. Sayers. January 24, 1902.

Record of Marks and Brands, Vol I. Hill County Courthouse. Hillsboro, Texas.

Varnell v. State. Court of Appeals of Texas. Opinion and Witness Testimonies. June 28, 1888.

Voucher. Texas State Penitentiaries. Expenses for Transporting Tom Varnell to Prison. June 19-20, 1885.

Warranty Deed. I. A. Varnell to Adeline Varnell McGee. 70 Acres. John Mills Head Right Survey. Book Q, Page 98. Hill County Court Records.

Warranty Deed. T. P. Varnell to F. L. Varnell. 985 Acres of land. Vol. 12, Page 444. March 12,1883.

Warranty Deed. I. Bassinger to T. P. Varnell. One Acre Lot. Town of Rienzi. Jan. 10, 1903.

Interviews:

Griffin, Lina Pearl Templeton. Written transcript of Interview by Jerry Templeton. Undated. Dublin, Texas.

Holland, Harry Frank. Long Time Resident of Abbott, Texas. Aug. 22, 1997 and Aug. 26, 2006.

McGee, Lane. Grandson of Adeline Varnell McGee by Jerry Templeton. Transcript of Interview. March 11, 2000.

Pendergrass, Ruby Templeton. Written transcript of Interview by Marian Pendergrass. Undated. Tx

Bios: *Robert W. Keen*. U. S. Work Projects Administration, Federal Writers' Project (Folklore Project, Life Histories, 1936-39); Manuscript Division, Library of Congress Copyright undetermined.

Turner, Thomas E. Written Transcript of Interview. Dec. 9, 1998. Waco, Texas.

Wallace, Sam. Grandson of Nellie Ferguson (sister of Oscar

Ferguson). Nov. 9, 2006. Hillsboro, Texas.

Newspapers:

Dallas Daily Herald

"Waco: Most Horrible Double Crime." March 7, 1883.

Dallas Morning News.

"Texas Justice On Trial." Oct. 15, 1885.

"T. P. Varnell Captured." Oct. 19, 1885.

"News From Waco. Tom Varnell." Oct. 22, 1885.

"News From Waco. Tom Varnell." Oct. 25, 1885.

"News From Waco. Tom Varnell Escape." Nov. 14, 1885.

"News From Waco. Tom Varnell Escape." Nov. 15, 1885.

"Local News from Waco. Tom Varnell Escape." Nov. 18, 1885.

"Tom P. Varnell On the Road." Nov. 20, 1885.

"Hillsboro." Nov. 21, 1885.

"The Varnell Case." Nov. 29, 1885.

"Waco Local Matters. Tom Varnell." Dec. 5, 1885.

"The News of the Day. State. Tom Varnell." Dec. 6, 1885.

"Waco Local News. Miss Emma Land." Dec. 6. 1885.

"Tom Varnell's Trial." Dec. 6, 1885.

"Waco. A Jailor Vetoes a Break for Freedom." Dec. 8, 1885.

"The Local News From Waco. The Varnell Case." Dec. 12, 1885.

"The News of the Day. Varnel Refused Bail." Dec. 12, 1885.

"A Dull Day at Fort Worth. Tom Varnell Brought To Jail." Dec. 13, 1885.

"Cleburne. Judge Hall." Dec. 13, 1885.

"Local News From Waco. Counsel for Tom P. Varnell." Dec. 15, 1885.

"Capt. S. C. Upshaw. Tom Varnell Case." Jan. 12, 1886.

"Tom Varnell's Case." Jan. 28, 1886.

"Four Men Capture a Train." Feb. 1, 1886.

"Itaska Items. Tom P. Varnell Case." March 7, 1887.

"Bloody Altercation." March 28, 1887.

"Tom P. Varnell." June 15, 1887.

"Admitted To Bail. Thomas P. Varnell." July 27, 1887.

"Thomas P. Varnell Case." April 7, 1888.

"Nine Years' Imprisonment." April 8, 1888.

"Varnell Will Appeal." April 10, 1888.

"Motion Overruled – Gone to Austin." April 15, 1888.

"The State Press. Brenham Banner." April 16, 1888.

"A Reversal in the Varnell Case." July 2, 1888.

"Varnell Gives Bond." July 12, 1888.

"Tom Varnell Falls From Horse." Aug. 3, 1888.

"Suit Compromised and Court Notes." Oct. 12, 1888.

"The Varnell Case. A Cause Celebre." Sept. 13, 1889.

"The Varnell Case." Sept. 26, 1889.

"Varnell Murder Case on Trial." March 26, 1890.

"Varnell Murder Case." March 28, 1890.

"No Verdict in the Varnell Case." March 29, 1890

"The Varnell Jury Disagrees." April 1, 1890.

"An Exciting Scene. A Life Struggle for the Possession of a Pistol." Feb. 18, 1891.

"Sensation at Hillsboro." March 29, 1891.

"Defense of the Courts." May 1, 1891.

"Defending the Courts." May 31, 1891.

"Drake and Varnell Cases." April 1, 1891.

"Gave Him the Slip." April 2, 1891.

"Tom Varnell Case. A Disagreement Between Judges Hurt and White." Dec. 24, 1891.

"Tom Varnell Case." Oct. 26, 1892.

"Varnell Case." Dec. 10, 1892.

"The Varnell Appeal." Dec. 14, 1892.

"The Varnell Case." March 7, 1893

"Criminal Cause Celebre. Finding in the Tom Varnell Case Affirmed." April 23, 1893.

"Varnell Sad and Nervous." April 25, 1893.

"Varnell Case." April 28, 1893.

"Tom Varnell Escapes." May 13, 1893.

"Ellis County. Reward." May 13, 1893.

"Escape of Varnell." May 14, 1893.

"Excitement Over Varnell's Escape." May 14, 1893.

"Recapture of Tom Varnell." May 15, 1893.

"In the Tom P. Varnell Case." June 13, 1893.

"Varnell Mandate." June 15, 1893.

"En Route to the Pen." June 20, 1893.

"Tom P. Varnell Starts for the Penitentiary." June 20, 1893.

"Tom Varnell in Stripes." June 24, 1893.

"Sheriff Tom Bell." Nov. 2, 1894.

"Tom Varnell." June 28, 1895.

"The Case of Tom Varnell." July 16, 1898.

"Man Killed at Abbott." July 27, 1903.

Fort Worth Daily Gazette

"Horrible Crime." March 7, 1883.

"Waco: Miss Land Passes Through." March 8, 1883

"Hill County: Misses Land." March 11, 1883

"Texas Topics: $1000 Reward." March 23, 1883

"Tom Varnell Captured." Oct. 19, 1885.

"A Burning Shame: Tom Varnell, the Ruffian and Murderer Breaks Jail." Nov. 13, 1885.

"Hillsboro: One of the Jail-Breakers Caught." Nov. 15, 1885.

"Varnell Has Vamoosed." Nov. 18, 1885.

"Tom Varnell Advised to Surrender Himself." Nov. 18, 1885.

"Tom Varnell Surrender." Nov. 20, 1885.

"Waco. Tom Varnell." Nov. 21, 1885.

"Criminal Callings." Nov. 30, 1885.

"Railings. What the Railroads are Doing in Fort Worth and Elsewhere in the World." Dec. 8, 1885.

"Waco. A Synopsis of the Testimony in the Habeas Corpus

Case of Tom Varnell." Dec. 8, 1885.

"Tom Varnell's Trial." March 27, 1888.

"Hillsboro. The Exciting Trial of Tom Varnell." April 6, 1888.

"State Vs Tom P Varnell." April 8, 1888.

"Varnell Case." April 2, 1890.

"Final Finding." March 30, 1891.

Hillsboro Reflector.

"Tom P. Varnell: The Other Side of the Land Matter." Advertisement. Undated (c. 1883)

"Excitement On Train," Feb. 1, 1886.

"Hubbard City Items. Miss Ella Land." June 17, 1886.

"Prisoners in Jail." March 5, 1887.

"District Court." March 31, 1887.

"Personal. Mrs. F. L. Varnell." April 28, 1887.

"The Trial of Tom P. Varnell." June 16, 1887.

"Criminal Cases." Oct. 13, 1887.

"Trial of Tom P. Varnell." Oct. 27, 1887.

Hillsboro Mirror

"Varnell Case Affirmed." April 26, 1893.

"Varnell Case." May 3, 1893.

"Deaths. Mrs. F. L. Varnell." Feb. 23, 1916.

National Police Gazette, The.

"Wanted By Judge Lynch." June 9, 1883. New York City.

Socorro Buillion News.

"How They Took the Scoundrel In." Oct. 17, 1885.

Waco Daily Examiner.

"The Varnell Murder." Jan. 11, 1876

"On The Mash." Nov. 30, 1881.

"From Hubbard City: Atrocious Murder of Mr. Land by Tom Varnell." March 7, 1883.

"Murder Most Foul: A Daughter Outraged and Her Father Murdered." March 7, 1883

"Varnell's Victim." March 9, 1883.

"Varnell's Refuge in Hill County." March 17, 1883.

"From Hubbard City: Supposed Capture of Tom Varnell in Fort Bend County." March

23, 1883.

"From Hillsboro: Surrender of George Walker to the Sheriff." March 30, 1883. p. 1.

"Varnell's Companion Surrenders." March 20, 1883.

"The Irony of Truth: *Texas Siftings* Appeal to "Colonel" Varnell." March 30, 1883.

"For Safe Keeping." April 11, 1883.

"Varnell in Hoc." Oct. 20, 1885.

"They Slip Out." Nov. 17, 1885.

"Varnell Surrenders: He Arrives in Waco With Sheriff Bell." Nov. 20, 1885.

"Round About Town. Tom Varnell." Nov. 20, 1885.

"Tom Varnell Taken to Hillsboro." Dec. 11, 1885.

"Facing the Music." Dec. 13, 1885.

Waco Daily Times Herald

"Tom Varnell Killed at Abbott Yesterday." July 27, 1903.

"Tom Varnell Was Well Known in Waco." July 28, 1903.

"Some Particulars of the Varnell Killing." July 28, 1903.

Waco Day.

"Varnell on the Loose." September 29, 1884.

"Thomas P. Varnell." March 30, 1891.

Waxahachie Enterprise.

"Tom Varnell Murder Case." April 12, 1889.

"Tom Varnell on Trial." March 28, 1890.

"Varnell Convicted." April 4, 1891.

"Varnell Escapes." May 19, 1893.

"Varnell in Stripes." June 21, 1893.

"Career of Tom Varnell." Aug. 1, 1903.

News articles without attribution:

"Horrible Murder: A Prominent Citizen Brutally Assassinated."

(Isaac Varnell murder)

"Tom P. Varnell Attends a School Exhibition on Wednesday Evening."

"Tragedy at Hobart."

Maps:

New Mexico. 1886.

Official Map The State of Texas. 1882. Under Direction of A. W. Spaight. Rand, McNally & Co.

Rusk Penitentiary. Schematic of Cells. Kanmacher & Denic, Contractors.

Sanborn Map. *Hillsboro*. 1880. http://sanborn.umi.com/sanborn/image.

Sanborn Map. *Hillsboro*. 1900. http://sanborn.umi.com/sanborn/image.

Sanborn Map. *Waco*. 1885. http://sanborn.umi.com/sanborn/image.

Sanborn Map. *Waxahachie*. 1893. http://sanborn.umi.com/sanborn/image

Waxahachie Jail. Schematic. Floor Plan.

Texas Bird's-Eye Views. *Fort Worth in 1886*.

Texas Bird's Eye Views. *Waco in 1892*.

West Central States and States of the Plains, Southern Division. *Railraod Map*. 1887.

Magazine & Periodicals:

"A Brief Description: Magdalena." No Publication Date Given.

Ashcroft, Bruce. "Miner and Merchant in Socorro's Boom Town Economy, 1880-1893." *New Mexico Historical Review*. April 1988.

"Ellis County Jail – 1888." by John Hancock. Waxahachie High School. 1978.

"Medicinal Old-Tyme Remedies." *Living in Pioneer Times: How*

Our Ancestors Lived Not So Long Ago; 2003, p. 26-30.

Waco Prostitution. Vertical File. The Texas Collection. Baylor University.

Proclamations:

Reward: $200.00 by Governor John Ireland. March 21, 1883.

Resolution of Respect and Resolution on the Murder of Jonah Land. Hubbard City Masonic Lodge. S. H. Barber, Secretary. On file at the Hubbard City Library. March 24, 1883.

Unpublished Sources:

Nancy Martin Nixon. *Descendants of William Varnell, Sr.* Genealogy. Unpublished. 1995.

Web Sites:

General Libraries of the University of Texas at Austin and the Texas State Historical Association. *Handbook of Texas Online.* http://www.utexas.edu/handbook/online. (accessed on various dates)

Heritage Quest Online. United States Census Records, 1850-1920. http://persi.heritagequestonline.com/hqoweb/library/do/census/search/basic. (accessed various dates)

Author's Note: A complete listing of all sources for this book would take up extensive space. I've chosen to list mostly those sources that will help the reader follow Tom Varnell's story as it unfolded in the media.

Author's Biography

A sixth-generation Texan, Sherri Knight grew up on a dairy farm in rural Erath County located in North Central Texas. She attended Lingleville and Dublin public schools before graduating from Stephenville High School (at age 16) and eventually Tarleton State University with degrees in English and history plus a Masters in Education. Ms. Knight took her all-level teaching certificate throughout the state of Texas making stops at Houston, Mineral Wells, Callisburg, Childress, Tolar, San Antonio (17 years) and Mansfield school districts, completing 31 total years in the classroom. Her numerous awards include Outstanding History Teacher— UTSA Regional History Fair, Outstanding Teaching of the Humanities presented by the Texas Council for Humanities, Teacher of the Year—East Central High School (San Antonio), National Endowment for the Humanities Scholar, Fulbright-Hays Scholar, Fulbright Summer Abroad, and Texas Exes Award for Excellence in Education, University of Texas at Austin. Ms. Knight coached students to excel in History Fair at both state and national levels. Outside of teaching, Ms. Knight also has a background as a legal secretary and is the former state director for Texas Women Western Artists and a contributor to their publication, "The Western Breeze" and "Texas Art Circles." Ms. Knight is a member of Women Writing the West. Today, Ms. Knight lives in her hometown of Stephenville, Texas, with her husband, Arden, and is currently working or her next book centered around the history of the district court of Erath County.